Creative Modelling with Lotus 1-2-3™

Creative Modelling with Lotus 1-2-3™

Second Edition

Mary Jackson
London Business School

JOHN WILEY & SONS
Chichester · New York · Brisbane · Toronto · Singapore

Reprinted May 1991

Other Wiley Editorial Offices

John Wiley and Sons, Inc., 605 Third Avenue,
New York, NY 10158–0012, USA

Jacaranda Wiley Ltd, G.P.O. Box 859, Brisbane,
Queensland 4001, Australia

John Wiley and Sons (Canada) Ltd, 22 Worcester Road,
Rexdale, Ontario M9W 1LI, Canada

John Wiley and Sons (SEA) Pte Ltd, 37 Jalan Pemimpin 05-04,
Block B, Union Industrial Building, Singapore 2057

Library of Congress Cataloging-in-Publication Data:

Jackson, Mary, 1936–
Creative Modelling with Lotus 1-2-3 / Mary Jackson. — 2nd ed.
p. cm.
ISBN 0-471-92407-5 (pbk.)
1. Lotus 1-2-3 (Computer program) 2. Electronic spreadsheets
3. Business—Data processing. I. Title.
HF5548.4.L67J33 1989
005.36′9–dc20 89–16600
CIP

British Library Cataloguing in Publication Data:

Jackson, Mary, *1936–*
Creative Modelling with Lotus 1-2-3™. — 2nd ed.
1. Microcomputer systems. Spreadsheet packages :
LOTUS 1-2-3™
I. Title
005.36′9

ISBN 0-471-92407-5

Typeset by Woodfield Graphics, Fontwell, Sussex, England.
Printed and bound in Great Britain by Courier International, Tiptree, Colchester.

Contents

Acknowledgements

My thanks go to participants on various London Business School courses for sharing my enthusiasm for 1-2-3 and trying out much of the material in the book. In particular, I would like to thank Mike Staunton and Angela Aubertin for their help and also Derek Stone for his insights concerning the budget worksheet. Above all, I am grateful to my husband Peter for his unfailing interest and encouragement and to the rest of my family for their patience with this enterprise.

Preface

This revised edition of *Creative Modelling with Lotus 1-2-3* takes advantage of the improvements and changes that have occurred in the Lotus 1-2-3 software package over the last few years. The book was originally written when the first release of 1-2-3 was widely used. Nowadays, many more people use Release 2 of the software, which contains several improvements and enhancements, in particular, the regression routine. This has led me to revise the material in Chapters 9 and 10 on Relationships and Forecasting to take advantage of the new regression routine in 1-2-3.

However, it is still the case that most of the material in the book can be implemented by users of either version of 1-2-3. If you are working with the first version, you may however, find it more straightforward to work with a disc of .WKS files (as opposed to the present CM disc with its Release 2 .WK1 files). This can be obtained by writing to: The Software Editor, John Wiley & Sons Ltd, Baffins Lane, Chichester, West Sussex, PO19 1UD, UK.

Since writing this book, Release 3 of 1-2-3 has arrived although it is still not yet widely available. The spreadsheet modelling heart of 1-2-3 has not changed fundamentally and .WK1 files can be used with this version. From what is known of the Lotus policy of 'upwards compatibility', it is likely that .WK1 files will be compatible with any future releases.

One further difference between this edition and the previous one is the inclusion of a chapter on investment appraisal. Chapter 12 has been added to fill the need for a description of the net present value and the 1-2-3 special functions that calculate these discounted cashflow measures.

With this edition, I have included on the disc more datafiles for illustrative purposes than with the earlier edition. Some of the datafiles correspond to the 'finished spreadsheet model' for a particular application and can be examined after working through the instructions in a particular chapter. The disc is a 5.25 inch disc: it can be exchanged for a 3.5 inch disc from John Wiley & Sons at the address given above.

CHAPTER 1

Introduction

1.1 The rise of spreadsheets

The 80s have witnessed the widespread dispersion of personal computers (PCs) and spreadsheet software. The first electronic spreadsheet, VisiCalc started being sold in the USA in late 1979. Its spectacular success led to a whole new breed of spreadsheet software.

Hard on the heels of the spreadsheets have come the 'integrated' software packages, that is, software that integrates separate applications on one disc. Staying in the environment of one piece of software, a user can carry out some spreadsheet modelling, switch to graphics, access a database, produce some text and print a graph. Of these 'integrated' packages, Lotus 1-2-3 has been widely sold, well received, and the market leader for many years.

The main application area has been in financial modelling, that is, in budgeting and planning. The scope for the use of products like 1-2-3 is much wider than financial modelling. One of the purposes of this book is to suggest some other fruitful avenues, for example, in sales forecasting, in statistical analysis, in analysing surveys, in handling personnel records as well as to throw new light on the process of building well planned financial models.

The innovative feature in the acceptance of spreadsheets has been that the manager builds a 'personalized' model and carries out the modelling himself. He decides on the logic of the model, and in effect he writes the program himself. This is possible because of the flexibility, the versatility and above all because of the ease of use of the software. Whilst computers have long been accepted as on-going tools for professional analysis, it has taken the advent of the spreadsheet to turn the computer into a means of personal model development for managers. The spreadsheet has been responsible for a new activity called 'professional personal computing'.

The trend is for the microcomputer and spreadsheet software to become personal investigative tools, for analysts, specialists, and managers alike. The enormous modelling potential and easy interchange with visual images provide an extension of the management mind. One purpose of this text is to try to accelerate this process by suggesting a range of ways in which the software, in particular Lotus 1-2-3, can be applied.

1.2 What is a computer spreadsheet?

A spreadsheet package contains the electronic equivalent of a pencil, an eraser and a large paper worksheet ruled with lines to give rows and columns. It can be used to solve problems quickly much as you would use a calculator in conjunction with your paper worksheet. The monitor screen connected to the microcomputer acts like a window displaying different areas of the worksheet. One position or 'cell' is uniquely defined by highlighting (or a flashing 'cursor') and this indicates where the pencil is currently pointing. At any position in the worksheet, you can enter words or numbers. In 'cells' where you want to perform a calculation, you enter a formula. The software responds immediately by carrying out the calculation automatically and displaying the results. A powerful recalculation facility jumps into action each time you make an entry in the worksheet, updating every cell with the new information. In consequence, you can perform calculations more rapidly and you can therefore try out many more options.

So by the term spreadsheet we mean software which allows calculations on a matrix of cells, with facilities for manipulating rows and columns of entries and 'copying' of formulae, and with automatic recalculation.

1-2-3 provides a giant electronic worksheet with 256 colums. The earliest version of 1-2-3 (Release 1) contained 2048 rows: the next version (Release 2) contains 8192 rows. Release 3, due in 1989, contains 256 worksheets each of 256 columns and 8192 rows. As well as the spreadsheet features described above, 1-2-3 has graphics routines which are truly easy to master and rapid to produce results. It can also be used for keeping records through its database facilities. The software is a prime example of the integrated spreadsheet modelling package, which typically encompasses database and graphics facilities, and may also include word processing and communications.

1.3 What spreadsheets are good at

Spreadsheet software is most effective when the analysis in hand can be structured into calculation sequences carried out systematically on rows and columns. Spreadsheet modelling is easiest to construct when there are lots of simple formulae, applied to a fixed number of rows (or columns). This is the structure of much financial and accounting analysis. The row structure is the same, month by month, year by year. The calculations are simple: addition, subtraction, and multiplication, etc. In the context of spreadsheets, common operations across rows and down columns mean that the underlying formulae can be replicated easily using a few keystrokes.

Equally, spreadsheets perform to great advantage when the underlying models contain many interrelated cells. For example, many profit projections take as their starting point some assumed sales values. Many of the cost items, direct labour, materials and direct overheads relate to sales as do the promotional and advertising expenses. Each time an entry is changed, the entire spreadsheet is rapidly recalculated. It is this facility that allows the 'what-if' questions to be so speedily answered.

The main selling feature of spreadsheets is their suitability for answering 'what-if' questions. Given a set of assumptions about the future, it is always necessary to explore what would happen if the assumptions were to change. The ease with which sensitivity analysis can be carried out has made the spreadsheet a true 'decision support system' for managers.

Compared to other computer software, the spreadsheets are proverbially easy to use. The software tends to be well documented and it is 'user-friendly'. For example, the user is prompted as to what to do next, and prevented as far as possible, from losing his work. The software tends not to 'crash' easily or 'hang' in an uncommunicating state. Most novices find they work productively right from the start.

70 per cent of sales revenue. Fixed costs are expected to be £1100 per quarter. We now enter this data for the first quarter into the worksheet in simple stages much as we would on paper. (In the keying instructions that follow, you type only the characters, etc., set out on the left hand side of the page: the right hand side explains what is going on.) Remember to start entering data from READY mode. To get back to READY mode at any stage, press Escape one or more times.

(a) Sales volume

With the pointer over A1, type:

Sales Volume	which is a LABEL as shown by the mode indicator
→	(the right arrow key) which enters the label and moves the pointer on to B1.

Ignore the fact that letters from the label in A1 run over into cell B1. We shall adjust the column width to accommodate our labels in due course.

Continuing (with the pointer over B1), type:

100	which is a VALUE as shown by the mode indicator
(↵)	which means 'Press Return'. This enters the value and leaves the pointer over B1.

Notice that pressing Return puts what you have typed into a cell and leaves the pointer over the same cell: pressing an arrow key after typing out some characters both enters the characters and moves the pointer to the adjacent cell.

Mistakes. If you notice a mistake whilst the entry is still displayed on the control panel, it can be corrected using the Backspace key to delete characters in the usual way.

If you do not notice the mistake until you have entered it into a cell, you can simply retype the entry and re-enter it. 'Overtyping' is often the quickest way to correct mistakes.

In addition, you can do 'on-line' editing with the Edit key as will be explained in Section 2.7. (In any case, mistakes in labels can be edited at a later stage.)

(b) Price

In the same way, enter the label, Price, in cell A2 and the value, 30, in cell B2.

At this stage your screen display should look somewhat like Figure 2.5.

	A	B
1	Sales Volume	100
2	Price	30

Figure 2.5 First entries in the worksheet

(c) Sales revenue

Again in the same way, enter the label, Sales Revenue, in cell A3 and move the pointer to cell B3. Ignore the 'spill over' of the label into B3.

To enter the value of sales revenue, we can use values already entered in the worksheet, namely the sales volume (in B1) multiplied by the price (in B2). The asterisk * is used to denote multiply. So with the pointer on B3, type:

+B1*B2 a formula, which 1-2-3 interprets as a VALUE.

Press Return to enter this formula in cell B3.

Notice the need to start the entry with a + sign, so that 1-2-3 interprets the entry as a value (currently the value 3000). Without the +, B1*B2 would be displayed as a label since the expression starts with an alphabetic character.

(Try typing B1*B2 (↵) into position B3. The mode indicator shows that this is a LABEL. Now correct the entry in B3 by typing in +B1*B2 (↵) where once again (↵) denotes 'Press Return'.)

Look at the display. The worksheet shows the number 3000 in B3. The control panel shows the actual contents of B3: namely the formula +B1*B2. Entering the formula (as we have done) is preferable to keying in the value 3000, since sales revenue will be calculated correctly if we choose to change the sales level in cell B1 or the price in B2 at a later stage.

(d) Variable costs

Variable Costs are estimated to be 70 per cent of sales revenue in this exercise.

Enter the label V Costs into A4 and with the pointer over B4, type:

.7*B3 (↵)

This formula expresses costs as 70 per cent of sales. Interpreting the symbols, it says:

take proportion .7 of the contents of cell B3 and put it in cell B4. The entry is a value since the first character is the decimal point.

If preferred you may enter 70% rather than the decimal .7. It is, however, crucial to key in the % sign.

(e) Fixed costs

Enter the label F Costs in A5 and the quarterly value, namely 1100 in B5.

Notice that the characters must be numeric not upper case alphabetic characters.

(f) Profits

Lastly, enter the label Profits in A6 and the formula for profits in B6. The formula takes the form +B3−B4−B5, i.e. sales revenue less variable and fixed costs.

Notice that, as with Sales Revenue, the formula for Profits must start with + as it is to be interpreted as a value.

Figure 2.6 shows the worksheet displayed on your screen at this stage. The underlying formulae are also indicated in Figure 2.6. You can see these formulae appear one by one in the control panel as you move the pointer from cell to cell down column B.

```
          A              B
1  Sales Volume         100
2  Price                 30
3  Sales Revenue       3000   ←  +B1*B2
4  Variable Costs      2100   ←  0.7*B3
5  Fixed Costs         1100
6  Profits             -200   ←  +B3-B4-B5
```

Figure 2.6 Entries for the first quarter

For practice, express Profits as a percentage of Sales Revenue and put the appropriate label and value in row 21 of the worksheet. The / sign is used for division. Figure 2.7 shows one possible solution.

```
          A                   B
21 · Profits/Sales %     -6.66666   ←  100*B6/B3
```

Figure 2.7 Profits/Sales ratio in row 21

Since we shall not use this percentage in the following development, we will 'erase' the label and formula entries. For Figure 2.7, the entries were in cells A21 and B21. To blank out this 'range' of cells, described as range A21.B21, the steps are:

/ to get the main command menu:

Worksheet Range Copy Move File Print Graph Data System Quit

R to choose Range giving the Range menu:

Format Label Erase Name Justify Protect Unprotect Input Value Transpose

E to choose Erase

A21.B21 (↵) as the range of cells to be erased.

Notice that the cell addresses A21 and B21 are separated by a period . (or full stop).

To blank out a single cell, put the pointer over the cell in question and type:

/ R E (↵) to Range Erase the cell 'pointed' to.

2.6 Column width

On loading 1-2-3, the columns in the worksheet are set to 9 spaces wide (the so-called 'default' setting). This is why some of the labels we entered appear abbreviated in the current display. 1-2-3 has commands for altering the width for the worksheet as a whole ('globally') or simply for individual columns.

To display the labels properly, column A needs to be at least 14 characters wide. Sales Revenue requires 13 spaces and add one for a margin. The Worksheet Column

Set-Width command will be used to Set column A to 14 characters wide leaving the remainder of the worksheet at its current setting. The sequence of choices from the menus is therefore Worksheet then Column then Set-Width. So with the pointer in column A, type:

/ W C	to start the Worksheet Column command
S	to Set-Width (or press Return to confirm the choice Set-Width)
14 (↵)	for the column width of 14 characters.

To summarize, the sequence of keystrokes to change the width of a column to (say) 14 characters is:

/ W C S 14 (↵)

Notice when you point to a cell in column A, the entry contents include the current width display denoted by (F14).

As well as the command just used, (/ W C etc.), which controls the width of a single column, there is the 'global' version which applies generally or globally across the worksheet. This latter command (/ W G C etc.) controls the width of all columns whose widths have not been set individually by the / W C command.

Alternative: pointing and expanding the pointer

To illustrate the alternative way of working with 1-2-3 via arrow keys, we will Set the Column width by 'pointing' and 'expanding' the pointer, issuing commands without using the letter keys. Start with the pointer in column A and type:

/	to get the main menu of commands, namely:

Worksheet Range Copy Move File Print Graph Data System Quit

(↵)	to confirm the choice Worksheet
→ → →	to choose Column (from the Worksheet menu)
(↵)	to issue the command
(↵)	to choose Set-Width
→ → → → →	to choose the appropriate column width by 'expanding' the cell pointer to indicate the desired width
← ← ← ← ←	to return to the new setting of 14 spaces
(↵)	to enter the width setting

2.7 More on editing

As well as 'overtyping' an entry to correct a mistake, one of the special function keys, the (f2/Edit) key, can be used. The editing procedure is to point to the cell which needs correcting, press the Edit key, make corrections and lastly press Return to enter the corrected label. In making corrections, the horizontal arrow keys and the Delete character key may be required.

To illustrate some of the editing facilities, we will improve the labels in the worksheet, turning V into Variable, F into Fixed and changing the Profits label.

With the pointer over A4, press the edit key. Notice that the mode changes to EDIT and the cell entry, V Costs, appears on the input line with the flashing cursor.

Use the left arrow key to move the cursor to the left until it is positioned under the space between V and Costs as shown below:

'V_Costs

Type in 'ariable' (the letters only) to complete the label. Then press Return to enter the amended label.

Next amend the label in A5, F Costs, to read Fixed Costs, using the Edit key. Notice that when typed in, characters appear immediately to the left of the cursor position.

Now, to illustrate the Delete character key, let us change the label Profits to Profit. With the pointer on A6, press the Edit key. With the left arrow key, move the cursor under the 's' in Profits as shown below:

'Profits

Press the Delete character key to remove the 's'. Press Return to enter the label into cell A6.

Finally, to change the label into Quarterly Profit, press the Edit key, jump the cursor to the 'front' by pressing the Home key and then move one place to the right, as shown below:

'Profit

Now type in Quarterly and press Spacebar so that the label on the edit line is as shown below:

'Quarterly Profit

and press Return.

Change the label back to Profits before proceeding to the next Section. You may wish to correct other mistakes to practice using the Edit key.

2.8 Label display

You may have noticed that the labels entered into the worksheet are left-aligned. That is, they occupy the leftmost spaces of the cell (in contrast to the numeric values which are right-aligned). Point to any label cell, say A2 which contains the label Price. Look at the control panel at the top of the screen and notice that the entry starts with an apostrophe '. The 'label-prefix' character determines the alignment of the label within the cell. Unless instructed to the contrary, 1-2-3 aligns labels to the left, adding the ' prefix itself. The possibilities for label-prefixes are:

' apostrophe	left-aligned label
" double quote	right-aligned with one space left free
^ caret	centred label

You can change the format of a label or a range of labels either using the Edit key or using the Range Label command. For example, to change Profits from left to right-alignment, press the Edit key and move the cursor key to the beginning of the entry:

'Profits

You can do this in one jump if you press the Home key.

Press the Delete character key to remove the apostrophe and type the double quote, '', to enter the prefix for right-aligned labels. The input line should look like this:

''Profits

Press Return to enter the label.

The other approach is to use the command sequence:

/ R L	for the Range Label command
R	for Right-alignment and
A6 (↵)	to specify the cell.

Try aligning all the labels in column A, i.e. align the range A1.A6 to the right by typing:

/ R L R A1.A6 (↵)

Then for practice, change the format back to left alignment.

Notice also that to turn an expression such as 1985 or 2nd Quarter into a label as opposed to a value, you use a label-prefix, e.g. start the entry with the apostrophe key '.

2.9 More on formulae

So far the worksheet contains results for only one time period—for the first quarter of the year. Now, let us assume that the sales volume increases by 5 per cent each quarter. Let us start to build formulae for the second quarter.

One approach would be to enter the following formula in C1 by typing:

1.05*B1 (↵)	so that the entry in C1 is 5 per cent greater than that in B1.

If you dislike typing formulae, you can avoid some of the hassle by 'pointing' at the variables you want to insert in a formula rather than keying them in.

To see how this works, put the pointer over C1 and type:

1.05*	but don't press Return.

At this stage the flashing cursor on the control panel is waiting for your next input. Using the left arrow key move the cell pointer to B1 and watch what happens on the input line. B1 appears in the formula on the input line as the result of 'pointing' at cell B1. Notice that the mode indicator says POINT (as opposed to EDIT when the entry is being typed in).

Now press Return to enter the formula in C1.

Figure 2.8 shows the screen display at this stage of the modelling.

```
       A                     B          C
1  Sales Volume             100        105
2  Price                     30         ↑
3  Sales Revenue           3000       1.05*B1
4  Variable Costs          2100
5  Fixed Costs             1100
6  Profits                 -200
```

Figure 2.8 Sales growth in the second quarter

A further elaboration of the sales increase formula is worth exploring at this point. We have assumed that sales increase by 5 per cent or proportion .05 per quarter and have built this into the formula in C1. If we wish to explore the effect of different rates of increase, a preferable approach would be to construct the formula using a generalized figure for the rate. For example, as shown in Figure 2.9, the label Rate could be stored in A10 say and its value .05 keyed into B10. The formula in C1 would now be written as:

(1+B10)*B1

By changing the value in B10 from .05 to .1, .15, −0.1, etc., the effects of increases of 10 per cent, then 15 per cent, and then a decrease of 10 per cent can be modelled.

```
       A                     B          C
1  Sales Volume             100        105
2  Price                     30         ↑
3  Sales Revenue           3000     (1+B10)*B1
4  Variable Costs          2100
5  Fixed Costs             1100
6  Profits                 -200


10 Rate                    0.05
```

Figure 2.9 Alternative layout for sales growth

Notice the use of brackets in the formula. These ensure that the correct multiplier, 1+B10, is evaluated before multiplication takes place. It is good practice to get into the habit of using brackets in complicated formulae, to ensure the correct results. Notice also that the bracket key (is interpreted as the start of a value not a label.

2.10 Automatic recalculation

We will now see the advantages of keying in formulae as opposed to actual values for costs, profits, etc.

Move the cell pointer to B1, change the value for Sales Volume, for example to 200, press Return and watch the recalculation on the screen. Try several different values, e.g. in cell B1, type:

2000 (↵)

347.56 (↵)
600 (↵) etc. . . and finally

100 (↵)

Look at the way 1-2-3 instantaneously changes the corresponding values for Sales Revenue, Costs, and Profits.

Our worksheet is very small at this stage. Nevertheless you can anticipate how useful 1-2-3's rapid recalculation powers can be for a large worksheet.

2.11 Filing worksheets

It is most important to save your worksheet on disc from time to time. You may wish to stop at some intermediate point in developing a worksheet and turn to some other task. As with all computer work, it is extremely important to get into the habit of saving your work to disc regularly to guard against inadvertent errors. In addition, when you switch off your personal computer, all the information in the worksheet will be lost unless you have made a copy on disc. At the very least you must guard against possible disasters of losing your work through some fault of programming, e.g. you may inadvertently issue the Worksheet Erase command and lose the results of many hours of keying in formulae.

To save a 1-2-3 worksheet you will need a formatted disc for storing data. It is assumed in the following instructions that your 1-2-3 disc is in Drive A and your CM data disc in Drive B. It is also assumed that your copy of 1-2-3 is configured to save and retrieve files from Drive B. If this is not so, you may need to specify the Drive as well as the filename in the instructions given below.

Each worksheet you save to disc in 1-2-3 is stored in a worksheet 'file' and is given a 'filename' to identify it. Filenames may be up to 8 characters long but may only include alphanumeric characters and the underline character _, and should not have any spaces between characters. For example, MYDATA2 is an acceptable filename: MY DATA or DATA£6 are not.

Suppose we have chosen the filename MYDATA. When the spreadsheet is saved, 1-2-3 adds a file extension of the form .WK1 (WKS for Release 1 files), so that the full file specification including the path to the B Drive is:

B:\MYDATA.WK1

However if your copy of 1-2-3 has been correctly set up, with Drive B as the Startup Directory, it is only necessary to specify the filename MYDATA, not the Drive or the file extension.

The sequence of commands for saving a file is File followed by Save and then the filename. Therefore, to save your worksheet, type:

/ F — to choose File from the main command menu

S — to choose Save from the File menu

When prompted to 'Enter save file name' and shown the general specification: B:*.WK1, simply key in

MYDATA — or some other filename

(↵)   to make 1-2-3 save the file.

Watch the Drive B light come on to indicate that your worksheet file is being saved on disc.

If you get an ERROR message as you are trying to save a file, press Escape to cancel the error message. There are several possible explanations:

(i) Drive B may not be ready because it does not contain a disc or the door is not closed. If so, insert the CM disc, close the drive door and try again.

(ii) The Startup Directory may be specified as something other than the B drive. A quick solution is to change the 'current' directory to the B drive. To do this, use the command sequence / File Directory and specify the current directory as B:

Alternatively, refer to the Lotus tutorial and Reference Manual which give very clear instructions on specifying the Startup Directory to suit your particular computer configuration.

(iii) Your computer may not have a Drive B. Assuming 1-2-3 is on the hard disc, you should specify the Startup Directory or current directory as A: and place the CM disc in Drive A. Notice that in saving a file, when specifying the filename on the control panel, the Escape key can be used to erase any unwanted drive and directory designations.

To check that your worksheet has been satisfactorily saved, you may like to List the files currently saved on the data disc. Type:

/F L W   to List the Worksheet Files on disc

When the alphabetically listed filenames appear on screen, (CALLS, CTV, etc), point to MYDATA. Full details of the MYDATA file, the date and time when it was saved and its size (in bytes) are displayed on screen. Press Return to end the display. (If you do not see MYDATA, or the filename you chose, you must go through the steps to File Save once again.)

Once you are sure that your worksheet has been saved, you can Erase the Worksheet currently displayed on your screen and retrieve the copy filed on the data disc. Type:

/W E Y   to Erase the Worksheet

/F R   to Retrieve the file.

When prompted to 'Enter name of file to retrieve:', either type:

MYDATA (↵)   or whatever,

or point to the filename displayed on the control panel and press Return.

2.12 On-line help

Much of the detail in previous sections, for example, editing keys and label-prefix keys, is hard to remember, even at the end of this 'hands-on' session. Luckily, some help is always at hand if you keep your 1-2-3 disc available in the disc drive. Access to this 'help' facility is via the (f1/Help) key.

To illustrate its use, assume we have embarked on some editing so press the Edit key. However, in EDIT mode, we have forgotten how the various keys operate. One solution is to press the Help key. 1-2-3 responds by suspending the editing and displaying a screen of information, in this case about EDIT mode. Access to other related topics, Fixing Typing Mistakes, Indicator Modes, is possible using the arrow keys and pressing Return to choose a topic. Also there is a general Help Index which can be selected. At any point, you can return to your 1-2-3 worksheet by pressing Escape.

No matter what manipulations you are carrying out with 1-2-3, you have access to this 'on-line' help. In response to the Help key, 1-2-3 suspends whatever operation is in progress and provides some relevant information. Pressing Escape returns you to the manipulations in progress when Help was called for. At the very least, this reduces the amount you need to remember in working with 1-2-3.

When you have finished looking at the Help screens, you may wish to take a break from 1-2-3. To do this elegantly, you can use the Quit command. But note, 1-2-3 does not automatically 'save' your spreadsheet when you quit. You need to use / File Save (as was described in the previous section). If you do this, 1-2-3 will suggest the filename used previously (MYDATA) and you simply press Return to agree to this filename. You then choose Replace to overwrite the previous version of the file with the more recent version, and the file is saved to disc. (Alternatively if you wish to keep the old file, Cancel the command. A different filename will ensure that both the old and the more recent versions are preserved.) In this instance, you saved your worksheet before looking at the Help facility. So unless you have made any changes subsequently, you need not issue the File Save command before ending. In any case, you may prefer to proceed to Chapter 3.

Note: For reference, a datafile called MD2 (short for MYDATA Chapter 2) is included on your CM disc. It contains the MYDATA spreadsheet as it should appear at the conclusion of this chapter.

CHAPTER 3

Expanding the Worksheet

One of the most powerful features of 1-2-3 is the Copy command. This allows values and formulae to be duplicated rapidly in other parts of the worksheet, saving much repetitious typing.

Most of this chapter is devoted to explaining how the Copy command works. Although the command is easy to issue, planning for its efficient use can take a little more time.

Formulae are usually copied to groups of cells or 'cell ranges' which you need to know how to specify. In addition formulae can be copied from single cells or from groups of cells (if they form cell ranges).

In the copying formulae, 1-2-3 adjusts them according to their position in the spreadsheet. You need to know what adjustments 1-2-3 will make to any formulae.

You also need to learn how to write formulae to take advantage of 1-2-3's copying facility. This requires an understanding of the difference between 'relative' and 'absolute' cell addresses.

1-2-3 contains a range of other commands which help in manipulating and controlling the expanding spreadsheet. In this chapter, formatting commands for changing the way entries are displayed and worksheet commands for inserting rows and 'freezing' titles are explained.

1-2-3 has several built-in calculation routines called @. Of particular use is the SUM function which calculates the sum of row (or column) entries. A close relative is the AVG function which gives the average value of a list of entries. (The Reference Manual contains a complete list of these @ functions and the Help key allows you to explore what expressions are available.)

3.1 Cell ranges

In 1-2-3 terms, a cell range (or more simply a range) is a group of one or more cells in a rectangular block. At one extreme, a single cell can be a 'range' so can a row (or column) of adjacent cells. Figure 3.1 gives examples of groups of cells that qualify as ranges as well as examples of groups that do not.

In copying a formula to a group of 'destination' cells, 1-2-3 asks you to specify these cells in terms of a range. Most commonly, a range is defined by the addresses of two diagonally opposite corners of the range. For example, the range from column D to column M along the first row of the spreadsheet would be specified by typing:

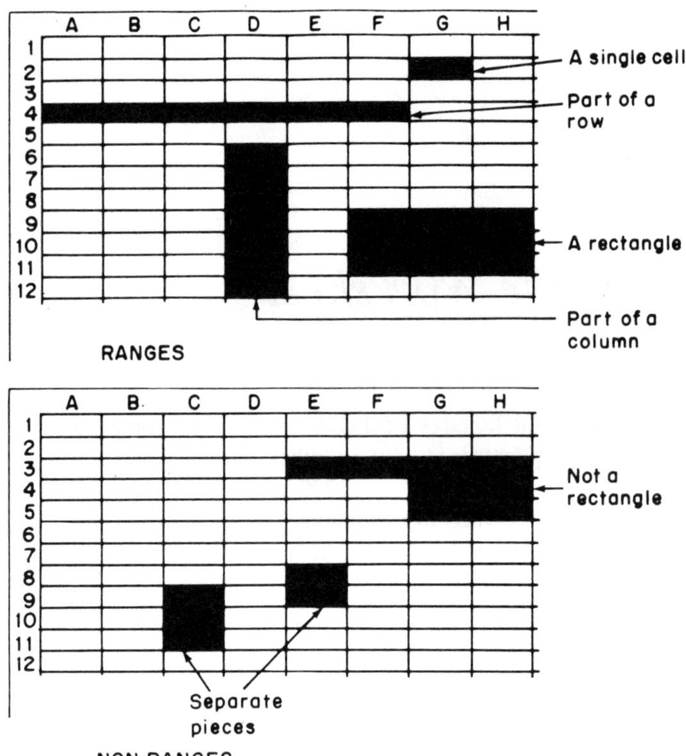

Figure 3.1 Ranges and non-ranges

D1.M1

with one or more full stops (or periods) separating the beginning and ending cells.

Other examples of range definitions are shown in Figure 3.2. Notice in particular that an individual cell, say D2, can be expressed in range form as D2.D2 or D2..D2. Although we shall not want to write a cell address in this way, 1-2-3 frequently uses this form for a single cell in prompts given in the control panel.

As with the writing of formulae in Section 2.9, you can reference the cells by typing in their addresses or by 'pointing' to them with the cell pointer.

3.2 Copying a single cell

The Copy command is the cleverest part of 1-2-3 and it can be used in many ways. We will illustrate some of this variety in expanding the simple worksheet developed in Chapter 2. At the end of that chapter, we had developed the formulae and values for the first quarter's profits. We will now make profit projections for the next 11 quarters.

If you are starting with an empty worksheet at this stage, it would be good practice to retrieve the file you saved at the end of Chapter 2. To do this, type:

/ to get the main command menu

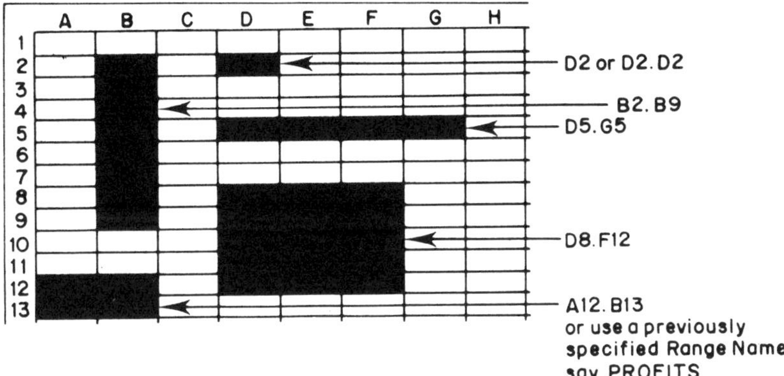

Figure 3.2 Range definitions

F R to choose File then Retrieve

MYDATA (↵) your file name (either type or 'point' to the filename).

(Note that ↵ is the symbol meaning 'press Enter' or 'press Return'.)

Make two amendments to the worksheet. Firstly, type the formula in C1 in its old form:

1.05*B1

Secondly, use the Range Erase command to blank out cells A10 and B10 if you still have the sales growth data stored there. That is, type:

/ R to choose a Range command

E A10.B10 (↵) to Erase cell range A10.B10.

Alternatively, if you do not have the file, retype the entries so that the screen display looks like Figure 3.3. (The formulae to be entered in cells B3, B4, and B6 are shown in the figure to the right of column B.)

```
        A                 B         C
1  Sales Volume          100       105  ← 1.05*B1
2  Price                  30
3  Sales Revenue        3000  ←    +B1*B2
4  Variable Costs       2100  ←    .7*B3
5  Fixed Costs          1100
6  Profits              -200  ←    +B3-B4-B5
```

Figure 3.3 Worksheet (MYDATA) saved at end of Chapter 2

Remember, in what follows that you can always escape from any mistakes or difficulties by pressing the Escape key a few times to get back to READY mode. If you do this, watch how 1-2-3 takes you back step by step through your previous choices. It is not always necessary to go right back to READY: often you can pick up the command sequence at some earlier stage.

First, you will learn how to copy a single value, then a single formula, then lastly a range of formulae in a single operation.

Copying a value

Let us suppose that the price (in B2) is not expected to change over the next 11 quarters. We therefore want to copy the price across the second row of the worksheet for 11 columns. To do this, put the pointer over the cell to be copied, B2, and type:

/ C to start the Copy command.

Notice that the control panel prompts you saying:

Enter range to copy FROM:B2 . . B2

The flashing cursor has moved into cell B2, waiting for you to confirm that B2 is the cell to copy FROM. So type:

(↵) to confirm that the contents of B2 are to be copied.

The control panel now tells you to:

Enter range to copy TO: B2

B2 is 1-2-3's suggested destination for copying the price—clearly not correct for the price is already entered in B2. Since we want to copy the price across the second row of the spreadsheet from column C to column M (the twelfth quarter), overwrite 1-2-3's suggestion by typing:

C2.M2 (↵)

The copying takes place almost instantaneously. To check the results, move the pointer over the cells in row 2. You should find that the value 30 has been entered in the cells from C2 across to M2.

Copying a formula

Suppose sales are expected to grow by 5 per cent, not only for the second quarter, but for the third quarter and so on over a period of three years. That is, the growth is 'compounded' over the twelve quarters, sales in any one quarter being 5 per cent higher than in the previous quarter. We can model this growth by entering the formula, 1.05*C1 into D1, 1.05*D1 into E1, etc. across to M1. Notice that the structure of the formulae is the same from quarter to quarter; all that changes is the cell address. The Copy command in 1-2-3 works in just this manner. Any cell reference in a formula is interpreted 'relative' to position when the formula is copied. So if the formula in C1, namely, 1.05*B1, is Copied using 1-2-3 into D1, E1,. . . , up to M1, i.e. across range D1.M1, the resulting sales growth should be modelled as required.

To do this, put the pointer on C1 and type:

/ C to start the Copy command.

The top line of the control panel shows the formula to be copied (1.05*B1). 1-2-3 prompts you saying:

Enter range to copy FROM:C1 . . C1

The flashing cursor has moved into cell C1, waiting for you to confirm that the formula in C1 is indeed the formula to be copied. So type:

(↵) to confirm that the formula in C1 is to be copied.

The input line now instructs you to:

Enter range to copy TO: C1

C1 is 1-2-3's suggestion for copying the formula—clearly not appropriate since the formula is already in C1. Since we want to copy to range D1.M1, we could simply type in the range D1.M1. As an alternative, we will point and 'expand' the pointer to specify where the formula is to be copied.

Point to cell D1, i.e. with the right arrow key, put the pointer on D1. D1 appears on the control panel to replace C1.

Press the full stop (or period) key to 'anchor the pointer'. The control panel responds with D1 . . D1.

Point to cell M1 with the right arrow key. (Watch the pointer 'expand' as it is moved across to cell M1. The highlighted range of cells show where the formula for sales volume is to be copied.) When the pointer reaches M1, the control panel reads D1 . . M1.

Press Return to enter this range, D1 . . M1.

Again, the copying occurs almost instantaneously. The results for the first few quarters are shown in Figure 3.4.

	A	B	C	D	E	F	G
1	Sales Volume	100	105	110.25	115.7625	121.5506	127.6281
2	Price	30	30	30	30	30	30
3	Sales Revenue	3000					
4	Variable Costs	2100					
5	Fixed Costs	1100					
6	Profits	-200					

Figure 3.4 Some results after copying the sales growth formula

Summary of the copying command

(i) Put the pointer over the cell with the formula for copying—here it was C1.

(ii) Type / C to start Copying the formula.

(iii) Type (↵) to confirm that the range for copying FROM is C1 and then enter the range of cells for copying TO, namely. D1.M1, the defining cells for the range separated by a full stop. Either key in the cell range or 'point', by anchoring and expanding the pointer.

(iv) Lastly, press RETURN.

Now move the pointer to see the effect of copying the formula in C1. Notice the numbers displayed in the worksheet and the underlying formulae shown on the control panel. (Some of these formulae are shown in Figure 3.5.)

As outlined earlier, in copying the formula in cell C1, 1-2-3 has adjusted it, relative to position. This adjustment of formulae is discussed more fully in Section 3.4.

	A	B	C	D	E	F	G
1	Sales Volume	100	1.05*B1	1.05*C1	1.05*D1	1.05*E1	1.05*F1
2	Price	30	30	30	30	30	30
3	Sales Revenue	3000					
4	Variable Costs	2100					
5	Fixed Costs	1100					
6	Profits	-200					

Figure 3.5 Formulae showing how the copy command works

3.3 Copying a range of formulae

The Copy command saves a lot of work in terms of typing in formulae. It can frequently be used to great effect to copy several formulae in the same operation. The formulae to be copied are specified as a range. This is illustrated by copying the formulae for Sales Revenue, Fixed and Variable Costs, and Profits across the twelve quarters in one copying operation. The entries in rows 3, 4 and 6 will be evaluated from formulae which are identical in structure to those in B3, B4 and B6, e.g. Sales Revenue is always the product of Sales Volume (row 1) and Price (row 2). The only difference is that cells addressed in the formulae are relative to position.

In telling 1-2-3 what ranges of cells are to be copied 'from' and copied 'to', the specification can either be keyed in (EDIT mode) or 'pointed at' by anchoring and expanding the pointer (POINT mode). You should choose whichever method suits you best.

Start as if the formula for Sales Revenue (in B3) is the one to be copied, i.e. with the pointer over B3 (and the formula +B1*B2 on the control panel). Then type:

/ C   to start the Copy command

In response to 1-2-3's request:

Enter range to copy FROM:B3 . . B3

type the range of formulae to be copied, namely:

B3.B6 (↵)   This is the EDIT mode approach.

(Alternatively, anchor the pointer (with a full stop) and expand it to B6, until the control panel shows range B3 . . B6, then press Return. This is the POINT mode approach.)

When 1-2-3 prompts you saying

Enter range to copy TO:B3

specify the destination range for copying, namely:

C3.M3

either by keying in or by pointing. Then watch 1-2-3 do the copying. Notice that it is only necessary to specify the 'copying range' for the first formula. The resultant

Nevertheless, some investment of time must be made in learning the basic rudiments. The point is that the spreadsheet solution to a problem might take longer the first time than simply using paper and pencil. However, if the same piece of analysis tends to crop up repeatedly, a generalized worksheet (called a 'template') can be developed for the problem. This can be used repeatedly in the future.

To solve problems in a spreadsheet environment, the user sometimes needs to know more about the calculation routines than is the case when using specialist computer software. For example, in calculating a correlation coefficient or estimating the seasonal factors for some sales data, it is necessary to know the formulae to use with 1-2-3: whereas with a specialist statistical package these quantities would be standard output. Sometimes the knowledge required to implement a technique with 1-2-3 helps in clarifying the technique: at other times, the intricacies of the calculations overwhelm the user with unnecessary detail. It is important to be clear where spreadsheet modelling is appropriate and where better returns are to be had from either a specialist package or a more conventional programming approach. There are also the 'structured' financial modelling languages which include more versatile ranges of calculation procedures than the spreadsheets, for example goal seeking and simulation procedures.

Turning to the integrated software like 1-2-3, this has the additional advantage that the user can switch from business modelling to graphics and back. This avoids the irritation of having to transfer data from one application to another encountering the computer's operating system en route. Also, the same procedures and commands tried and learnt in the spreadsheet context can be applied to database operations.

Speed and ease of use make for an exploratory, investigative form of analysis. It means analysis will be tried rather than ignored, simply because it is so easy to do and painless to carry out.

1.4 The objectives of this book

This book has been written to meet the requirements of managers who wish to use Lotus 1-2-3 in their business activities. It assumes no previous use of spreadsheet programs but it does assume that the reader has some knowledge of management techniques—particularly simple accountancy.

Perhaps the only drawback of 1-2-3 as compared with the earlier spreadsheets is that it is no longer possible to exploit its full potential by jumping straight in and picking up techniques as you go along. This is recognized by 1-2-3's authors who provide an introductory tutorial as part of the software package. There is also a comprehensive well written Reference Manual which is an excellent source of information. However, despite these aids, there remains a problem in learning how best to apply 1-2-3 to real-life business problems. This is because the emphasis in the Reference Manual is on describing and documenting commands and facilities rather than developing potential applications.

Creative Modelling with 1-2-3 takes the alternative approach of focusing throughout on applications and introducing 1-2-3 techniques as they arise in the solution of a particular problem. Thus throughout the book, the reader is invited to consider the '1-2-3 solution' to a series of practical and familiar management analyses.

As mentioned previously, 1-2-3 has been sold mostly into the financial planning market. However, it can be applied to many other problems. It should be viewed as the latest professional analysis tool in a series that starts with log tables and proceeds through slide rules and pocket calculators to electronic spreadsheets.

1.5 Scope and contents

The purpose of the book is to get you, the reader, to start using Lotus 1-2-3 as soon as possible. The book is written for you to read as you sit at your personal computer building a spreadsheet model. The descriptions of techniques are intended to be followed step by step and the developing spreadsheet is illustrated at each stage.

Chapters 2 to 4 concentrate on spreadsheet modelling and illustrate the main commands and facilities. The modelling context is the preparation of quarterly profit forecasts for the next three years from estimates of future sales levels of some product.

Chapter 2 shows how to model profits for the first quarter and introduces you to the basic skills of moving round the spreadsheet, making entries and issuing 1-2-3 commands.

The important Copy command is described in Chapter 3. It is used to expand the spreadsheet to give profit forecasts over twelve quarters. Different ways of formulating the relationships in the model are discussed, since these have implications for the way formulae are copied across the twelve quarters. Also, the Range commands for formatting areas of the spreadsheet are introduced. These formatting commands enable the spreadsheet entries to be displayed in different forms, for example, values can be displayed as currencies, and rates as percentages.

Chapter 4 is concerned with designing spreadsheets so that they can be used for sensitivity analysis; that is, seeing how sensitive profits are to changes in assumed values (such as sales levels).

Chapter 5 describes printing and producing various kinds of graph. Clearly, it is important to get hard copy of the important calculations and it is sometimes useful to get a listing of cell formulae to help in documenting a spreadsheet model. Often the main features in a spreadsheet can be demonstrated most vividly with a graph.

The remaining chapters of the book cover a variety of different applications. The book assumes that you have mastered the basic techniques of 1-2-3 by this stage and it suggests some promising areas for applying spreadsheet modelling.

The techniques mastered in Chapters 2 and 3 can be used in database applications. The rows of the spreadsheet can be used as individual records, for example as a set of personnel records. In Chapter 6, the special Data commands are described. These are used to sort the records in various ways and search out groups of records satisfying certain criteria.

Chapter 7 looks at the organization and summary of large sets of data, using simple statistical analysis. 1-2-3 has several special functions which calculate averages and measures of variability and a command for getting frequency distributions. Chapter 7 also explores some theoretical distributions to see how well these models fit actual observations. Some knowledge of elementary statistics is helpful in understanding one or two of the topics covered in this chapter.

Chapter 8 suggests how 1-2-3 can assist in the analysis of statistical data such as market research findings and sample surveys. It describes the special statistical calculation routines which can be used on the back of database procedures. Also covered are methods for evaluating findings for separate subgroups and 1-2-3's facilities for cross tabulating the data.

Chapter 9 looks at the relationships between different factors (or variables) and introduces some statistical methods of analysis. 1-2-3's regression facility is explained and the procedures for carrying out correlation and regression analysis are described. The ideas behind the techniques are explained in layman's terms. However, as with Chapter 7, some acquaintance with elementary statistics helps in getting the most out of this chapter.

Various approaches to sales forecasting are described in Chapter 10. With 1-2-3, it is relatively easy to smooth sales data either using moving averages or exponential smoothing. It is also possible to estimate the seasonal factors in sales data with a strong seasonal pattern.

Chapter 11 discusses financial planning models in some depth. Two different planning models are considered and many modelling techniques are described. The first model is a slightly more complicated version of the profit planning example used as the vehicle for learning 1-2-3. The second model, the so-called 'budget worksheet', has helped many non-accountants gain a useful insight into the relationship between the Balance Sheet and the Profit and Loss Account. The application highlights a valuable model for planning and sensitivity analysis.

The final chapter explores the concept of discounted cashflow. 1-2-3's useful special functions for calculating the net present value and internal rate of return are explained fully. Their use is demonstrated in an example concerning investment appraisal.

The sequence of the book is important, in that later chapters build on knowledge gained in earlier ones. If you have never used a spreadsheet, you will need to work steadily through the first four chapters. If you have used VisiCalc or a similar package, you can skim through Chapter 2, but you will need to read about the Copy and Range commands in Chapter 3, the Data Table facilities in Chapter 4 and the Graph commands in Chapter 5. If you are familiar with 1-2-3, you may wish to skip or skim the earlier chapters, perhaps starting to look at the applications in Chapter 6 onwards.

The text concentrates on applying 1-2-3 to problems and the use of certain commands and functions to achieve the objectives of the analysis. It does not aim to provide comprehensive documentation of every command and every facility in 1-2-3. The excellent 1-2-3 Reference Manual fulfils this role more than adequately at present. No assumption is made that you have read the Reference Manual but you will need to refer to it from time to time. It is an extremely well written work of reference.

Lotus 1-2-3 is available on a variety of microcomputers. The commands are given in more or less the same manner apart from the fact that certain keys are given different names on the different machines. In the text, the IBM PC, AT key names are given. These naming differences are only relevant in Chapter 2 when the special keys for 1-2-3 are discussed. Any ambiguity can be resolved by looking at the keyboard diagrams supplied by Lotus 1-2-3 with its software.

As your proficiency with 1-2-3 grows, you will want to work on some larger models or sets of data. To reduce the time spent keying data into your worksheet, some of these models are provided on the disc that accompanies the text. This disc (referred to in the text as the CM disc) is formatted for use on the IBM PC. To avoid accidents, you are advised to make a copy of the CM disc, retaining the Master disc as a backup. To do this, you need to refer to the documentation on your computer and its operating system (called DOS). The relevant procedures are those for disc-copying or copying files.

It is also assumed that you have performed the disc installation procedure described in your 1-2-3 documentation: that is, you have configured your copy of 1-2-3 for your particular combination of disc drives and printer. In particular, it is assumed that 1-2-3 will 'look' to a particular drive or directory to input and output data files—the 'Startup

Directory'. In the following text, the Startup Directory is assumed to be the B drive. This preserves the convention of working with the program disc on Drive A and the data disc on Drive B.

You can learn to use 1-2-3 in several different ways all involving some investment of time. If your personal computer and 1-2-3 are to hand, you can start straight away by turning to Chapter 2. If you prefer, you can first work through the Lotus tutorial (included in the 1-2-3 package) which teaches you some of the basics. When you feel ready, turn to Chapter 2 and start spreadsheeting!

CHAPTER 2

Simple 1-2-3 Worksheets

The chapter starts with a brief look at your keyboard to ensure that you can find the vital keys needed in running 1-2-3. The layout of the 1-2-3 worksheet is explained and the screen display in interpreted.

You start to get 'hands-on' experience with 1-2-3 by moving the cell pointer around the worksheet and issuing commands.

To use 1-2-3 for problem solving, you need to learn how to enter numerical values and labels into the spreadsheet and how to correct mistakes. You also need to know how to write formulae using relationships between cells. To increase your speed in manipulating 1-2-3 worksheets, you must learn to 'point' and to 'anchor and expand' the pointer much as you would point with your pencil to entries in a worksheet on paper.

Lastly worksheets have to be 'filed' (or saved to disc). It is important to learn how to do this and how to retrieve spreadsheets for further use.

2.1 Your keyboard

Before starting to learn 1-2-3, it is important to know the location and function of several vital keys. The layout of the keyboard for the IBM PC is shown in Figure 2.1 together with a brief introduction to the function of several special keys. To start, without pressing any keys, make sure you know the position of the following keys on your keyboard:

(i) Four arrow keys →, ←, ↑, ↓
These keys move the pointer around the worksheet. They are usually positioned to the right hand side of the typewriter section of the keyboard.

(ii) RETURN or ENTER
This key tells 1-2-3 you have selected a command or finished keying in an entry. It does a job similar to the 'carriage return' key on an electric typewriter: hence its name and the symbol on the IBM PC, (↵).

To simplify matters, the key is always referred to as Return in the following text. Often, the notation (↵) will be used as shorthand for 'press Return'.

(iii) SHIFT
As on a normal typewriter, this key produces capital (or 'upper case') letters and the upper symbols on the non-letter keys.

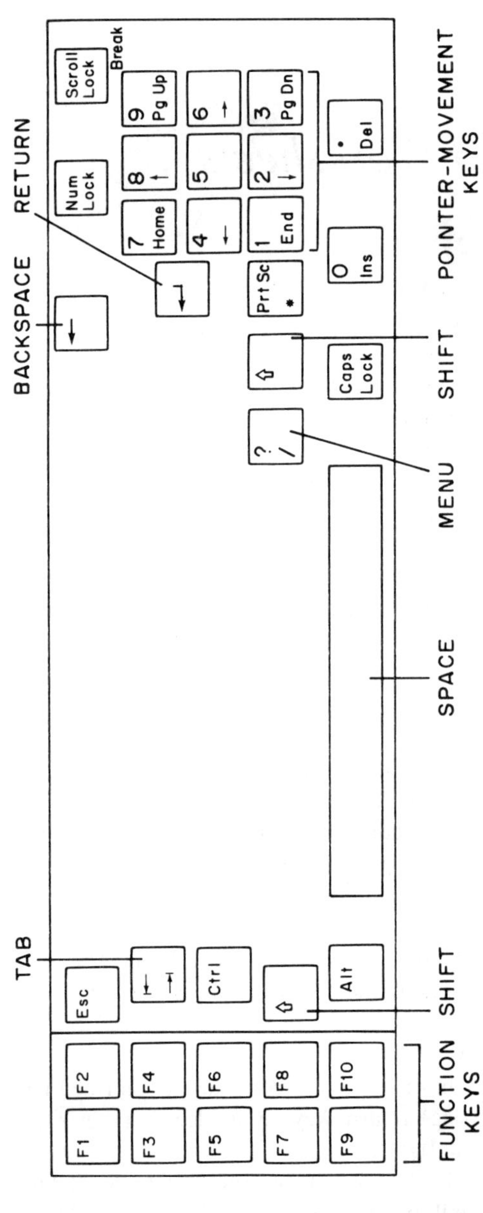

Figure 2.1 IBM PC keyboard

(iv) ESCAPE
This tells 1-2-3 to reverse its last operation or in other words to 'go back a step'. If pressed several times, Escape (ESC) returns you to 'READY' mode. In addition, if a flashing ERROR message occurs, pressing Escape will cancel the error message and return you to READY mode.

(v) BACKSPACE
This erases the last character typed or, when pointing, frees the pointer from a previous setting and returns it to its original location.

(vi) The slash key /
This is referred to as the Menu key as it gives access to the main 1-2-3 menu of commands. It is used to start a 1-2-3 command sequence.

(vii) * (asterisk) and / (slash) are used for multiply and divide respectively.

There are also the 'function keys' for which a plastic template is provided by Lotus to indicate their particular function in the 1-2-3 environment. For example, the fifth one, denoted (f5/GoTo) jumps the pointer to a specific cell in the worksheet.

The name and facility offered by each of the function keys will be described as the need to use them arises. They are summarized for reference in Figure 2.2 which also includes other special keys and key combinations.

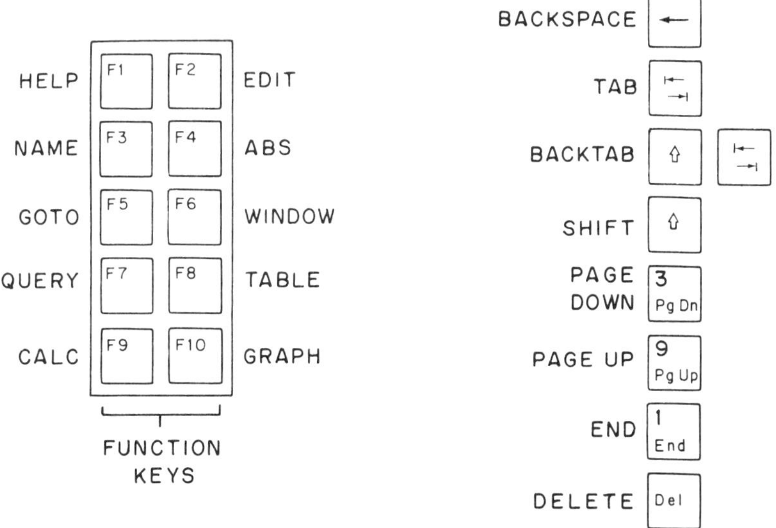

Figure 2.2 Function keys and other special keys

2.2 Window on the worksheet

After loading 1-2-3, the initial screen display should look like Figure 2.3, the upper illustration.

The major part of the display is the worksheet itself, devoid of any entries at this stage. The worksheet can be thought of as a rectangular grid with rows and columns intersecting

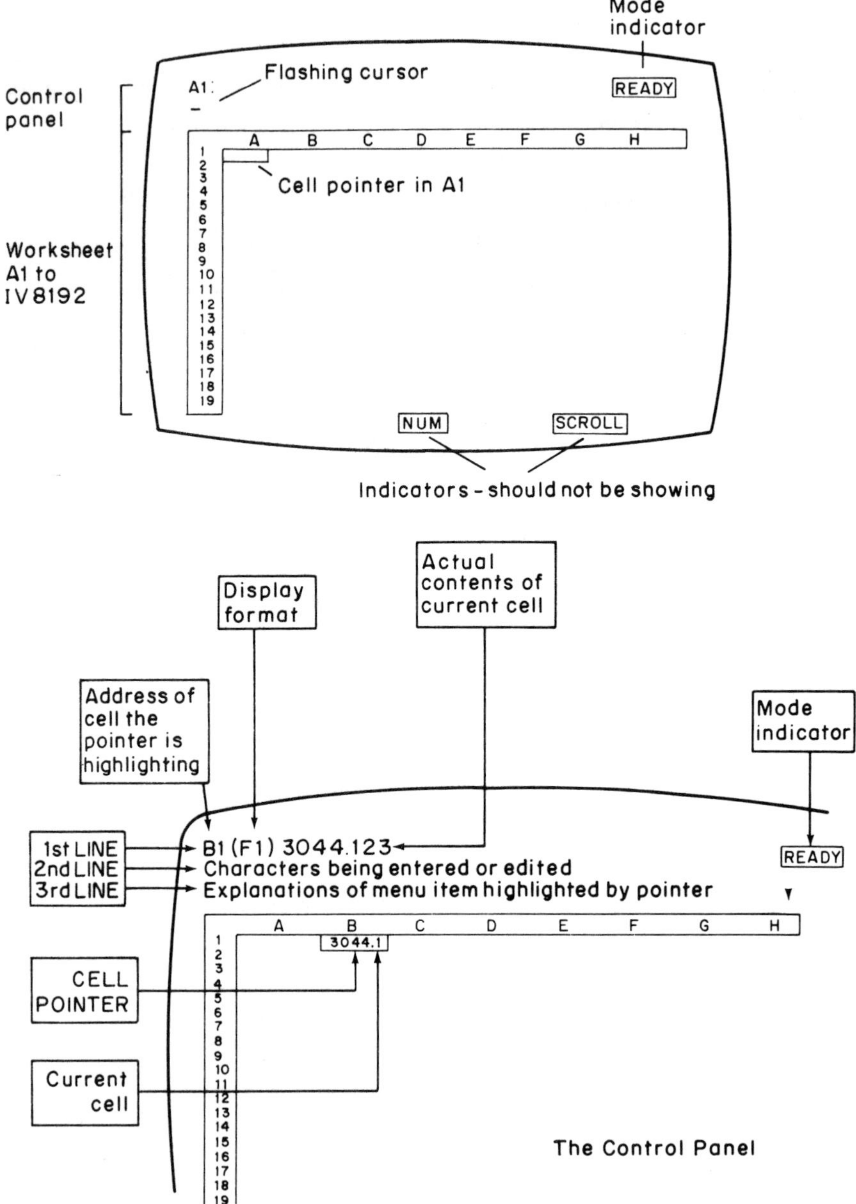

Figure 2.3 Screen display—control panel after use

to give many small rectangles called cells. Rows are numbered 1, 2, 3,. . . and columns labelled A, B, C,. . . Z, AA, AB,. . . The screen acts like a window displaying only a small part of the worksheet at any time. At this stage, it is displaying only the top left hand corner of a much bigger worksheet.

Each cell in the worksheet has a unique reference (its address) consisting of its column and row coordinates, e.g. A3, D7, M26, AG31,. . .. Notice that the column marker is always given first, as in chess. Information entered into the cells can be text ('labels'), numbers ('values'), or formulae which can be either text or values. The contents of cells can be used in formulae by means of their cell addresses as will be explained later in the chapter.

At the top of the screen, above the border of letters A, B, C,. . . is a special display area called the control panel. This area shows what is currently happening in the worksheet, e.g. the entries being keyed in, the 1-2-3 commands in progress, etc. Currently, the flashing 'cursor' in the top left hand cell and the 'mode' indicator on the right hand side indicate that 1-2-3 is READY for us to take action of some kind.

On first loading 1-2-3, the top left hand cell in the worksheet (address A1) has a rectangular highlight (the cell 'pointer') over it. Notice that address A1 is shown in the top left hand position of the control panel above the worksheet. In working on the spreadsheet, this pointer can be moved around to other cells. Once positioned over a particular cell, information keyed will be entered into this cell. (If we compare 1-2-3 with the 'paper and pencil' spreadsheet, the pointer is the electronic equivalent of the position of your pencil.)

Having examined the worksheet and control panel layout, we are now ready to start interacting with 1-2-3. In doing so, it is a good idea to watch the screen display (rather than concentrate exclusively on the keyboard). This is because 1-2-3 'prompts' you step by step via the control panel so that you are rarely in doubt as to what to do next.

Note: For 1-2-3 to work properly, the Num and Scroll Lock keys should not be 'on'. If your screen display says 'NUM' or 'SCROLL' press the corresponding key to remove the message from the screen.

2.3 Moving the cell pointer

The four arrow keys move the cell pointer around the spreadsheet—in single moves if the arrow keys are pressed lightly, in a continuous movement if the arrow key is held down. As the pointer reaches the edge of the screen, the window moves with the pointer so that other areas of the spreadsheet are displayed.

Try moving the cell pointer horizontally pressing the right hand arrow several times. If you have problems moving the pointer, make sure that your mode indicator says READY. If not, press the Escape key once or more to return to READY mode. Now hold the arrow key down to speed up the process. Now try moving the cell pointer up and down the screen using the 'up' and 'down' arrow keys. The program beeps at you if you hit one of the boundaries of the spreadsheet.

Adjacent to the arrow keys are the 'Page Up' and 'Page Down' keys (denoted Pg Up and Pg Dn). A 1-2-3 'page' consists of a block of cells of the size of the screen display. Pressing one or other of these keys makes the pointer 'jump' to the next page, i.e. the next block of rows in a vertical direction.

The equivalent key for jumping from page to page in the horizontal direction is the Tab key (or the Shift key together with the Tab key). This key is denoted ⇆ on the IBM PC.

Experiment with the 'End' key situated adjacent to the pointer movement keys. The screen indicator END toggles on and off as the End key is pressed. Press End followed by the down arrow key to get rapidly to the bottom boundary of the worksheet. The End key coupled with one of the arrow keys can be used for 'big' jumps in this way.

Experiment to see the size of the spreadsheet. How far can you move or jump the cell pointer horizontally? How far does the worksheet stretch vertically? Notice that the address of the current pointer position is always shown on the top line of the control panel.

Finally to return to the top left hand corner of the worksheet, cell A1, press the Home key. This is usually the fastest way of returning the pointer to cell A1 in a large spreadsheet.

The (f5/GoTo) key

Rather than move step by step around the spreadsheet, it is also possible to 'jump' to a specific cell by means of the GoTo key. This is the special function key, f5, which will be denoted by (f5) below to indicate 'press f5'.

Start with the pointer on A1 in READY mode. To move to cell M56, press the (f5/GoTo) key and then type in the address M56 followed by Return as follows:

(f5) M56 (↵)

where (↵) is a 'shorthand' way of writing 'press Return' or 'press Enter'. Notice what happens to the screen at each stage. On pressing the GoTo key, the second line (the 'input' line) of the control panel reads:

Enter address to go to: A1

and the mode indicator says POINT. Type M56 and watch this address appear on the input line. The adjacent flashing cursor tells you that 1-2-3 is waiting for some input from you. On pressing Return, the second line of the control panel goes blank and the pointer jumps to cell M56. The mode is now READY (for your next action).

Practice moving the pointer using the GoTo key and the arrow keys. See how the screen acts as a window displaying only a small part of the 1-2-3 worksheet.

Try entering the word Lotus in a number of positions. Use the keyboard as a normal typewriter. To get the capital L for Lotus, hold down the Shift key and then press the L key. On completing the word Lotus, enter it into the cell by pressing Return. Use the pointer movement keys or the (f5/GoTo) key to move to another cell and enter Lotus again. If you encounter any difficulty, get back into READY mode by pressing the Escape key one or more times.

Finally press the Home key to return to the top left hand corner of the worksheet.

2.4 Commands: erasing the spreadsheet

The next step is to start building a small spreadsheet. However, to ensure that we start with a 'clean slate', we need to clear out or 'erase' any unwanted entries. To do this, we use a simple sequence of 1-2-3 commands to achieve a 'Worksheet Erase'. Before carrying this out, we shall look at the way commands work in general.

To issue any 1-2-3 command, you start by pressing the slash key, /, noticing that on some keyboards you may also need to hold down the Shift key to obtain /. On pressing /, a command 'menu' is shown on the second line of the control panel. The menu includes options such as 'Worksheet', 'Copy', 'File', 'Quit' and one of the options is highlighted, with brief details of the option set out on the line below. The highlight (or 'menu pointer') can be moved to other options using the arrow keys. To issue the command which is highlighted, you simply press Return. This often leads to a second menu where the procedure is similar. Alternatively, you can issue a command from a menu by keying the first letter of the command.

Let us try to issue the command sequence to Erase the Worksheet. (If difficulties arise in what follows, you can always 'jump' out of the command sequence by pressing Escape one or more times until the mode indicator returns to READY.) To start issuing a command, the mode indicator must be showing READY. If not, press Escape once or more until the mode is READY.

The steps are:

(i) Press the slash key /
Notice that the mode indicator has changed from READY to MENU.

(ii) Look at the second line of the control panel. 1-2-3 prompts you with a list of the ten possible commands at this stage:

Worksheet Range Copy Move File Print Graph Data System Quit

The menu pointer (or highlight) is currently over the Worksheet command and below it on the third line is a list of the options on the Worksheet menu, namely:

Global, Insert, Delete, Column, Erase, Titles, Window, Status, Page

You can issue a command in 1-2-3 in two ways: either by keying in the first letter of the required command (here W for Worksheet) or by moving the menu pointer until it highlights the required choice and then pressing Return. You move the menu pointer with the horizontal arrow keys.

Try moving the highlight noticing how the third line of the control panel changes, at each stage listing the option(s) associated with each command.

Put the pointer back over Worksheet and press Return. (Alternatively, type W—upper or lower case is immaterial—but do not press Return after the 'W'.)

(iii) Now the second line reads:

Global Insert Delete Column Erase Titles Window Status Page

and since the highlight is over the Global option, the third line explains that the purpose of this is to

Set worksheet settings.

However, the option we want is 'Erase' so move the highlight over Erase and press Return (or press the 'E' key—upper or lower case), to get the next prompt from 1-2-3:

No Yes
Do not erase the worksheet; return to READY mode

Move the menu pointer over Yes (or press the 'Y' key to say Yes to 1-2-3)

and the current worksheet is erased.

When you are familiar with 1-2-3 and the keyboard, you will probably find using keystrokes is a faster way of issuing commands than pointing with the arrow keys. For example, to Erase the Worksheet, the sequence of keystrokes explained above is simply:

/W E Y

Notice that it is not necessary to remember these keys since 1-2-3 prompts you at each stage. Also, it is immaterial whether lower or upper case letter keys are used.

2.5 Typing entries into the spreadsheet

We will now start building a small worksheet to illustrate how data is entered and manipulated in 1-2-3.

Two types of entry will be made—'labels', which are non-numeric (most often text) and 'values', which are essentially numeric. It is usually not necessary to tell 1-2-3 which kind of entry is being made. If the first keystroke is a letter of the alphabet, 1-2-3 assumes that the entry is a label and the mode indicator displays the message LABEL: if it is a number or an arithmetic sign such as + or − or an opening bracket, (, 1-2-3 assumes that a value is being entered, and the indicator shows VALUE. There are ways of getting round this as we shall see.

For the labels, you may wish to use the Shift key to get capitals for reasons of appearance, but this is of no consequence in the operation of 1-2-3. It is also unimportant whether you refer to cells using capital letters or not, e.g. both A1 and a1 refer to the same cell.

Our illustrative worksheet takes the form of a simple projection of sales, costs, and profits derived from a single product over twelve quarters. Figure 2.4 shows part of the worksheet as it will look when you have completed it. However, to start at the beginning. . .

Quarter	1	2	3	4	5	6
Sales Volume	100	105	110	116	122	128
Sales Revenue	3,000	3,150	3,308	3,473	3,647	3,829
Variable Costs	2,100	2,205	2,315	2,431	2,553	2,680
Fixed Costs	1,100	1,100	1,100	1,100	1,100	1,100
Profits	(200)	(155)	(108)	(58)	(6)	49

Planning	Values
Sales Growth	5.0%
Price	30
Cost of GS	70%
Fixed Costs	1100

Figure 2.4 Completed worksheet—first six quarters

Suppose the sales volume for product ABC in the first quarter is expected to be 100 units and the price per unit is £30. Each unit costs £21 to make, so variable costs represent

values should tie up with those in Figure 3.6. Notice that the fixed costs get copied as a constant.

	A	B	C	D	E	F	G
1	Sales Volume	100	105	110.25	115.7625	121.5506	127.6281
2	Price	30	30	30	30	30	30
3	Sales Revenue	3000	3150	3307.5	3472.875	3646.518	3828.844
4	Variable Costs	2100	2205	2315.25	2431.012	2552.563	2680.191
5	Fixed Costs	1100	1100	1100	1100	1100	1100
6	Profits	-200	-155	-107.75	-58.1375	-6.04437	48.65340

	A	H	I	J	K	L	M
1	Sales Volume	134.0095	140.7100	147.7455	155.1328	162.8894	171.0339
2	Price	30	30	30	30	30	30
3	Sales Revenue	4020.286	4221.301	4432.366	4653.984	4886.683	5131.018
4	Variable Costs	2814.200	2954.910	3102.656	3257.789	3420.678	3591.712
5	Fixed Costs	1100	1100	1100	1100	1100	1100
6	Profits	106.0860	166.3903	229.7098	296.1953	366.0051	439.3054

Figure 3.6 Results for 12 quarters after copying

3.4 Formulae—relative and absolute addressing

At the end of Section 3.2, we made the point that in copying formulae, 1-2-3 adjusts them 'relative to position'. For example, the formula for Sales Revenue, +B1*B2 in cell B3 becomes +C1*C2 when it is copied into cell C3, etc. So in copying the B3 entry across row 3 of the worksheet, the formula entered into a particular cell is the product of the entry two rows above and the entry one row above.

Sometimes, we do not want cell addresses changed relative to position. It would be more efficient to hold the price in one location (e.g. cell B2) rather than duplicate the value across the second row. The Sales Revenue formulae in the cells of row 3 would always refer to B2 for the price but look to the entry two rows above for Sales Volume.

We can achieve this kind of copying with 1-2-3 if the price cell B2 is given its 'absolute' address in the Sales Revenue formulae. That is, we write B2 as $B$2 so that the formula in B3 becomes:

+B1*$B$2

When 1-2-3 copies this formula across row 3, $B$2 will always take the value contained in cell B2 whereas the sales volume (B1) will be copied relative to position.

Let us try this in the worksheet. First, we need to clear out the contents of cells C2 to M3 using the Range Erase command. Next, the new version of the Sales Revenue formula is entered into B3. Lastly, the formula is copied into cells C3 to M3. So the steps are:

(i) To Erase the cell Range C2.M3, start with the pointer on C2 and type:

/ R E C2.M3 (↵)

(ii) Edit or re-enter the formula for Sales Revenue in cell B3, so that it becomes:

+B1*$B$2

The worksheet looks like Figure 3.7 at this stage.

	A	B	C	D	E	F	G
1	Sales Volume	100	105	110.25	115.7625	121.5506	127.6281
2	Price	30					
3	Sales Revenue	3000					
4	Variable Costs	2100	0	0	0	0	0
5	Fixed Costs	1100	1100	1100	1100	1100	1100
6	Profits	-200	-1100	-1100	-1100	-1100	-1100

Figure 3.7 Worksheet with changed formula for Sales Revenue

(iii) Copy the formula to cell range C3 to M3, i.e. with the pointer on cell B3, type:

/ C (↵) to Copy FROM B3

C3.M3 (↵) TO cell range C3.M3.

Moving the pointer, look at the formulae in row 3. Because B2 was referred to by its absolute address ($B$2), it has been copied unchanged in the formula across row 3. The results are shown in Figure 3.8. The Profit figures are of course unchanged, since we merely changed the method of copying a formula.

	A	B	C	D	E	F	G
1	Sales Volume	100	105	110.25	115.7625	121.5506	127.6281
2	Price	30					
3	Sales Revenue	3000	3150	3307.5	3472.875	3646.518	3828.844
4	Variable Costs	2100	2205	2315.25	2431.012	2552.563	2680.191
5	Fixed Costs	1100	1100	1100	1100	1100	1100
6	Profits	-200	-155	-107.75	-58.1375	-6.04437	48.65340

Figure 3.8 Results when price (B2) is 'absolutely' addressed ($B$2)

Strictly speaking, it would have been sufficient to use the 'mixed' address $B2 in the copying operation above. Column B is absolutely addressed, whereas row 2 is relatively addressed. The following examples, which relate to a formula in cell C8, say, try to make the reason for this clear.

(i) Relative
In the formula +B*B2 in cell C8, the 'B2' term really means 'the value six rows above and one column to the left'.

(ii) Mixed
In the formula +B1*$B2 in cell C8, the '$B2' means 'the value in column B six rows above'.

(iii) Absolute
In the formula +B1*$B$2, the '$B$2' means 'the value in cell B2' irrespective of where the formula is positioned in the spreadsheet.

So in copying the formula containing B2 for Sales Revenue across the row immediately below, the mixed address $B2 would be adequate. In this case, the row position of the formula relative to the row position of cell B2 does not change. However, when you start using 1-2-3, it is possibly best to avoid the mixed form of address until some experience in writing formulae is gained.

In the previous operation, we used the Range Erase command to clear out the unwanted entries in row 3. This was done to avoid confusing old and new versions of the Sales Revenue formula. Notice that it is not strictly necessary to use / Range Erase for these cells as previous entries are automatically 'erased' by a new entry 'typed over the top'. This continues to be the case when a new entry is copied across to a range of cells which already hold entries.

3.5 Other useful commands in 1-2-3

At this point, the presentation of the worksheet could be much improved by adding headings and rounding the numbers say to the nearest integer. This section contains some new commands which help with headings: the next section concentrates on formatting the numbers in various ways.

Insert/Delete

First, we will insert two rows at the top of the worksheet to allow for headings for each quarter and a dividing line. The command is Worksheet Insert Row, so with the pointer over A1 type:

/ W I R	to Insert one or more blank Rows in the Worksheet above A1.

1-2-3 prompts saying:

Enter row insert range:A1 . . A1

To indicate that two blank rows are required at the top of the worksheet, specify by typing or pointing:

A1.A2 (↵)	to indicate that rows are required in row positions 1 and 2.

Move the pointer around the spreadsheet to see how 1-2-3 has adjusted the formulae now that the addresses of the various entries have changed.

Headings: Data Fill

Next, we will number the twelve different quarters across the top of the spreadsheet. The Data Fill command helps us to add simple headings like 1,2,3,. . . Notice that the command results in headings that are values though, not labels.

Put the label Quarter into cell A1, then move the pointer onto B1. Then type:

/ D F	to start the Data Fill command
B1.M1 (↵)	as the range to be filled
1 (↵)	to specify 1 as the 'starting' value for the first quarter
(↵)	to confirm 1 as the 'step' or increment
(↵)	to confirm 8191 as the 'stop'.

The headings should look like those in Figure 3.9 although the values in the worksheet are different because no formatting has been carried out yet. (The headings go up to quarter 12 in column M not up to quarter 8191. The cell range B1.M1 overrides the stopping value.)

	A	B	C	D	E	F	G
1	Quarter	1	2	3	4	5	6
2	------------------	--------	--------	--------	--------	--------	--------
3	Sales Volume	100	105	110	116	122	128
4	Price	30					
5	Sales Revenue	3000	3150	3308	3473	3647	3829
6	Variable Costs	2100	2205	2315	2431	2553	2680
7	Fixed Costs	1100	1100	1100	1100	1100	1100
8	Profits	-200	-155	-108	-58	-6	49

	A	H	I	J	K	L	M	N
1	Quarter	7	8	9	10	11	12	Total
2	------------------	--------	--------	--------	--------	--------	--------	--------
3	Sales Volume	134	141	148	155	163	171	1592
4	Price							
5	Sales Revenue	4020	4221	4432	4654	4887	5131	47751
6	Variable Costs	2814	2955	3103	3258	3421	3592	33426
7	Fixed Costs	1100	1100	1100	1100	1100	1100	13200
8	Profits	106	166	230	296	366	439	1125

Figure 3.9 Worksheet with 'fixed' format (F0)

Repeating labels \ key

To get dotted lines, etc, consisting of a repeated symbol such as the dash -, the \ key is used. Notice that this is not the same as the slash key, /, used for starting 1-2-3 commands. To put a dotted line under the headings, put the pointer on A2 and type:

\—(↵) to repeat the symbol—across A2.

Next copy cell A2 across from B2 to M2, i.e. with the pointer on A2, type:

/ C (↵) B2.M2 (↵)

At this stage your worksheet should have a dividing line between the headings and the quarterly calculations.

To summarize, the keystrokes to Insert two rows at the top of the worksheet, to number the quarters, and to draw a dotted dividing line are:

(i) Put the pointer on A1, then type:

/ W I R A1.A2 (↵)

(ii) With the pointer on A1, type:

Quarter →

With the pointer on B1, type:

/D F B1.M1(↵) 1 (↵) (↵)(↵)

(iii) Put the pointer on A2, then type:

\ – (↵)

/ C (↵) B2.M2 (↵)

Deleting rows or columns can be done in a similar fashion to inserting them. The command sequence is / W D C followed by the range of Columns (or rows) to be deleted.

3.6 Formatting screen display

To make the worksheet easier to read, the numbers can be presented in different ways with the Range Format command. Currently, the values in the spreadsheet are in 'general' format but other possibilities are 'fixed' format (in which a fixed number of decimal places are permitted) and 'currency' (with the appropriate monetary units and commas).

First, let us round the values in the worksheet to the nearest integer (i.e. use Fixed Format with no decimal places). Put the pointer over B3 (the first cell with a value) and type:

/ R F for the Range Format command.

The options are:

Fixed Scientific Currency, General +/– Percent Date Text Hidden Reset

You can explore each of the options by moving the menu pointer across to reveal the details of each option on the line below. The most useful are Fixed, Currency and the comma format shown as ',' on the menu.

When you have finished, type:

F to choose the Fixed format and

0 (↵) for the number of decimal places

B3.M8 (↵) as the range to be formatted

Your worksheet should look like that of Figure 3.9 (excluding column N) at this stage. Each cell in the range B3.M8 contains the (F0) display format. This shows up on the control panel as part of the contents of the cell when the cell is pointed at. The worksheet is much more clearly displayed and none of the accuracy in the figures has been lost. In fact, whatever display format is chosen, 1-2-3 remembers the values with full precision (and that can be up to as many as 15 decimal places). By / Range Format Reset, the original General format can be retrieved.

One further point on formats when cell entries are copied should be made. When / Copy is applied to formatted cells, the format as well as the entry is copied.

For practice, try changing the values in the spreadsheet using the Fixed format with 2 decimal places (denoted by (F2) in the control panel) and then try the Currency and so-called ',' formats. The Currency form includes the $ sign which may or may not be appropriate (Release 2 supports a wide range of different currency symbols. Explore the Worksheet Global Default Other International command in your Lotus Reference Manual if you need to change the currency symbol.) The ',' format adds commas to separate the hundreds and thousands, etc., and uses brackets to indicate negative values. The Percent format permits values stored as proportions such as .05 to be displayed as percentages (5%). We shall use this format in the next chapter.

You may also find it entertaining to look at the 'Text' format, which reveals all the formulae underlying your worksheet. (The present column-widths in the spreadsheet are not adequate for displaying some of the entries. Individual columns can be adjusted with the Worksheet Column command described in Chapter 2.)

After experimenting with the different displays, return to the integer format (i.e. Fixed with 0 decimal places denoted by F0). Also modify any column widths that may have been changed in the recent experimentation. Your spreadsheet should look once again like that of Figure 3.9 though without the column of totals. These will be constructed in the next section.

Remember to save your work to disc from time to time using the File Save sequence. This is described in detail at the end of Section 3.8.

3.7 1-2-3 special functions

As well as commands, 1-2-3 also contains some special functions which can be thought of as calculation routines already programmed. These functions are accessed by typing the function flag @ (called 'at'). One very frequently needed function is the sum function for totalling the elements in a row or in a column. This is explained below.

@SUM

Suppose we want to calculate total sales, costs, and profits over the twelve quarters. To get Total Sales Volume, put the pointer over N3 and type:

@SUM (B3.M3)

and then press Return.

The cell range B3.M3 can be specified by typing or pointing. This formula sums the Sales Volume entries in row 3 from B3 to M3, i.e. twelve quarters' sales.

Display the Total Sales Volume figure in integer form like the sales figures in the worksheet, i.e. with the pointer over N3, type:

/ R F F	for Range Format Fixed
0(↵)	for no decimal places
(↵)	to confirm the range N3 . . N3.

Sales Revenue, Variable and Fixed Costs, and Profits can be summed in the same manner. Alternatively, the formula for Total Sales Volume in cell N3 can be copied to cells N5, N6, N7, and N8 (the range N5.N8) to obtain these totals. 1-2-3 copies the sum function relative to position since the range of cells to be summed was addressed relatively when we entered the original formula into N3. Notice that the format (F0) in cell N3 is also copied together with the formula.

As an exercise, copy the formulae for totals so that the worksheet contains totals for Sales Revenue, Variable and Fixed Costs, and Profits.

Tidy up the worksheet by adding the heading Totals in N1 and extend the dotted line. If the values in column N are not displayed as integers, use the Range Format Fixed command to make these totals consistent with the rest of the worksheet.

To extend your knowledge of 1-2-3 functions, try to put average quarterly figures for sales, costs, and profits in column O either by constructing a formula using the totals in column N or using the average function (@AVG) which works in a similar fashion to the sum function.

3.8 Freezing titles

One difficulty in interpreting the worksheet is the disappearance of the main labels (or titles) in scrolling the window. It often helps to 'fix' or freeze either vertical or horizontal titles or possibly both. In 1-2-3, this is the Worksheet Titles command. Try it on your worksheet. Put the pointer on B3 and type:

/ W T to freeze Worksheet Titles.

The prompt line says:

Both Horizontal Vertical Clear

Press Return (or type B) to freeze titles both above and to the left of the current pointer position.

Move the pointer across the spreadsheet to the right to see how the titles remain as the screen scrolls.

One slightly irritating feature of fixed titles is that access to the frozen title area is only possible using the GoTo key. This can result in a double set of titles. Although this allows 'frozen' cell entries to be accessed and modified as required, some skilled pointer work is needed to return the spreadsheet to its original single title form. If you find this feature annoying, you can Clear the fixed titles by going through the Worksheet Titles command sequence again. This time, choose the Clear option (i.e. / W T C).

As we shall see in Chapter 4, splitting the screen into 'windows' makes a large worksheet easier to view. This is often more of an improvement than fixing the titles.

The final spreadsheet should have opening and closing quarters, Totals, and Averages looking something like Figure 3.10.

	A	B	J	K	L	M	N	O
1	Quarter	1	9	10	11	12	Total	Average
2	----------------	------	------	------	------	------	------	------
3	Sales Volume	100	148	155	163	171	1592	133
4	Price	30						
5	Sales Revenue	3000	4432	4654	4887	5131	47751	3979
6	Variable Costs	2100	3103	3258	3421	3592	33426	2785
7	Fixed Costs	1100	1100	1100	1100	1100	13200	1100
8	Profits	-200	230	296	366	439	1125	94

Figure 3.10 Worksheet with two ranges displayed

Remember to save your worksheet to disc before moving on to Chapter 4. To conserve space on your disc, it is good practice to store this worksheet under the same name as before, i.e. MYDATA or whatever. The improved worksheet will overwrite the version previously saved to disc. For this reason, if you give a filename used on a previous 'File Save', 1-2-3 asks whether you want to Cancel the command or Replace the existing file. Usually, you want to Replace the file with the new version. On the other hand, if you wish to keep the old file, Cancel the command. A different filename will ensure that both worksheets are preserved.

In saving the spreadsheet, 1-2-3 will also store the various format settings and fixed titles as well.

3.9 On-line help

Finally, to consolidate on some of the topics touched on in this chapter, press the (f1/Help) key to get the Help screen. Start by pointing at 'How to Use Help'. Go on to the Help Index and use the arrow keys to choose 'Moving the Cell Pointer'. Follow on to 'Pointing to Ranges' and then return to the Help Index. You may also find it informative to look at the screens called 'Formulas' and '@ Functions'.

In working with 1-2-3, you may have encountered an error message displayed at the bottom of the screen. These error messages are explained on a Help screen called Error Messages. If 1-2-3 'beeps' at you and displays an error message, press Return, or Escape to READY mode. A second Help Screen called Error Message Index lists the different error messages. However, you will need to delve into your Reference Manual if you are uncertain how to correct the 'error' in question.

Note: Datafile MD3 on your CM disc contains the MYDATA spreadsheet as it should appear at the conclusion of this chapter. You may wish to explore it if you had any difficulty in implementing the instructions in this chapter.

CHAPTER 4

Designing Worksheets

In this chapter, we discuss some important ideas about structuring 1-2-3 worksheets so as to make them more relevant in analysis. In order to exploit the power of 1-2-3, it is suggested that general models should be constructed which do not depend on a particular set of data.

In the following paragraphs, the separation of planning and computed values is explained. Some useful 1-2-3 commands such as the Worksheet Window and Move are introduced and the structured Data Table approach to sensitivity analysis is explained. Lastly, a simple graph is produced by 1-2-3, anticipating the fuller treatment of graphical display in Chapter 5.

We assume by now that you have grasped many essential 1-2-3 skills. It should no longer be necessary to spell out every sequence of keystrokes in great detail. For this reason, you are encouraged to keep your eyes on the screen, and follow 1-2-3's prompts. You will have noticed that 1-2-3 'remembers' your previous inputs for cell ranges, etc. If 1-2-3's suggested responses are correct, you merely press Return to confirm. If not, type the desired response 'over the top'.

In the following text, the illustrative figures should be your models, rather than lists of keystrokes. In manipulating and changing the worksheet layout, formulae 'on the page' are changed in the worksheet and rapidly become 'out of date'.

By the end of Chapter 4, you will have met most of the frequently used spreadsheet building commands. The Graph, Print, and Data commands will be covered in the next two chapters. Other commands will be introduced in the application chapters. The 1-2-3 Reference Manual gives very full coverage of the total set of commands and procedures.

4.1 Planning spreadsheets

In planning, assumptions are made and the consequences evaluated on the basis of the assumptions. For example, in the worksheet exercise of the last two chapters, profit was calculated assuming a 5 per cent growth rate in quarterly sales. In addition, the price was assumed to be £30 and the cost of goods sold was taken as 70 per cent of sales. These assumptions are embedded in the formulae of the worksheet. We can change the assumptions and recalculate profits. However, as the spreadsheet is structured at present, to do so would take almost as long as starting again from scratch.

In Section 2.9, an alternative approach was suggested for modelling sales growth. Rather than write a formula for growth in terms of the particular 5 per cent rate, a cell was specified to hold the current value (it was in fact cell B10). The formula for sales growth in the second quarter used the address B10 rather than the 5 per cent value. If this formula were to be copied, the resulting spreadsheet would contain formulae referencing cell B10 for the rate of growth. It would then be a trivial matter to change the value stored in B10 to examine the effect on profits of a whole range of possible growth rates, e.g. 2 per cent, 4 per cent, 10 per cent, etc. The recalculation of the whole worksheet to obtain the profits could be left to 1-2-3's rapid calculation facility. This type of experimentation with a 'parameter' or 'planning value' (here growth rate) is called sensitivity analysis. A more down to earth name is 'what-if' analysis.

As well as testing the sensitivity of profits to sales growth, we may wish to ask 'what-if' questions about the effect of the cost of goods sold, or the price or the level of fixed costs all of which may represent assumptions about the future. This has implications for the way we structure 1-2-3 worksheets. The layout needs to be planned with these 'what-if' questions in mind so that it is a simple task to change assumed values.

One good approach is to group these planning values together in a separate area of the worksheet. The rest of the worksheet will contain 'computed values', that is, values computed on the basis of the 'planning values'. It is then an easy task to change the planning values and discover the effect on the computed values.

Conventionally, these planning values are grouped at the top of the worksheet or scattered down amongst the cells of the first few columns. Neither of these approaches seems entirely satisfactory. In particular, it prevents the proper use of the Titles facility, which allows titles to be frozen so that they do not scroll off the screen. With planning values at the top, the frozen 'titles' area has to span the planning values which leaves little of the screen 'unfrozen' for entering values and formulae. A better approach is to put the planning values below or to the right hand side of the 'computed values'. The layout can be organized so that the planning values are grouped together say one or two 'pages' down (or across) the worksheet from the A1 cell.

In Chapter 3, absolute addressing was discussed. The Sales Revenue formula was written in terms of the Price (B2) using its absolute address ($B$2). When the Sales Revenue formula was copied across the spreadsheet, the location of the Price entry did not change relative to position as usually happens when formulae are copied. Since most formulae in spreadsheets are copied, any 'planning value' will usually need to be absolutely addressed when it appears in formulae.

These ideas will be illustrated by improving the layout of the worksheet which we have been building in the last two chapters. We shall also use various 1-2-3 facilities to help carry out sensitivity analyses.

4.2 Restructuring the spreadsheet

First retrieve the datafile saved at the end of the previous chapter. With your CM data disc in Drive B, type:

/ F R	to Retrieve the File called
MYDATA	or whatever you have named it.

Notice that 1-2-3's response to the File Retrieve command is to display a selection of filenames on the control panel. Instead of typing in MYDATA, you can use the pointer movement keys to search through the filenames until MYDATA is highlighted. Then simply press Enter to retrieve this file.

Your worksheet should be similar to that shown in Figure 4.1. If the titles are fixed, clear them at this stage (/ W T C).

	A	B	C	D	E	F	G
1	Quarter	1	2	3	4	5	6
2	----------------	----------	----------	----------	----------	----------	----------
3	Sales Volume	100	105	110	116	122	128
4	Price	30					
5	Sales Revenue	3000	3150	3308	3473	3647	3829
6	Variable Costs	2100	2205	2315	2431	2553	2680
7	Fixed Costs	1100	1100	1100	1100	1100	1100
8	Profits	-200	-155	-108	-58	-6	49

	H	I	J	K	L	M	N	O
1	7	8	9	10	11	12	Total	Average
2	----------	----------	----------	----------	----------	----------	----------	----------
3	134	141	148	155	163	171	1592	1334
4								
5	4020	4221	4432	4654	4887	5131	47751	3979
6	2814	2955	3103	3258	3421	3592	33426	2785
7	1100	1100	1100	1100	1100	1100	13200	1100
8	106	166	230	296	366	439	1125	94

Figure 4.1 Worksheet (MYDATA) saved at end of Chapter 3

Press the Tab key to jump across a 'page' and look at the second six quarters, then press Shift and Tab together to jump back.

We will proceed to revamp the worksheet so that it will look like Figure 4.2. The main steps are to group the planning values at the bottom of the worksheet and then to express sales and costs in terms of the planning values. The steps are:

	A	B	C	D	E	F	G
1	Quarter	1	2	3	4	5	6
2	----------------	----------	----------	----------	----------	----------	----------
3	Sales Volume	100	105	110	116	122	128
4	Sales Revenue	3,000	3,150	3,308	3,473	3,647	3,829
5	Variable Costs	2,100	2,205	2,315	2,431	2,553	2,680
6	Fixed Costs	1,100	1,100	1,100	1,100	1,100	1,100
7	Profits	(200)	(155)	(108)	(58)	(6)	49
9	Planning	Values					
10	----------------	----------					
11	Sales Growth	5.0%					
12	Price	30					
13	Cost of GS	70%					
14	Fixed Costs	1100					

	H	I	J	K	L	M	N	O
1	7	8	9	10	11	12	Total	Average
2	----------	----------	----------	----------	----------	----------	----------	----------
3	134	141	148	155	163	171	1,592	133
4	4,020	4,221	4,432	4,654	4,887	5,131	47,751	3,979
5	2,814	2,955	3,103	3,258	3,421	3,592	33,426	2,785
6	1,100	1,100	1,100	1,100	1,100	1,100	13,200	1,100
7	106	166	230	296	366	439	1,125	94

Figure 4.2 Worksheet set out with planning values

1. Set out the planning values as shown in Figure 4.3, the left hand display.

	A	B
10	Planning	Values
11	------------------------	
12	Sales Growth	0.05
13	Price	30
14	Cost of GS	0.7
15	Fixed Costs	1100

	A	B	
10	Planning	Values	
11	------------------------		
12	Sales Growth	5.0%	← (P1)
13	Price	30	
14	Cost of GS	70%	← (P0)
15	Fixed Costs	1100	

Figure 4.3 Planning values as entered (LHS) and with display format (RHS)

Start with a heading such as Planning Values in cells A10 and B10 and a dotted line in cells A11 and B11. Group the planning values in cells B12 to B15 with labels in column A. Put the Sales Growth rate (.05) into B12, Price (30) into B13, Cost of Goods Sold proportion (.7) into B14 and Fixed Costs (1100) into B15. Put the associated labels into column A. The Sales Growth and the Cost of Goods Sold entries are best displayed in percentage format (/ Range Format Percent etc.). The display formats and the way the numbers appear on the screen is shown in the right hand display of Figure 4.3. Notice that the entries are unchanged (e.g. 0.05 for Sales Growth). The display format (P1) merely affects the appearance on the screen (5.0%). Refer back to Section 3.6 for Range Formatting or, after you have issued the command / R F P for Percent Format, press the Help key.

2. Adjust the Sales Volume formula in C3. This is best done with the Edit key, deleting and inserting the relevant characters or it can be retyped. (Remember when editing that the Home key jumps the cursor to the front of the entry and the Delete character key removes unwanted characters.) The Sales Volume formula in C3 becomes:

(1+$B$12)*B3

Copy the formula FROM C3 across TO the range D3.M3, i.e. type:

/ C C3 (↵) D3.M3 (↵)

3. Amend the Sales Revenue formula in B5 in terms of the Price now situated in cell B13. Using the Edit key, change the formula to:

+B3*$B$13

4. Amend the Variable Costs formula in B6 using the Cost of Goods Sold proportion in cell B14. It becomes:

+$B$14*B5

5. Change the Fixed Costs entry in B7 to the form:

+$B$15

One way to do this is to type + then 'point' to the cell B15. To make the address that has appeared on the control panel absolute, press the Absolute key (f4/Abs), then press Return to enter the formula.

6. Copy the formulae in cell range B5.B7 across to range C5.M5, i.e. type:

/ C B5.B7 (↵) C5.M5 (↵)

7. Delete the Price row (row 4) from the worksheet since the Sales Revenue formula now refers to the planning value (B13). With the pointer in row 4, type:

/ W D R (↵) to Delete the Row with the pointer in

8. Finally, use the ',' format for range B3.O7 to make the numbers easier to read. That is, type:

/ R F , to put the ',' Format on the Range

B3.O7 (↵)

The worksheet should look roughly like that of Figure 4.2 now. If any cells are displaying an error message, you should check that the formulae in your worksheet correspond to those in Figure 4.4 and correct them where necessary. (For interest, you can display the formulae in your worksheet with / Range Format Text. You may have to alter the Column widths to see whole formulae on the screen. When you have finished checking your formulae, use / Range Format to change back to the format of your choice and set the Column widths back to 9 characters.)

	A	B	C	D	E
1	Quarter	1	2	3	4
2	----------------	----------------	----------------	----------------	----------------
3	Sales Volume	100	(1+$B$11)*B3	(1+$B$11)*C3	(1+$B$11)*D3
4	Sales Revenue	+B3*$B$12	+C3*$B$12	+D3*$B$12	+E3*$B$12
5	Variable Costs	+$B$13*B4	+$B$13*C4	+$B$13*D4	+$B$13*E4
6	Fixed Costs	+$B$14	+$B$14	+$B$14	+$B$14
7	Profits	+B4-B5-B6	+C4-C5-C6	+D4-D5-D6	+E4-E5-E6

Figure 4.4 Formulae in worksheet

Notice that because the Price row has been deleted, the cell addresses below row 3 have been adjusted. Consequently, they no longer correspond exactly with the formulae entered before the row was deleted.

This completes the restructuring for the present. It is now easy to change the Sales Growth or Price or whatever and examine the effect on Profits. But before asking 'what-if' questions in this way, you may like to consider the suggestions made in the next section.

Now is the time to save your worksheet with the / File Save sequence. After modifying the worksheet as described in the following sections, you may wish to return to this basic structure rather than reverse all the changes you are about to make.

4.3 Windows

It would be much easier to judge the effect of changes in the planning values were it possible to see the final profits figures adjacent to the planning values. One approach is to set up a pair of cells, say B16 and B17, to contain the Total and Average Profits figures. To do this, the entries for B16 and B17 would be +N7 and +O7 respectively. Suitable labels would be entered in adjacent cells and the formats of cells B16 and B17 adjusted. Figure 4.5 shows the results of these modifications.

	A	B	C	D	E	F	G
1	Quarter	1	2	3	4	5	6
2	----------------	--------	--------	--------	--------	--------	--------
3	Sales Volume	100	105	110	116	122	128
4	Sales Revenue	3,000	3,150	3,308	3,473	3,647	3,829
5	Variable Costs	2,100	2,205	2,315	2,431	2,553	2,680
6	Fixed Costs	1,100	1,100	1,100	1,100	1,100	1,100
7	Profits	(200)	(155)	(108)	(58)	(6)	49
9	Planning	Values					
10	----------------	--------					
11	Sales Growth	5.0%					
12	Price	30					
13	Cost of GS	70%					
14	Fixed Costs	1100					
15	----------------	--------					
16	Total Profit	1,125	← +N7				
17	Average Profit	94	← +O7				

Figure 4.5 Total and average profit on screen with planning values

A more exciting way to display the Total Profits figures and planning values together is to split the screen into two 'windows'. For this we use the Worksheet Window command. The screen is split to the left hand side of the current pointer position.

To achieve a sensible split, point to a cell one column in from the right of the screen, probably in column F, and type:

/ W W   to start the Worksheet Window command

V   to split the screen vertically.

The pointer, currently in the left hand window can be 'jumped' into the right hand window using the (f6) function key called the Window key. To get Totals and Averages lined up in the right hand window, jump the pointer into the right hand window and press the right arrow key until column N with Totals comes into view. The screen should now look like Figure 4.6.

Now try asking those 'what-if' questions. For example, jump to the left hand window, change the Sales Growth to .075 and the Price to £25 and watch the effect on the right hand screen. Explore the effect on final profits of higher/lower prices and/or higher/lower growth rates, etc.

There are many possibilities and some structured search process would be helpful. The Data Table approach described next helps in recording the results of sensitivity analyses in an orderly fashion. Before leaving this section you should return to a single window using the command sequence / Worksheet Window Clear.

4.4 Data tables

The Data Table command allows you to organize sensitivity analyses systematically and record the results in a table. Either one or two factors can be varied in the sensitivity analysis. For example, you can study the effect on profits of varying the Sales Growth rate

	A	B	C	D	E	N	O
1	Quarter	1	2	3	4	Total	Average
2	----------	----------	----------	----------	----------	----------	----------
3	Sales Volume	100	105	110	116	1,592	133
4	Sales Revenue	3,000	3,150	3,308	3,473	47,751	3,979
5	Variable Costs	2,100	2,205	2,315	2,431	33,426	2,785
6	Fixed Costs	1,100	1,100	1,100	1,100	13,200	1,100
7	Profits	(200)	(155)	(108)	(58)	1,125	94
9	Planning	Values					
10	----------	----------					
11	Sales Growth	5.0%					
12	Price	30					
13	Cost of GS	70%					
14	Fixed Costs	1100					
15	----------	----------					
16	Total Profit	1,125					
17	Average Profit	94					

Figure 4.6 Worksheet 'split' into two windows

(one 'input') or of varying both Sales Growth and Price simultaneously (two 'inputs'). We will look at each possibility in turn.

Data Table 1

The Data Table occupies a rectangular range of cells and this 'table range' has to be specified. First, we will look at a Data Table with one input, which is called in 1-2-3 parlance a 'Data Table 1'. The first table will be set up in row 21 onwards. We will explore the effect on quarterly profits (in row 7) of different growth rates, i.e. the Input cell is B11 where the current rate of 5% is stored.

The proposed layout for the Data Table is shown in Figure 4.7. Headings and underlining occupy rows 21 and 22. The Data Table proper starts in row 23 where the formulae for quarterly profits (including average and total profits) are entered. These profit formulae are linked to those in row 7 by entering in cell B23 the formula:

+B7

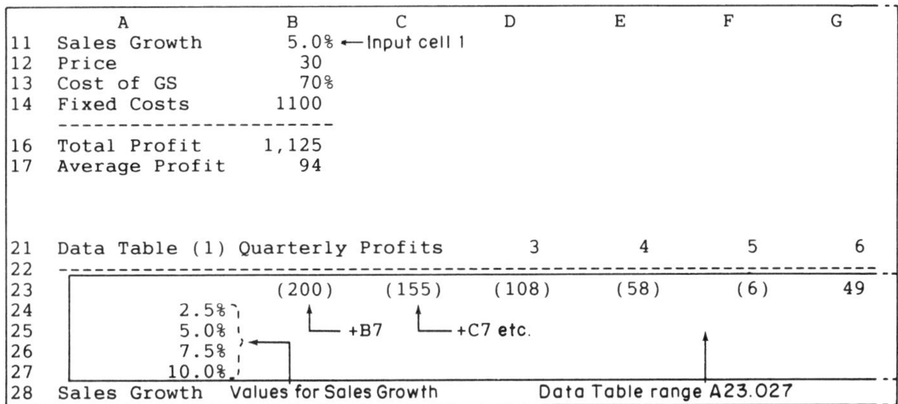

	A	B	C	D	E	F	G
11	Sales Growth	5.0%					
12	Price	30					
13	Cost of GS	70%					
14	Fixed Costs	1100					
	----------	----------					
16	Total Profit	1,125					
17	Average Profit	94					
21	Data Table (1) Quarterly Profits			3	4	5	6
22	----------	----------	----------	----------	----------	----------	----------
23		(200)	(155)	(108)	(58)	(6)	49
24	2.5%						
25	5.0%						
26	7.5%						
27	10.0%						
28	Sales Growth						

Figure 4.7 Data Table for profits with Sales Growth as input

The entry in B23 is then Copied TO range C23.O23.

The values currently displayed in the cells of row 23 assume a 5 percent growth rate.

Notice that cell A23 is left empty. This is necessary for the Data Table command to work properly.

In cells A24 to A27, different values for the Sales Growth are entered—in Figure 4.7, the values .025, .05, .075 and .1 have been keyed in. By adding the Percent Format (P1), these values are displayed as percentages with one decimal place. The sensitivity analysis involves calculating 14 profit figures (12 quarterly figures plus the Total and Average) for each of four Growth rates. The Data Table occupies rows 23 to 27 in columns A across to O, hence the 'table range' is A23.O27.

The procedure is as follows:

With the pointer on A23, type:

/ D T 1	to start the Data Table 1 command
A23.O27 (↵)	to specify the Table range
B11 (↵)	to define Sales Growth as Input cell 1.

The mode indicator indicates WAIT while the sensitivity analysis is performed. To make the resultant table of values easier to read, display the profit figures in ',' format, i.e. type:

/ R F , 0 (↵)	to Format Range
B24.O27 (↵)	in ',' format to the nearest integer.

The results are shown in Figure 4.8. With the low growth rate there is an overall loss (of £784), whereas for a growth rate of 7.5 per cent Total Profits treble. However, high growth is unlikely without some change in price. We can look at the effect of varying both factors with the 'Data Table 2'.

	A	B	C	D	E	F	G
21	Data Table (1)	Quarterly	Profits	3	4	5	6
22	-----	-----	-----	-----	-----	-----	-----
23		(200)	(155)	(108)	(58)	(6)	49
24	2.5%	(200)	(178)	(154)	(131)	(107)	(82)
25	5.0%	(200)	(155)	(108)	(58)	(6)	49
26	7.5%	(200)	(133)	(60)	18	102	192
27	10.0%	(200)	(110)	(11)	98	218	349
28	Sales Growth						

Figure 4.8 Results for first six quarters with different Sales Growth

Data Table 2

With two 'inputs', we must restrict our interest to one formula in any one table. Suppose we choose Total Profit in N7. The proposed layout for the Data Table with two inputs, Sales Growth and Price, is shown in Figure 4.9. The table proper starts in cell D11, with the formula for Total Profits:

+N7	entered in cell D11.

	A	B	C	D	E	F	G
1	Quarter	1	2	3	4	5	6
2	------------	------------	------------	------------	------------	------------	------------
3	Sales Volume	100	105	110	116	122	128
4	Sales Revenue	3,000	3,150	3,308	3,473	3,647	3,829
5	Variable Costs	2,100	2,205	2,315	2,431	2,553	2,680
6	Fixed Costs	1,100	1,100	1,100	1,100	1,100	1,100
7	Profits	(200)	(155)	(108)	(58)	(6)	49
9	Planning	Values	Input cell	Data	Table (2)		
10	------------	------------		------------	------------	------------	------------
11	Sales Growth	5.0% ← 1		1,125 ←	25	30	35
12	Price	30 ← 2		2.5%			
13	Cost of GS	70%		5.0%	+N7		
14	Fixed Costs	1100		7.5%			
15	------------	------------					
16	Total Profit	1,125			Data table range D11.G14		
17	Average Profit	94					

Figure 4.9 Data Table for profits with Sales Growth and Price as inputs

Sales Growth is the Input cell number 1, and three values, .025, .05, and .075 are set out in cells D12 to D14. They are displayed as percentages (P1). Price is Input cell number 2, and three prices of interest, 25, 30, and 35 are set out in Row 11. The value of the Total Profits for each combination of growth and price is calculated when the Data Table command is invoked.

Having entered the formula and specimen growth and price values as shown in Figure 4.9, the procedure is as follows:

With the pointer on cell D11, type:

/ D T 2 — to start the Data Table 2 command.

Type:

D11.G14 (↵) — as the Table range

B11 (↵) — to make Sales Growth the Input cell 1

B12 (↵) — to make Price the Input cell 2.

To make the resulting table of values easy to read, display the profit figures in ',' format to the nearest integer (,0) or Fixed format as integers (F0). Your results should tally with those shown in Figure 4.10. Notice that the results are numeric: the values in the cells are not formulae linked into the worksheet.

If you want to recompute the same table with table range and input cells, but a different selection of values for Price and Sales Growth, the steps are simple.

(i) Change the values in D12 to D14 and E11 to G11 as required.

(ii) Change any other cells in the worksheet if required. For example, the formula evaluated in the table could be changed to Average Profit by entering +O7 into the table cell D11.

(iii) Press the special Table key, (f8/Table) and the whole table will be recalculated.

	A	B	C	D	E	F	G
1	Quarter	1	2	3	4	5	6
2	-------------------	------	------	------	------	------	------
3	Sales Volume	100	105	110	116	122	128
4	Sales Revenue	3,000	3,150	3,308	3,473	3,647	3,829
5	Variable Costs	2,100	2,205	2,315	2,431	2,553	2,680
6	Fixed Costs	1,100	1,100	1,100	1,100	1,100	1,100
7	Profits	(200)	(155)	(108)	(58)	(6)	49
9	Planning	Values		Data	Table (2)		
10	-------------------	------		------	------	------	------
11	Sales Growth	5.0%		1,125	25	30	35
12	Price	30		2.5%	(2,853)	(784)	1,285
13	Cost of GS	70%		5.0%	(1,262)	1,125	3,513
14	Fixed Costs	1100		7.5%	618	3,381	6,145
15	-------------------	------					
16	Total Profit	1,125		Total Profits for each Growth-Price Combination			
17	Average Profit	94					

Figure 4.10 Total profits for different Sales Growth-Price combinations

To avoid confusion with the Data Table in row 21, add the label Data Table (2) in cell D9 before proceeding.

4.5 Move

Another useful command for manipulating the layout of the worksheet is the Move command. This moves a block of cells from one part of the spreadsheet to another. Furthermore, it will adjust any formulae in the block to reflect the new layout. We will illustrate its use by moving the second sensitivity table, called 'Data Table (2)' from its present location (in range D9.G14) to A30, i.e. to the 'next page' underneath the first.Data Table.

With the pointer on D9, type:

/ M   to start the Move command.

1-2-3 says:

Enter range to move FROM: D9..D9

Anchor the pointer over D9 by pressing the full stop key and expand the pointer to cover the range D9.G14 before pressing Return (or simply type the range: D9.G14).

1-2-3 then says:

Enter range to move TO:

Point to cell A30 and press Return (or simply type the 'range': A30).

Although the table seems to have disappeared, it is in row 30. To see its new location, press the 'Page Down' key to jump down a 'page' or use the down arrow key.

Jump back to A1 by pressing the Home key.

The Move command gives great flexibility in designing the layout of the worksheet as modelling proceeds. Some care must be taken in deciding the destination for a block of cells because any existing entries in the destination range (only specified by the top left hand cell) will be overwritten.

4.6 Range names

1-2-3 commands often involve cell ranges. Pointing and anchoring and expanding the pointer reduce the need to key in the ranges. Also, 1-2-3's ability to hold in memory and prompt with the last-used range helps in entering ranges.

A further facility which reduces the need to remember or work out cell ranges is the Range Name command. Frequently used ranges are given names. In further operations, these ranges can be referred to by their names. For example, the range B3.M3 which contains the Sales Volumes can be named (say) SALESVOL. To do this, type:

/ R N	to start the Range Name command
C	to Create the name for the range
SALESVOL (↵)	
B3.M3	to define the range that goes with name SALESVOL.

We will use this range name in the next section. In any further 1-2-3 operation, the range B3.M3 can always be referred to as SALESVOL.

Note that in POINT mode, pressing the Name key (f3/Name) allows the required name to be chosen from a menu rather than keyed in. This is sometimes helpful if several ranges are named, but the name of a particular range is only dimly remembered.

4.7 Graphing results

Lastly, to demonstrate how it is possible in 1-2-3 to flip from spreadsheet to graph and back, we will plot the quarterly Sales Volumes and Profits using the Graph command. Since graphing techniques are dealt with at length in Chapter 5, this treatment will be kept simple.

The sequence of choices from the Graph menu is circular and you are continually returned to this menu. You can get back to READY mode by choosing Quit from the menu, or by pressing Escape a few times. The procedure is:

1. Type:

/G	to start the Graph command.

This gives the Graph menu with the following options:

Type X A B C D E F Reset View Save Options Name Quit.

2. Choose the option Type which leads to a menu of graph Types from which you choose Line.

3. From the Graph menu, choose X, the horizontal axis and specify the X range as cell range B1.M1 (i.e. the number of the Quarter 1, 2, 3. . .).

4. From the Graph menu, choose A, the first series to be plotted and specify the A range of data as SALESVOL, the range of quarterly Sales Volumes 'named' earlier. (Either type in the name SALESVOL or press the Name key (f3) and choose from the menu (of one name in this case!).)

5. From the Graph menu, choose B, the second series to be plotted and specify the B range as B7.M7, i.e. the quarterly Profits.

6. From the Graph menu, choose View to go to the graph. Press any key to return.

7. To improve the graph you can add labels. To do this, choose Options and then Legends and type suitable legends for your data. (We shall look further at these Options in Chapter 5.)

Figure 4.11 shows one such graph of Sales Volume and Profits against Time. When you have finished viewing the graph, Quit or Escape will return you to READY mode.

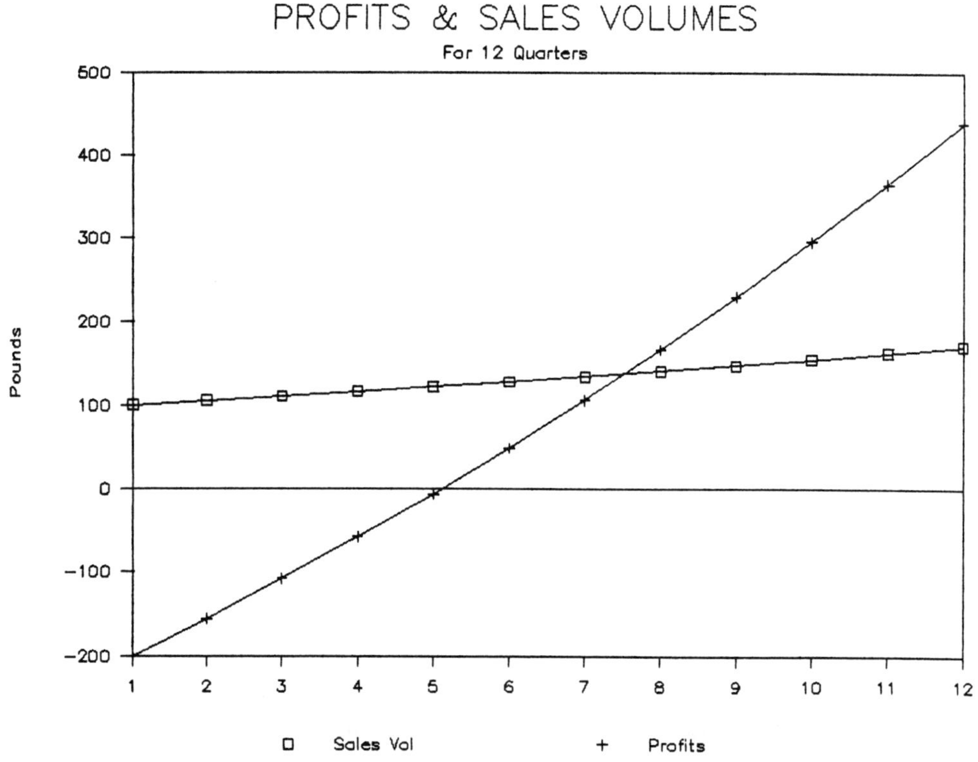

Figure 4.11 Results for first 12 quarters graphed

Changing the planning values will change the Sales Volumes and Profits but not their locations. Once specified, the graph settings will hold for different values. To see the graph with the changed planning values, you merely press the (f10/Graph) key.

Graph techniques are explained more fully in Chapter 5. In the meantime, remember to save your worksheet on your data disc under the filename MYDATA.

Note: Datafile MD4 on your CM disc contains the spreadsheet with the graph that results from following the instructions in this chapter. Since MD4 was saved to disc after the graph was set up, the graph settings are retained, and the graph can be viewed again via the Graph key.

CHAPTER 5

Graphs and Printed Worksheets

During the course of analysis and at its conclusion, we frequently want 'hard copy', for example, a print-out of the spreadsheet resulting from the modelling in Chapters 2 to 4. With 1-2-3, a print-out can be obtained at any stage, if a printer is connected to the microcomputer. If not, a file containing specifications for printing can be saved for printing at a later stage. For reference, a print-out of the formulae in the worksheet can also be obtained.

Sometimes the numeric formatting and printing facilities can be used to explore different forms of presentation for numerical data. Often the meaning of a table of data is not immediately apparent because insufficient thought has been put into presenting the data clearly. Certain simple rules of data display can improve the presentation markedly. These rules are easy to implement with 1-2-3. They are discussed in the context of a table of regional sales statistics.

Often graphs can be used to convey the meaning of some data very vividly. With 1-2-3, it is easy to produce simple graphs quickly. These can be improved and made more sophisticated using the extensive set of graphics commands. Various types of graph can be built—bar charts, line graphs, and XY scatter plots and several sets of data can be graphed at once. Moreover, graphs can be 'named' for reviewing and saved for printing.

In this chapter, we discuss 1-2-3's graphing and printing facilities. We illustrate something of what is possible with reference to the spreadsheet model of Chapters 2 to 4 and the regional sales statistics outlined in Section 5.3.

5.1 Printing worksheets

In this section, you will print the worksheet illustrated in Figure 4.10, that is, the Quarterly Profit figures and the Data Table in rows 9 to 14. This will involve specifying the range or ranges of cells to be printed, spacing chunks of output and deciding options such as borders and headings. The 'Options' menu will be discussed more fully in the next section. The rest of the 'Print' menu choices will be outlined in this section.

First retrieve the file saved at the end of Chapter 4. That is type:

/ F R	to Retrieve the File called
MYDATA	or whatever you named it.

The spreadsheet contains entries which spread across 15 columns in all, most of which are 9 characters wide. Unless your printer can cope with 140 characters width, it is not possible to print the whole spreadsheet across horizontally. A sensible division would be to print the labels in column A together with the first 6 quarters' figures (i.e. columns A to G inclusive), then to print columns H to O inclusive immediately below or on a new page.

Before starting the print command, make sure your printer is on. It also helps to start with the pointer on A1. Then type:

/ P to start the Print command

P to send output to the Printer.

(Alternatively, F if you want to delay printing and make a print File instead.)

In the following, we assume the output is sent to a printer.

The Print menu should now be displayed in the control panel. It consists of Range Line Page Options Clear Align Go Quit

The sequence of choices with this menu is circular: in 1-2-3 jargon, it is a 'sticky' menu. On choosing any particular sequence, say Range, you are always eventually returned to the Print menu again, until you choose Quit (or press Escape). With Quit, you are returned from MENU to READY mode.

Looking at the Print menu, the Range option currently highlighted entails specifying the range(s) to be printed. Line and Page position the printed output on the printer stationery. Choosing Line advances the printer one line whereas Page moves the printer to the head of the next page. (Choosing Line and observing the printer respond with a 'line feed' action is one way of checking that your printer is communicating with 1-2-3.) The 'Options' possibilities are explored in the next section.

Once specified, 1-2-3 'remembers' printing specifications. You may wish to clear out some or all of the print settings. Clear is the Print menu choice to delete these settings. The Align option resets 1-2-3's line number and page counters back to 1, so that the printer behaves as if it were at the top of the page. In practice, choosing Align then Go ensures that short pieces of output are not interrupted by the blank lines that signal the end of the page. (You do not usually need the Align option unless you interrupt 1-2-3 sessions using the form feed control on your printer.)

To print the spreadsheet, choose Range, specify the first range for printing as A1.G17 and then choose Go.

The result should be that the first part of the spreadsheet is printed.

For clarity, choose Line a couple of times to leave a gap before printing the second part of the spreadsheet.

Again, choose Range, and 1-2-3 will respond in POINT mode with the expanded pointer showing your previous Print range. If appropriate, you would merely press Return. However, the required range is different, namely H1.O7. Either key in this range (EDIT mode), that is type:

H1.O7 (↵)

or continue in POINT mode. To specify the range by pointing, 'unhook' the pointer anchor cell by pressing Escape or Backspace (this frees the printer). Then point to H1, anchor the pointer by pressing full stop, then expand the pointer to O7. The control panel shows H1 . . O7 so press Return. Lastly choose Go. The printed output should now look like Figure 5.1.

```
Quarter                  1        2        3        4        5        6
---------------------------------------------------------------------------
Sales Volume           100      105      110      116      122      128
Sales Revenue        3,000    3,150    3,308    3,473    3,647    3,829
Variable Costs       2,100    2,205    2,315    2,431    2,553    2,680
Fixed Costs          1,100    1,100    1,100    1,100    1,100    1,100
Profits              (200)    (155)    (108)     (58)      (6)       49

Planning      Values                Data     Table  (2)
-----------------------             ---------------------------------------
Sales Growth          5.0%            1,125       25       30       35
Price                   30             2.5%  (2,853)    (784)    1,285
Cost of GS             70%             5.0%  (1,262)    1,125    3,513
Fixed Costs           1100             7.5%      618    3,381    6,145
-----------------------
Total Profit         1,125
Average Profit          94

        7        8        9       10       11       12    Total  Average
---------------------------------------------------------------------------
      134      141      148      155      163      171    1,592      133
    4,020    4,221    4,432    4,654    4,887    5,131   47,751    3,979
    2,814    2,955    3,103    3,258    3,421    3,592   33,426    2,785
    1,100    1,100    1,100    1,100    1,100    1,100   13,200    1,100
      106      166      230      296      366      439    1,125       94
```

Figure 5.1 Print-out of file MYDATA

In summary, the steps to print out the worksheet of Figure 4.10 are:

/ P P	to choose Print and to send the output to the Printer (rather than to File)
R A1.G17 (↵)	to specify the first print Range
A	to Align, i.e. reset the line counter to 1
G	to Go, i.e. print the first range
L L	to give two blank lines
R H1.O7 (↵)	to specify the second print Range
G	to Go, i.e. print the second range.

If the range you specify does not fit on one printed page, 1-2-3 will cut off the extra columns and print them on the next 'page' of output.

Assuming that the printer can cope with the range actually displayed on the screen at any one time, use of the Tab key can simplify the specification of each print range for a wide worksheet. The start of each new print range can be defined by unhooking the pointer, pressing Tab once to jump one page across the spreadsheet, to point to the start of the next print range.

5.2 Print options

Printed output can be augmented with borders, extra text, and page numbers, and the page format (page length, size of margins, etc.) can be altered to suit particular requirements. These options can be accessed through the Print Options submenu. Of particular interest are the Header and Footer choices which set header and footer lines of text for inclusion in the output. The Borders option allows you to attach a particular column and/or row to a print range to form a 'border'. For example, in printing out the spreadsheet from Chapter 4, it might be desirable to attach the labels in column A to the second six months' figures. Also a title or Header such as MYDATA PRINT-OUT could be added.

To achieve this, column A is specified as the print border via the Borders option. Starting from the Print menu, with the print Range specified as H1.M7, type:

O — to get the Options submenu

B C — for Borders that are Columns

and point to column A to indicate the Border.

Similarly, from the Options submenu, choose Header and enter a Header line such as:

MYDATA PRINT-OUT @

then Quit the Options submenu.

From the main Print menu, choose Align (to ensure that the printer starts from the 'top' of the page) and then Go. The print-out should look like Figure 5.2 (The @ symbol translates into the current date, if the 1-2-3 session was started with the current date or if the computer has an internal clock.)

Note: It is a good idea to Clear out print settings such as the Borders after printing. These settings tend to be overlooked, when the time arrives for different ranges to be printed out. In consequence further print-outs can inadvertently end up with unexpected borders.

```
MY-DATA PRINTOUT    22-Jan-89 <-----------------------------
Column A as Border      Print range H1.M7               ----Header line
Quarter                    7         8         9        10        11        12
--------------------------------------------------------------------------------
Sales Volume             134       141       148       155       163       171
Sales Revenue          4,020     4,221     4,432     4,654     4,887     5,131
Variable Costs         2,814     2,955     3,103     3,258     3,421     3,592
Fixed Costs            1,100     1,100     1,100     1,100     1,100     1,100
Profits                  106       166       230       296       366       439
```

Figure 5.2 Print-out with border and header

To keep a record of a particular piece of modelling, you can print out a one cell per line 'listing' of all the entries in the spreadsheet—numbers, formulae, and labels. For example, the Cell-Formulas of the MYDATA worksheet, starting in column B when listed out look like Figure 5.3. To obtain this listing, specify the print Range as B3.D7 say. From the Options submenu, choose the 'Other' option and then choose the Cell-Formulas as the form of output required.

```
B3: (,0) 100
C3: (,0) (1+$B$11)*B3
D3: (,0) (1+$B$11)*C3
B4: (,0) +B3*$B$12
C4: (,0) +C3*$B$12
D4: (,0) +D3*$B$12
B5: (,0) +$B$13*B4
C5: (,0) +$B$13*C4
D5: (,0) +$B$13*D4
B6: (,0) +$B$14
C6: (,0) +$B$14
D6: (,0) +$B$14
B7: (,0) +B4-B5-B6
C7: (,0) +C4-C5-C6  <-- Formula
D7: (,0) +D4-D5-D6
 ^    ^
 |    └-------------- Display format
 └------------------- Address
```

Figure 5.3 Listing of formulae in MYDATA

Once again, refer to the 1-2-3 Reference Manual for further details on printing. Alternatively, issue the Print command, then press the Help key (f1) and browse through the Help screens on the Print command and associated topics.

5.3 Data presentation

Often, the table of numbers emerging from some spreadsheet analysis is not in a form that is immediately communicable to others. Frequently the figures need rounding and the rows and columns need reordering before the message in the data is clearly revealed.

A few simple rules have been found to work wonders in communicating tables of numbers. In particular:

1. Round numbers to two 'effective' digits.

2. Give row and/or column averages in the table to provide a visual focus.

3. Order rows and/or columns by the size of these averages or some other measure of size (keeping to the same order if there are several similar tables).

4. Put figures to be compared into columns rather than rows, with values in descending size order as far as possible.

Effective digits means digits that vary in the set of values under scrutiny. With the sales figures, rounding to two effective digits results in 34.4 rounding to 34 and 25.8 rounding to 26. (With index numbers such as 117.4 and 134.9 where the base year is 100, rounding to two effective digits produces 117 and 135. The initial 1's are not 'effective digits' because they do not vary from reading to reading.) Rounding to two effective digits results in the sales figure, 305.7 rounding to 310 as contrasted with 34.4 rounding to 34. In other words, when the readings in a table differ greatly, readings are rounded to different numbers of digits. This is sometimes called variable rounding.

Adherence to the rules above for data presentation does not have to be slavish: their purpose is to simplify the mental arithmetic which has to be applied to the table and to help in the perception of patterns. In practice, applying the rules almost always results in tables that are easier to read.

Fortunately, 1-2-3 has a range of formatting, rounding, and sorting procedures that make applying the rules of data presentation relatively easy. These include the Range Format commands which allow the cells to be formatted and rounded in a variety of ways, the special functions @ROUND and @AVG, and the Data Sort and Move commands which allow columns and rows to be reordered.

To illustrate what is possible, consider the regional sales results in Figure 5.4. The main features of the sales figures, trends, differences between regions, etc. are not immediately obvious. One difficulty is that the sales regions have been ordered alphabetically which in no way helps us to understand the numerical information. Also the data is too detailed and undigested.

```
         A          B          C          D          E
1  Regional Quarterly Sales Data              (000s)
2  ------------------------------------------------------
3  REGION          Q1         Q2         Q3         Q4
4  Central       34.4       32.1       27.7       32.2
5  N East       148.6      139.6      144.3      166.5
6  N West       305.7      284.4      245.3      377.8
7  South         25.8       29.2       24.9       27.8
8  S East       256.7      242.1      212.9      243.0
9  S West        68.5       73.3       67.9       84.6
```

Figure 5.4 Regional sales data (file QSALES)

In contrast, look forwards to Figure 5.7. The regions have been ordered by average size of sales, numbers have been rounded, and marginal averages are shown. The pattern in the figures is clear: the decline in sales over three quarters was reversed in the fourth quarter and this last quarter increase in sales was more marked in the North West region than elsewhere. The line graphs of Figure 5.10 shows these features clearly.

We will work through the intervening steps. You can key in the sales figures as shown in Figure 5.4. Alternatively, you can enter the data using the CM disc that accompanies this text. The worksheet file that contains the regional sales data is called QSALES. So with this disc in Drive B type:

/ F R to Retrieve a File

1-2-3 responds by putting the names of the first eight worksheet files (drawn from the disc) on the control panel. You choose the file to retrieve either by typing its name or by pointing with the highlight (much as you choose commands from the command menu). If QSALES appears on the control panel, point to it and press Return. If QSALES is not on the control panel, keep pressing the down arrow key until it appears. Then point to it and press Return as before.

The data disc that comes with the text contains several worksheet files. You can 'list' the files on the screen at any time by issuing the File List Worksheet command (/ F L W). From the listing, pressing any key will return you to the worksheet currently in use.

To improve the presentation of the regional sales data, row and column averages will be added. First, extend the dotted line across cell F2 (\ –) and add a dotted line in row 10 (\ – and Copy).

Next enter the row and column labels Average in cells A11 and F3 respectively. The special function @AVG calculates the average of the entries in a range of cells. So in cell F4, type:

@AVG (B4.E4)

and Copy this formula into cell range F5.F9 (i.e. / C F4 (↵) F5.F9 (↵)).

In cell B11 type:

@AVG (B4.B9)

and Copy this into cell range C11.F11.

Next display the numerical values to the nearest whole number, i.e. with the pointer on cell B4, type:

/ R F	to Format a Range
F 0 (↵)	in Fixed format with 0 decimal places
B4.F11 (↵)	the range to be formatted.

The display should look like Figure 5.5 at this stage.

```
         A           B           C           D           E           F
 1  Regional Quarterly Sales    Data       (000s)
 2  ------------------------------------------------------------------
 3  REGION          Q1          Q2          Q3          Q4     Average
 4  Central         34          32          28          32          32
 5  N East         149         140         144         167         150
 6  N West         306         284         245         378         303
 7  South           26          29          25          28          27
 8  S East         257         242         213         243         239
 9  S West          69          73          68          85          74
10  ------------------------------------------------------------------
11  Average        140         133         121         155         137
```

Figure 5.5 Rounded sales data with average values

The next step is to sort the rows by average sales level with the largest values at the top of the table. This helps comparisons that rely on mental arithmetic. The particular 1-2-3 command is / Data Sort which is explained much more fully in Chapter 6. To use this command, the range of rows to be sorted must be specified and the 'Primary key' or column label on which the sorting is performed must be specified. Here the location of the Primary-Key is F3 (Average) since this is the 'fieldname' of the column on which the sort will be performed. The rows to be sorted are defined as the range A4.F9. So with the pointer on A4, type:

/ D S	to start the Data Sort command
D	to choose the Data-Range option

A4.F9 (↵) to specify the range of cells for sorting

P to choose the Primary-Key option

F3 (↵) to specify that the sort is on size of average

D (↵) to choose Descending order of sort

G to Go.

The resulting table should resemble Figure 5.6.

	A	B	C	D	E	F
1	Regional	Quarterly	Sales	Data	(000s)	
2	----------	----------	----------	----------	----------	----------
3	REGION	Q1	Q2	Q3	Q4	Average
4	N West	306	284	245	378	303
5	S East	257	242	213	243	239
6	N East	149	140	144	167	150
7	S West	69	73	68	85	74
8	Central	34	32	28	32	32
9	South	26	29	25	28	27
10	----------	----------	----------	----------	----------	----------
11	Average	140	133	121	155	137

Figure 5.6 Sales data ordered by row average

For reference purposes, datafile QS on your disc contains the spreadsheet at this stage. If you encountered any difficulty with the Data Sort operation, you may like to retrieve this file.

The Data Sort operation can only be applied to rows (not columns). In this quarterly sales example we would not want to interfere with the sequence of the quarters anyway. However, the rearrangement of columns could easily be done by moving columns (/ M) and inserting and deleting blank columns (/ W I or / W D). Note that some care is required with the formulae for row averages. These will display as ERRORS if the defining columns Q1 or Q4 are 'moved'. However, row averages can easily be re-entered when column moves are complete.

Finally, certain cells need to be further rounded if we are to work with two effective digits. For example, the sales figure 257 consists of three digits and needs to be rounded to 260 to reduce the 'information' to two effective digits.

The special function

@ROUND (x,n)

rounds the value x to the number of digits specified by n. If n is zero, rounding is to the nearest integer; if n is 1 to 1 decimal place; if n is -1 to the nearest 10. So for example, @ROUND (B5, −1) would give 260 in place of the current entry in B6, namely 257.

To use @ROUND avoiding 'circular' cell references, first copy the entire table complete with headings and labels into say row 21. That is, with the pointer on A1, type:

/ C A1.F11 (↵) A21 (↵)

to Copy from range A1.F11 to A21.

Now with the pointer on B24, the North West sales in the first quarter, type:

@ROUND (B4, −1) (↵)

and watch 306 round to 310. Copy this formula from B24 across to range C24.F24.

Next, copy the formulae in range B24.F24 down to rows 25, 26, and 31. (The figures for the other regions—S West, Central, and South are already rounded to two effective digits.) The worksheet now consists of a pair of tables like Figures 5.6 and 5.7 where the lower table has entries all of which have been rounded to two digits (so-called 'variable' rounding).

	A	B	C	D	E	F
21	Regional Quarterly Sales Data (000s)					
22	------------					
23	REGION	Q1	Q2	Q3	Q4	Average
24	N West	310	280	250	380	300
25	S East	260	240	210	240	240
26	N East	150	140	140	170	150
27	S West	69	73	68	85	74
28	Central	34	32	28	32	32
29	South	26	29	25	28	27
30	------------					
31	Average	140	130	120	160	140

Figure 5.7 Sales data after variable rounding to 2 digits

The pattern of sales and the differences between the regions are now much more visible. However, communication can be greatly enhanced if the results are presented graphically as well as in a table. The next sections illustrate how graphs can be set up quickly and how they can be named and saved with a worksheet, or alternatively saved for printing.

Before proceeding to Section 5.4, remember to save your worksheet file. (You may need to put your own data disc into Drive B if it is not present already.) If Drive B is empty, you will probably get an 'error message'. You can recover the situation by hitting the Escape key. If the disc in your Drive is 'write protected', you will also get an error message displayed. In most cases, you 'withdraw' from an error message, by hitting the Escape key. So, with your data disc in Drive B, type:

/ F S QSALES1 (↵)

to save your worksheet under the file name QSALES1 say. (Once again, your CM disc already contains a datafile QS1 which should tie up with QSALES 1.)

Instead of continuing with the full set of data and the intermediate analysis, we could 'extract' the numerical values to be graphed and set up a second worksheet file. To illustrate, the numerical results in the range of cells A21 to F31 will be saved in a separate worksheet file using the File Xtract command. This command allows parts of spreadsheet files to be saved. (An associated command File Combine allows existing spreadsheet files to be combined with spreadsheets currently held in memory. Together, the File Xtract and File Combine commands provide considerable flexibility for file handling in 1-2-3.)

The steps are as follows. Start by pointing to the start of the data to be extracted, cell A21. Then type:

/ F X V to File Xtract Values

(Values result in numerical entries: in contrast, Formulae will save the syntax of the formulae, although the cell addresses will be subtly altered.)

In response to the request for an Xtract file name, type:

QSALES2 (↵)

and finally

A21.F31 (↵)

the range of cells whose numerical values are to be extracted and stored in file QSALES2.

You may wish to examine the new file QSALES just saved. Retrieve the file and check that it contains numerical results only (no formulae), the figures being those displayed in Figure 5.7. We will use QSALES2 as the starting point for exploring the graphics capability in 1-2-3.

(To avoid any difficulties which may occur with the File Xtract command, your data disc contains file QS2 which should be identical to QSALES2. If in doubt, use datafile QS2 in the ensuing sections on graphics.)

5.4 Overview of 1-2-3 graphics

The graph command in 1-2-3 enables you to construct a graph for the numbers in a row or column of the spreadsheet rapidly and painlessly. 1-2-3 does the scaling and plotting automatically. For example, in Chapter 4, the Graph command was used to produce a simple line graph of quarterly sales and quarterly profits with data taken from the spreadsheet.

Different types of graph are available with 1-2-3—line graphs like Figure 4.11, bar charts, stacked bar graphs, pie charts which are essentially univariate, and XY (or scatter) graphs which are bivariate. Several sets of data can be displayed at the same time—in Chapter 4 both sales volume and profits were graphed simultaneously and you can specify up to 6 data ranges at once.

To define a graph, you specify the graph type and the cell range(s) in which the data to be plotted are stored. With this minimal information a graph can be produced. It is relatively easy to add labels to axes, 'legends' when several graphs are displayed at once, and titles at the top of the graphs.

Having once defined a graph, it is possible to change some of the data (keeping its location in the worksheet unchanged) and redraw the graph simply pressing the Graph Key (f10). 1-2-3 remembers your most recent graph settings, e.g. the most recent graph type, the data ranges to be plotted, the axis labels, etc. This is called the 'current graph' and can be redrawn by pressing the (f10/Graph) key from READY mode.

If you save a spreadsheet with / File Save, the 'current' graph is also saved. We shall see this when we retrieve the file saved at the end of Chapter 4, namely MYDATA, which contains the setting for the simple graph in Figure 4.11. In addition, graph settings can be saved under 'graph names' so that different graphs can easily be redrawn for particular spreadsheets. If the worksheet is subsequently saved to disc, the named graphs will also be saved for re-viewing when the worksheet is next retrieved.

It is also possible to print graphs using the 1-2-3 PrintGraph program. You need to save an intermediate 'graph file' on disc. Subsequently you can print the graph using the 1-2-3 PrintGraph disc.

5.5 Bar charts

In this section, we will build a bar chart to represent the regional sales data of Section 5.3. We start by producing graphs for the North West region alone, and then plot the data for all 6 regions on the same graph.

Either key in the data shown in Figure 5.7 or retrieve the file saved at the end of Section 5.3, namely QSALES2. In the following description, the quarterly sales data are assumed to be in rows 4 to 9, exactly as in QSALES2. If the alignment of the data is different in *your* spreadsheet, retrieve datafile QS2 and work with this file instead.

The Graph menu, like the Print menu considered in Section 5.1, is a circular or 'sticky' menu: you make a choice and are returned to the menu for a further choice. To return to READY mode, you either choose Quit or press Escape a few times. To start graph building, the procedure has the following steps:

1. Type:

/ G   to start the Graph command.

This gives the Graph menu with the following options:

Type X A B C D E F Reset View Save Options Name Quit

2. Choose the option Type which leads to a menu of graph types from which you choose Bar.

3. From the Graph menu, choose X, and specify the X-axis range as B3.E3. Consequently, the horizontal (or X-) axis will be labelled Q1, Q2, etc.

4. From the Graph menu, choose A, the first data range to be plotted and specify it to be the quarterly sales in the North West region, i.e. cell range B4.E4.

5. From the Graph menu, choose View to go to the graph of sales in the North West region.

You should see a bar graph somewhat like that of Figure 5.8. The vertical axis is automatically labelled from 0 to 400, and the 'bars' sit on top of the chosen X-axis labels. (For the simplest graph of all, it is not necessary to specify the X-axis range at all.) When you have finished looking at the graph, press any key to return to the spreadsheet.

The graph can be improved by adding labels, but first we will build the graph for all the sales ranges, i.e. for several data ranges. The essential step is number 4 in the above list. That is, from the Graph menu, choose B, and specify it as the South East region sales, i.e. cell range B5.E5. Then choose C, and so on until all 6 ranges have been specified.

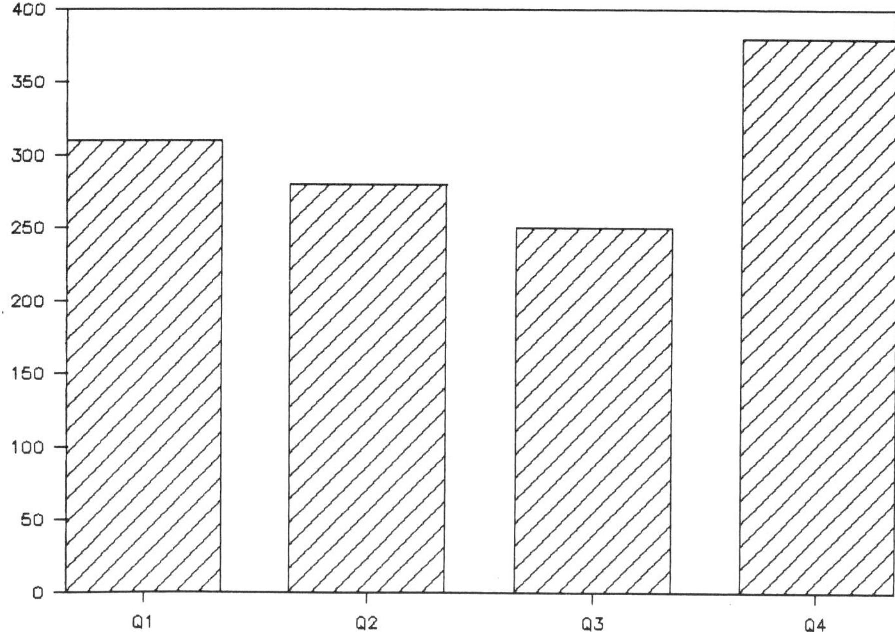

Figure 5.8 First bar chart of North West region sales

Finally, View the graph. It should now look like the bar chart of Figure 5.9. Each sales region has its own shading pattern. If preferred, the bars can be stacked one on top of each other by selecting the Stacked-Bar type of graph. Alternatively, a Line graph can be specified, leading to a display such as that shown in Figure 5.10.

The Line graphs can be drawn in different ways. The Graph Options Format command sequence allows you to say how the line graphs are to be drawn and connected up. The possibilities are lines, symbols or both. Take care that you do not choose the option 'Neither' from this menu. If you do your graph will mysteriously disappear.

We will explore these possibilities in the context of scatter plots in Chapter 9.

5.6 Adding text and colour

The basic graph in Figure 5.9 can be improved by adding a title, some labels for the axes and for the patterns used to distinguish the different sales regions. To make these additions, choose Options from the main Graph menu. The Options submenu contains several choices—Titles and Legends among others.

Choose Titles and then First. Add your main title, say 'Quarterly Sales for Regions' and press Enter. Choose Titles again and then Second to add a subtitle in the same way. You can also add 'titles' for the vertical (Y-axis) and horizontal X-axis in the same manner.

Choose Legends from the Options submenu and then A. Add a brief description of the A data range, say NW, to indicate that this data is for the North West. Continue to add

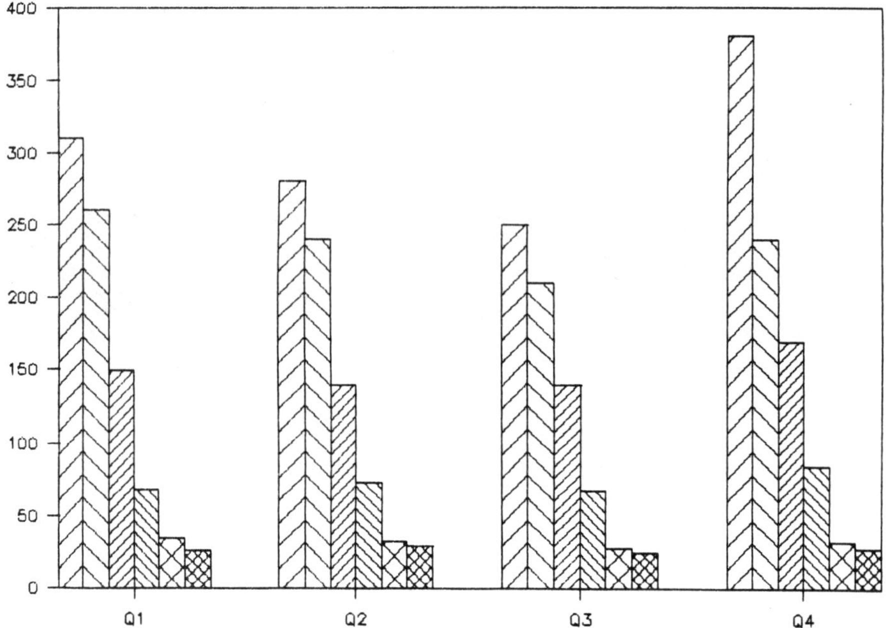

Figure 5.9 Bar chart comparing sales for 6 regions

'legends', SE, NE, etc., for the other data ranges. In this way, the meaning of the different shading patterns in the graph is made clear.

If you have a colour monitor, you may like to add colour to your graphs. On the Options menu, it is merely necessary to choose Color to achieve this effect: the other choice B & W displays graphs in black and white. (You may find the B & W display a better basis for printing graphs with some personal computer equipment.)

There are other choices on the Options menu, which give considerable flexibility in displaying data graphically. The Scale option allows you to scale the axes manually rather than leave 1-2-3 to do the scaling automatically. The Format option permits line graphs to be shown as lines or symbols or both. The Grid choice enables horizontal and/or vertical lines to be superimposed on the graph. Lastly, Data Labels can be added to the different data ranges in the body of the graph (as opposed to underneath).

Try adding the suggested legends, together with suitable titles. Your final graph should look something like Figure 5.11.

5.7 Naming graphs

When a graph is considered 'satisfactory', it should be given a name. This procedure ensures that the graph can be displayed again and printed if required. The command sequence Graph Name Create allows names to be associated with different graph settings. Several different graphs (in fact, different graph settings) can be named in this way and they will be retained

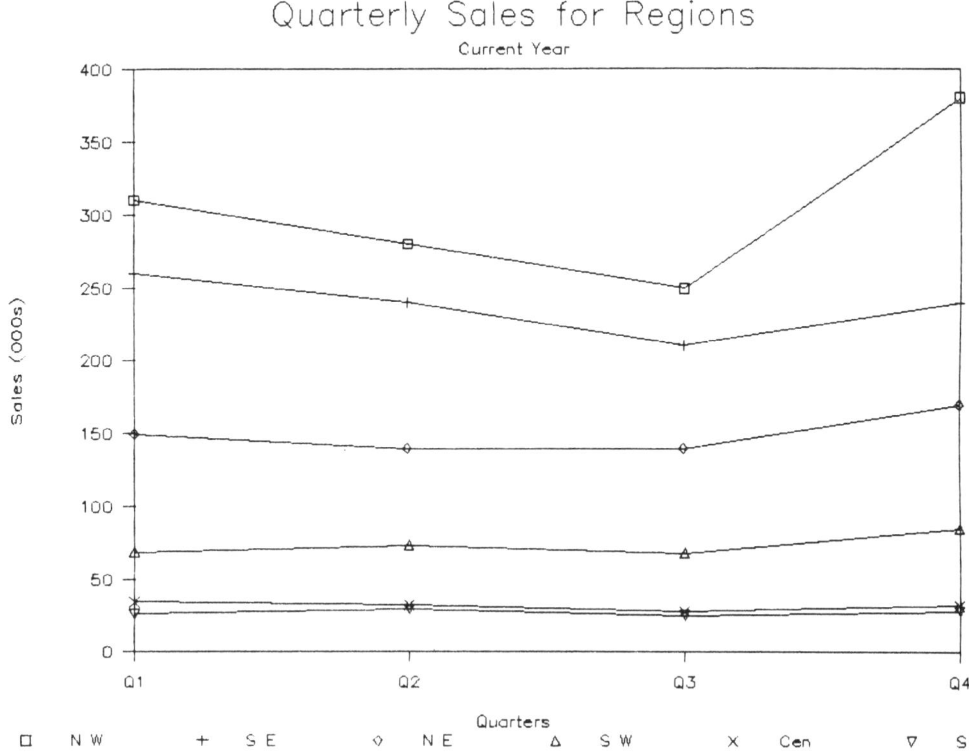

Figure 5.10 Line graphs comparing regional sales

when the worksheet containing them is 'file saved' to disc. Named graphs can be recalled to the screen with the command sequence Graph Name Use.

To illustrate, the bar chart of quarterly sales for regions will be named. From the Graph menu, view the current graph using the steps:

/ G V	to View the current graph

We assume that the graph on screen is somewhat like Figure 5.11. It will be given the name GRAPH1. Returning to the Graph menu, type:

N C	to Name Create
GRAPH1	the name attached to the current graph.

Returning to the Graph menu once more, type:

T L	to change the Type to a Line graph
V	to view the Line graph.

The current graph now corresponds to Figure 5.10. Clearly, respecifying the Type of graph could produce the bar chart again. However, since the bar chart was named, it can be named and used as follows:

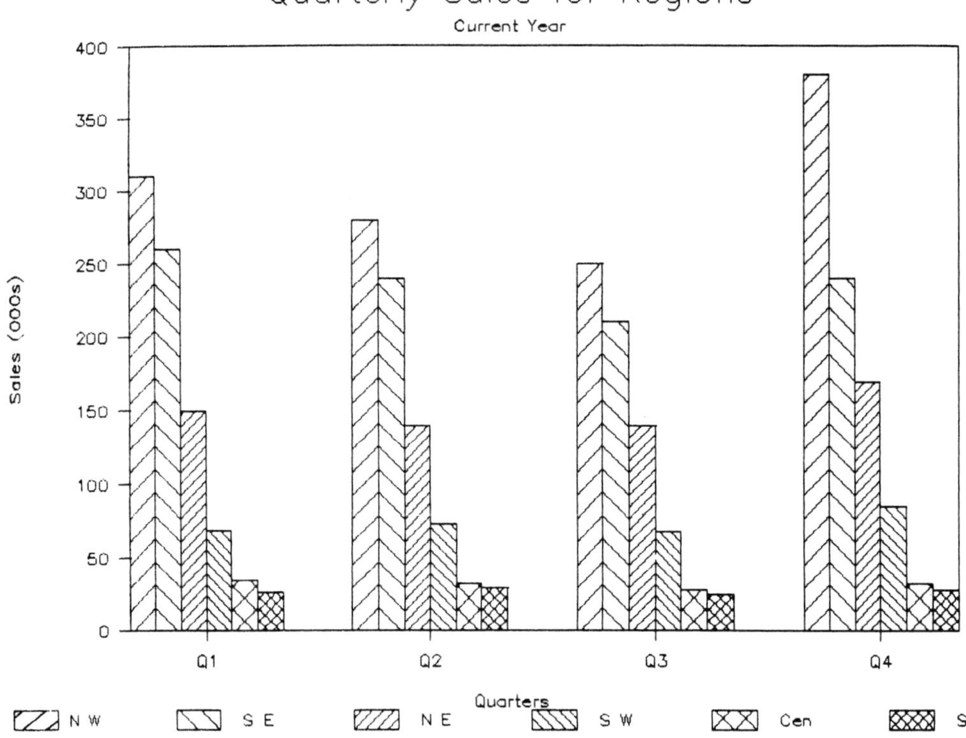

Figure 5.11 Bar chart with titles and legends

N U GRAPH1 — to Use the previously Named graph, i.e. to specify GRAPH1 as the current graph.

You may like to explore the naming procedure by setting up and naming other graphs associated with the quarterly sales data. Finally, remember to save your worksheet file using File Save to ensure that all named graphs can be recalled to the screen when you work on your spreadsheet at some future date.

Datafile QS3 on your disc represents the QSALES spreadsheet at this stage. It contains the two named graphs described in this section. You may wish to retrieve the file and access the named graphs from the Graph menu.

5.8 Saving a graph file for printing

There is another way of keeping a record of a graph: the special Save command on the Graph menu. This saves the graph details in a separate graph file in the form of a binary 'screen dump'. This file contains pixel by pixel information from which the graph can be reconstituted, but only for printing purposes.

Thus, to obtain a print-out of a graph, such as Figure 5.11, get the graph on screen from the Graph menu. Choose the Save option and give your graph file a suitable name such as

QSALES. 1-2-3 will make a graph file called QSALES.PIC on your disc for use with the PrintGraph program.

When your current modelling session with 1-2-3 is concluded, choose Quit to leave 1-2-3 and from the Access menu, choose PrintGraph. When you have accessed PrintGraph, choose Image-Select from the main menu and 'mark' the graph to be printed, as is described on the screen. When returned to the PrintGraph main menu, choose to Go and your graph will be printed.

Again, if you encounter any difficulties with PrintGraph, press the Help key (f1) and 1-2-3 will provide appropriate information. If you press Help, the Escape key returns you to the PrintGraph main menu. You may need to choose Settings to ensure that your hardware and software are correctly configured to produce a graph. One other useful choice on the Settings menu is Image and after that Scale. With this sequence of commands you can choose the appropriate size for your graph on printing out.

5.9 What-if graphing

Returning to 1-2-3 from PrintGraph, retrieve the worksheet saved at the end of Chapter 4 (MYDATA) and press the Graph key (f10) to view the graph built in Section 4.7.

If you look through the details of how the graph was constructed, you will see that Line graphs were specified. Profits and Sales Volumes were plotted each quarter on the basis of assumptions. For example, Sales Growth was assumed to be 5 per cent per quarter and the Cost of Goods Sold was taken as 70 per cent. If we change any of the assumptions, it is not necessary to redefine the graph because the cell location of the data to be plotted has not changed. Pressing the Graph key will reveal the new graph incorporating the changed assumptions. This could be dubbed 'what-if graphing'.

Try changing the Cost of Goods Sold to 60 per cent and the Sales Growth rate to 5.5 per cent per quarter. Press the Graph key to see the new graph.

You may also like to retrieve a finished version of the MYDATA spreadsheet, called MDFINAL, on your CM disc. This shows the MYDATA spreadsheet at the end of Chapter 4. It contains three named graphs. Graph 1 is the plot of Profits and Sales Volume shown in Figure 4.11. It is 'linked' into the spreadsheet model and can be used for What-if graphing as just described. In contrast, Graph 2 is based on a data table showing how the profits change as the sales growth assumption varies. This graph does not change as What-ifs are performed on the profits spreadsheet. Finally, Graph 3 shows the profits resulting from a set of best and worst value assumptions. The profit figures have been stored in the spreadsheet for each case: Most Likely, Best, Worst. They can then be graphed together for comparative purposes.

The companion volume, Advanced Spreadsheet Modelling, contains further detailed material on the use of graphs and sensitivity analysis.

Finally, remember to save your worksheet before moving on to the next chapter.

CHAPTER 6

Database Management

In previous chapters, we have concentrated on two of 1-2-3's capabilities, namely, spreadsheet modelling and graphics. In this chapter we turn to the third capability, namely database management. In the following sections, we investigate 1-2-3's special facilities for manipulating, searching, and controlling records.

A database is a collection of records, each with information organized under different headings or 'fields'. For example, a database could consist of names and associated addresses and telephone numbers, such as in a telephone directory. Or it could consist of part numbers with associated prices, suppliers, stock levels, and reorder quantities.

A database can be constructed using the rows of the 1-2-3 spreadsheet as records, and the columns as fields. Each record contains a group of associated entries, e.g. a name with associated address and telephone number. Corresponding information (e.g. telephone numbers) is entered in the same column (field) on each row (record). Figure 6.1 gives some examples of 1-2-3 structured databases. Notice that the first row of the database consists of labels identifying the different types of information. These are called field names.

The records in a database can be set up and maintained using 1-2-3 in exactly the same way as we have used 1-2-3 in spreadsheet modelling. 1-2-3 commands, explained in Chapters 2 to 4 can be used to modify and update the records. For example, additional fields can be added using / Worksheet Insert Column, and the contents of a record can be updated using the normal Edit facilities. For simple databases, that is, sets of records with easily classifiable information (particularly if it is numeric), 1-2-3 can be used most effectively to handle and organize data.

In this chapter, we shall use a small database of 50 personnel records. Information on current salary, commencement date of contract, department, and number of days absence from work is available for each employee. Figure 6.2 shows the database records in full. In the following paragraphs, we will illustrate a variety of ways in which the 1-2-3 Data commands can Sort and Query the personnel records. Since contract dates are included in the database, we shall also look briefly at 1-2-3's calendar arithmetic facilities.

6.1 Setting up the database

The records displayed in Figure 6.2 are already structured in a form suitable for entering into the 1-2-3 worksheet. All the data for an individual employee is set out on one row—this is a record. All the entries on, say, salary are set out in the same column,

PERSONNEL RECORDS XYZ Co

SURNAME	C NAME	SEX	SALARY	DEPT	CONTRACT
Carter	Tony	M	9552	Prod	Aug-77
Griffith	Tom	M	6192	Staff	Jan-72
Metzer	Tim	M	10704	Prod	May-73
Foxon	Tessa	F	11832	Sales	Aug-70
Brooks	Susan	F	8592	Staff	Nov-79
Iverson	Steve	M	7872	Sales	Oct-81
George	Steve	M	8304	Sales	Jan-73
Sutcliffe	Sam	M	13776	Mktg	Nov-83
Kingston	Rory	M	8016	Admin	May-77
Lochran	Robert	M	9120	Accts	May-77

ORDERBOOK DATABASE

ORDER NO	DEALER	ORDER DATE	DUE DATE	QUANTITY
1	216	07-Jan-89	01-Mar-89	75
2	214	09-Jan-89	15-Mar-89	20
3	215	10-Jan-89	07-Mar-89	50
4	207	16-Jan-89	01-Mar-89	55
5	209	16-Jan-89	04-Mar-89	45

STUDENT GRADES IN STATISTICS

NAME	MARK1	MARK2	AV MARK	EXAM	GRADE
Brown	65	70	33.75	30	64
Chesser	75	75	35.5	41	79
Chance	70	75	36.25	35	71
Condor	65	70	33.75	33	67
Constance	70	40	27.5	29	57

SURVEY RECORDS FOR DATABASE

NAME	SEX	SALARY	SERVICE	ATTITUDE
Cornell	Male	796	8	U
Dyer	Female	516	3	F
Day	Female	892	33	A
Westwood	Male	986	18	U
Smith	Male	716	9	A
Boyd	Male	692	12	A
Kirk	Female	656	12	U
Jackson	Male	1148	21	U

Figure 6.1 Four examples of databases

under the field name SALARY. The tabular layout and data can be copied straight into the 1-2-3 worksheet much as they are.

Try entering the field names, SURNAME, C NAME, SEX, and SALARY and the first two records (i.e. data for employees Carter and Griffith) as shown in Figure 6.3. This in principle is the way you would set up the database.

The file RECORD contains the full 50 'records' of which you have part-entered the first two. So now retrieve this file from disc and load it into the computer memory to complete the database. That is, type:

	A	B	C	D	E	F	G
1	PERSONNEL	RECORDS	XYZ Co				
2	--						
3	SURNAME	C NAME	SEX	SALARY	DEPT	CONTRACT	ABSENCE
4	Carter	Tony	M	9552	Prod	Aug-77	0
5	Griffith	Tom	M	6192	Staff	Jan-72	0
	Metzer	Tim	M	10704	Prod	May-73	2
	Foxon	Tessa	F	11832	Sales	Aug-70	0
	Brooks	Susan	F	8592	Staff	Nov-79	0
	Iverson	Steve	M	7872	Sales	Oct-81	0
	George	Steve	M	8304	Sales	Jan-73	0
	Sutcliff	Sam	M	13776	Mktg	Nov-83	1
	Kingston	Rory	M	8016	Admin	May-77	2
	Lochran	Robert	M	9120	Accts	May-77	7
	Wong	Philip	M	10704	Prod	Dec-78	1
	Hudson	Peter	M	10320	Sales	Apr-75	0
	Beattie	Paul	M	5880	Sales	Jan-79	0
	Thwaite	Ossie	M	8976	Admin	Jun-76	0
	Watson	Norman	M	18976	Accts	Oct-68	4
19	Franklin	Nick	M	16312	Staff	Apr-69	3
20	Yoshi	Nick	M	9288	Prod	Jan-72	0
21	Pope	Meg	F	9288	Prod	Apr-71	2
	Stewart	Mathew	M	18208	Accts	May-70	5
	Rose	Mary	F	6624	Accts	Apr-70	0
	Drosser	Martin	M	17560	Admin	Apr-70	3
	Abraham	Liz	F	8304	Sales	Jul-78	0
	Kent	Keith	M	8136	Accts	Jun-82	9
	Barnet	Katie	F	10320	Staff	Jan-73	4
	Blockley	Joyce	F	8592	Prod	Feb-76	4
	Jones	John	M	7056	Accts	Feb-73	4
	Matsura	Jo	F	7872	Staff	Oct-66	0
	Dudson	Jane	F	10104	Accts	Mar-75	5
	Kettle	James	M	11520	Accts	Jun-76	6
	Tolley	Helen	F	6768	Mktg	Aug-68	3
	Scarr	Hazel	F	8976	Admin	Jan-71	1
	Peabody	Harold	M	17288	Mktg	Jun-63	0
	Frost	Gordon	M	7560	Prod	Apr-69	1
	Waters	Fred	M	8304	Mktg	May-73	0
	Beecher	Fay	F	5880	Accts	Jan-71	2
	Lambert	Eve	F	9816	Admin	Mar-75	3
	Greene	David	M	7872	Sales	Mar-72	0
	Marris	David	M	7560	Prod	Sep-63	0
	Rodgers	David	M	8856	Accts	Nov-74	4
	Costain	Clodagh	F	8976	Admin	Jun-82	1
	Harper	Chrissie	F	10272	Accts	Jun-76	2
	Mantle	Chris	F	7056	Sales	Sep-78	4
	Herbert	Brigid	F	12984	Mktg	Nov-80	0
	Naylor	Brian	M	8448	Prod	Jun-65	2
	Asher	Brian	M	7248	Staff	Apr-71	2
	Turner	Bob	M	7560	Mktg	Nov-74	0
	Elliott	Beth	F	11352	Mktg	Dec-78	1
	Hartley	Anna	F	8304	Staff	Aug-77	0
	Bowlus	Andy	M	10272	Prod	Oct-67	0
53	Morris	Andrew	M	9552	Prod	Oct-76	2

Figure 6.2 XYZ personnel records in 1-2-3 layout

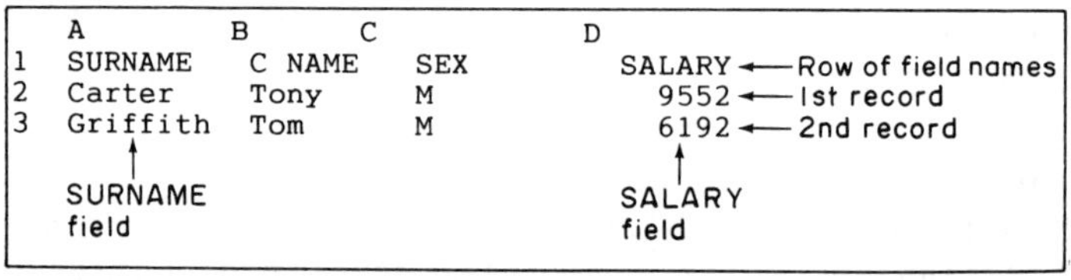

	A	B	C	D
1	SURNAME	C NAME	SEX	SALARY ← Row of field names
2	Carter	Tony	M	9552 ← 1st record
3	Griffith	Tom	M	6192 ← 2nd record
	↑ SURNAME field			↑ SALARY field

Figure 6.3 Entering the records

/ F R RECORD (↵) to File Retrieve the named datafile.

Your worksheet should look like Figure 6.2. Explore the records that are currently not displayed on the screen. The keys 'Pg Up' and 'Pg Dn' adjacent to the arrow keys allow you to 'jump' up and 'down' the spreadsheet in 'pages'.

6.2 Sorting the records

One major requirement of a database system is to be able to sort records in different orders. For example, suppose we require the employee records in alphabetical order or in order of salary size, department by department. To sort the records, three things must be specified:

(a) the range of records to be sorted,
(b) the 'Primary-Key' (the location of the selected field name) for sorting,
(c) the order of the sort, e.g. Ascending (smallest value first), or Descending (largest value first). Alphabetic order also counts as Ascending order.

(i) Sorting records alphabetically

The employee records start in row 4 and finish in row 53, i.e. the 'range' of the records to be sorted is A4.G53. It is important to specify this range correctly. If mis-specified as say A4.A53, only the Surnames will be reordered, and the rest of each record will be 'left behind' in the sort.
Note: Do not include the row with field names (row 3), only the rows to be sorted.

The Primary-Key for arranging the records alphabetically is 'SURNAME' so the selected field name is in A3.

The Sort order is A for Ascending (or alphabetic order which counts as Ascending). So type:

/ D S	to Data Sort
D	for Data-Range (or press (↵) to confirm Data-Range)
A4.G53 (↵)	to specify the Data-Range of records
P A3 (↵)	for the Primary-Key to be SURNAME in cell A3
A (↵)	for the Ascending (i.e. alphabetical) sort order
G	to Go, i.e. to perform the sort.

Check that the records are now in alphabetical order i.e. Abraham, Asher, Barnet, etc. Figure 6.4 shows the first 10 records after the alphabetic sort.

(ii) Sorting by department

Now, suppose that the records must be sorted in Department order. In sorting a second time, it is only necessary to enter changes, in this case the change of Primary-Key. So type:

/ D S	to Data Sort

	A	B	C	D	E	F	G
1	PERSONNEL	RECORDS	XYZ Co				
2	------------	------------	------------	------------	------------	------------	------------
3	SURNAME	C NAME	SEX	SALARY	DEPT	CONTRACT	ABSENCE
4	Abraham	Liz	F	8304	Sales	Jul-78	0
5	Asher	Brian	M	7248	Staff	Apr-71	2
6	Barnet	Katie	F	10320	Staff	Jan-73	4
7	Beattie	Paul	M	5880	Sales	Jan-79	0
8	Beecher	Fay	F	5880	Accts	Jan-71	2
9	Blockley	Joyce	F	8592	Prod	Feb-76	4
10	Bowlus	Andy	M	10272	Prod	Oct-67	0
11	Brooks	Susan	F	8592	Staff	Nov-79	0
12	Carter	Tony	M	9552	Prod	Aug-77	0
13	Costain	Clodagh	F	8976	Admin	Jun-82	1

Figure 6.4 First 10 records after alphabetic sorting

P E3 (↵) for the Primary-Key to be DEPT in E3

A (↵) for the order to be Ascending (or alphabetic)

G to Go.

Your records should now be ordered as indicated in Figure 6.5.

	A	B	C	D	E	F	G
1	PERSONNEL	RECORDS	XYZ Co				
2	------------	------------	------------	------------	------------	------------	------------
3	SURNAME	C NAME	SEX	SALARY	DEPT	CONTRACT	ABSENCE
4	Kent	Keith	M	8136	Accts	Jun-82	9
5	Kettle	James	M	11520	Accts	Jun-76	6
6	Watson	Norman	M	18976	Accts	Oct-68	4
7	Lochran	Robert	M	9120	Accts	May-77	7
8	Rodgers	David	M	8856	Accts	Nov-74	4
9	Beecher	Fay	F	5880	Accts	Jan-71	2
10	Rose	Mary	F	6624	Accts	Apr-70	0
11	Dudson	Jane	F	10104	Accts	Mar-75	5
12	Stewart	Mathew	M	18208	Accts	May-70	5
13	Harper	Chrissie	F	10272	Accts	Jun-76	2
14	Jones	John	M	7056	Accts	Feb-73	4
15	Costain	Clodagh	F	8976	Admin	Jun-82	1
16	Kingston	Rory	M	8016	Admin	May-77	2
17	Drosser	Martin	M	17560	Admin	Apr-70	3
18	Scarr	Hazel	F	8976	Admin	Jan-71	1
19	Thwaite	Ossie	M	8976	Admin	Jun-76	0

Figure 6.5 First 14 records after sorting by department

Notice that we did not specify the Data-Range as it was unchanged from the previous sort. 1-2-3 ‘remembers’ previous settings and will use these unless instructed to do otherwise.

(iii) Sorting by department then salary

It is possible to sort on a Secondary-Key as well as a Primary one. All records with the same Primary-Key entry (for example Admin) can be sorted with respect to a second field name. Suppose we require the employee records sorted firstly by department and within department by salary. The primary sort would be on department (with field name DEPT in cell E3) and the secondary sort on salary (with field name in cell D3).

As mentioned above, in sorting a second time it is only necessary to enter changes and new requirements, i.e. in this case the new Secondary-Key. The Primary-Key is unchanged as is the Data-Range. In specifying the details of the Data Sort, 1-2-3 always suggests the settings used on the last sort. If they are appropriate, you simply press (↵) to confirm. If 1-2-3's suggested setting is inappropriate, you type the correct entry 'over the top'.

So to sort the records on DEPT then SALARY, type:

/ D S — to Data Sort

Next, the Secondary-Key must be specified. So type:

S D3 (↵) D (↵) — for the Secondary-Key to be SALARY in D3 and the order of the sort to be Descending (largest salary first)

G — to Go.

Check that the order of the sort is as shown in Figure 6.6, e.g. Watson, Stewart, Kettle, etc.

	A	B	C	D	E	F	G
1	PERSONNEL	RECORDS	XYZ Co				
2	----------	----------	----------	----------	----------	----------	----------
3	SURNAME	C NAME	SEX	SALARY	DEPT	CONTRACT	ABSENCE
4	Watson	Norman	M	18976	Accts	Oct-68	4
5	Stewart	Mathew	M	18208	Accts	May-70	5
6	Kettle	James	M	11520	Accts	Jun-76	6
7	Harper	Chrissie	F	10272	Accts	Jun-76	2
8	Dudson	Jane	F	10104	Accts	Mar-75	5
9	Lochran	Robert	M	9120	Accts	May-77	7
10	Rodgers	David	M	8856	Accts	Nov-74	4
11	Kent	Keith	M	8136	Accts	Jun-82	9
12	Jones	John	M	7056	Accts	Feb-73	4
13	Rose	Mary	F	6624	Accts	Apr-70	0
14	Beecher	Fay	F	5880	Accts	Jan-71	2
15	Drosser	Martin	M	17560	Admin	Apr-70	3
16	Lambert	Eve	F	9816	Admin	Mar-75	3
17	Scarr	Hazel	F	8976	Admin	Jan-71	1
18	Thwaite	Ossie	M	8976	Admin	Jun-76	0
19	Costain	Clodagh	F	8976	Admin	Jun-82	1

Figure 6.6 Records after sorting by department then salary

For practice, order the male employees' records in ascending order of salary. The order should be—Beattie, Griffith, Jones, etc. Check your result with Figure 6.7.

6.3 Querying the records

Often, the objective is to search or 'query' the database for a particular record, or a group of records that satisfy a particular condition. For example, suppose we want to locate Carter's record or sort out employees with a bad attendance record or those whose salaries are due for review.

Having queried the database, 1-2-3 has several ways of dealing with the output: the records may simply be found (the Find option), they may be copied to another part of the worksheet (Extract) or they may be removed from the database (Delete).

	A	B	C	D	E	F	G
1	PERSONNEL	RECORDS	XYZ Co				
2	---------	---------	---------	---------	---------	---------	---------
3	SURNAME	C NAME	SEX	SALARY	DEPT	CONTRACT	ABSENCE
4	Beattie	Paul	M	5880	Sales	Jan-79	0
5	Griffith	Tom	M	6192	Staff	Jan-72	0
6	Jones	John	M	7056	Accts	Feb-73	4
7	Asher	Brian	M	7248	Staff	Apr-71	2
8	Frost	Gordon	M	7560	Prod	Apr-69	1
9	Marris	David	M	7560	Prod	Sep-63	0
10	Turner	Bob	M	7560	Mktg	Nov-74	0
11	Iverson	Steve	M	7872	Sales	Oct-81	0
12	Greene	David	M	7872	Sales	Mar-72	0
13	Kingston	Rory	M	8016	Admin	May-77	2
14	Kent	Keith	M	8136	Accts	Jun-82	9
15	Waters	Fred	M	8304	Mktg	May-73	0
16	George	Steve	M	8304	Sales	Jan-73	0
17	Naylor	Brian	M	8448	Prod	Jun-65	2
18	Rodgers	David	M	8856	Accts	Nov-74	4
19	Thwaite	Ossie	M	8976	Admin	Jun-76	0
20	Lochran	Robert	M	9120	Accts	May-77	7

Figure 6.7 Records after sorting by sex then salary

Before issuing the Data Query command, you must specify two or possibly three 'ranges':

(a) The range of records to be searched (or 'queried') which may or may not be the entire database. This is called the Input range.
(b) The conditions a record must satisfy to be selected, the so-called Criterion. The Criterion is expressed as a set of field names and conditions and is located in the Criterion range.
(c) If copies are required of the selected records, an area of the worksheet must be specified to receive the 'output', i.e. copies of the selected records. This is the Output range. It is only needed for the Extract option not for the Find option.
The Find option will be described in this section: the Extract option in the next section.

(i) Finding an individual record

First, we will track down Carter's record.

The Input range is the entire database, i.e. the range A3.G53, which includes the field names in row 3 together with the 50 employees' records.

The Criterion range will be set up adjacent to the database, in columns H across to N, starting in the third row of the worksheet, as shown in Figure 6.8. Although the Criterion range shown in the figure contains all the field names, this is not necessary. The Criterion range consists of at least two rows and some or all of the field names in the Input range.

Unless we want to Extract (i.e. get a copy of) Carter's record, there is no need to set up an Output range at this stage. (The Output rangc will be explained in Section 6.4.)

The Steps are:

(a) Set up the Criterion range by copying the field names from range A3.G3 to H3.N3 using the Copy command. To do this, type:

	A	B	C	D	E	F	G	H	I	J	K	L	M	N	
1	PERSONNEL	RECORDS	XYZ Co					CRITERION	RANGE						1
2	----------	----------	----------	----------	----------	----------	----------	----------	----------	----------	----------	----------	----------	----------	2
3	SURNAME	C NAME	SEX	SALARY	DEPT	CONTRACT	ABSENCE	SURNAME	C NAME	SEX	SALARY	DEPT	CONTRACT	ABSENCE	3
4	Beattie	Paul	M	5880	Sales	Jan-79	0							0	4
5	Griffith	Tom	M	6192	Staff	Jan-72	0								
6	Jones	John	M	7056	Accts	Feb-73	4								
7	Asher	Brian	M	7248	Staff	Apr-71	2								
8	Turner	Bob	M	7560	Mktg	Nov-74	0								
9	Frost	Gordon	M	7560	Prod	Apr-69	1								
10	Marris	David	M	7560	Prod	Sep-63	0								
11	Iverson	Steve	M	7872	Sales	Oct-81	0								
12	Greene	David	M	7872	Sales	Mar-72	0								
13	Kingston	Rory	M	8016	Admin	May-77	2								

Figure 6.8 Worksheet layout for Data Query (Find Carter's record)

	A	B	C	D	E	F	G	H	I	J	K	L	M	N	
1	PERSONNEL	RECORDS	XYZ Co					CRITERION	RANGE						1
2	----------	----------	----------	----------	----------	----------	----------	----------	----------	----------	----------	----------	----------	----------	2
3	SURNAME	C NAME	SEX	SALARY	DEPT	CONTRACT	ABSENCE	SURNAME	C NAME	SEX	SALARY	DEPT	CONTRACT	ABSENCE	3
4	Beattie	Paul	M	5880	Sales	Jan-79	0	Carter							4
5	Griffith	Tom	M	6192	Staff	Jan-72	0								
6	Jones	John	M	7056	Accts	Feb-73	4								
7	Asher	Brian	M	7248	Staff	Apr-71	2								
8	Turner	Bob	M	7560	Mktg	Nov-74	0								
9	Frost	Gordon	M	7560	Prod	Apr-69	1								
10	Marris	David	M	7560	Prod	Sep-63	0								
11	Iverson	Steve	M	7872	Sales	Oct-81	0								
12	Greene	David	M	7872	Sales	Mar-72	0								
13	Kingston	Rory	M	8016	Admin	May-77	2								

Criterion Range H3.N4

Input Range A3.G53

Figure 6.9 Layout for Data Query (Find records with 0 days absence)

/ C A3.G3 (↵)	to Copy FROM A3.G3
H3 (↵)	the starting cell where the field names are to be copied TO.

(b) Specify the Criterion for the query by typing Carter into cell H4.

Note: It is most important that Carter's name is keyed into the Criterion range so that its form is identical to that in the original database. It should start with a capital letter but be in lower case thereafter with no 'trailing' spaces.

It is equally important that the field names in the Input and Criterion ranges are identical. This is ensured by using the Copy command as described above to set up the Criterion range.

(c) Now carry out the Data Query. With the cursor on H4, type:

/ D Q	for Data Query
I	to choose the Input option (or press (↵))
A3.G53 (↵)	to specify the Input range
C H3.N4 (↵)	to specify the Criterion range and lastly
F	for 1-2-3 to Find the record.

By now, the pointer should be highlighting Carter's record.

(d) Press Escape to jump out of the FIND mode and press Escape again several times (or Q for Quit on the Menu) to return to READY mode.

If you encounter any problems in carrying out this Data Query, retrieve the file (/ F R) called RECORD1 and continue on from step (b) above.

The (f7/Query) Key

If the Input and Criterion ranges remain the same (although the Criterion itself alters), the Data Query procedure can be repeated by simply pressing the (f7/Query) key.

To practice this, try to find Pope's record. This can be done quickly by changing the name in cell H4 of the Criterion range and then pressing the (f7/Query) key. Press Escape to return to READY mode.

(ii) Finding a group of records

Next let us track down employees who have not been absent from work this year.

The Input and Criterion ranges remain unchanged (although the actual criterion must be modified). Thus, the steps are:

(a) Use the Range Erase command to erase the name in cell H4 and type 0 into N4 under the field name ABSENCE. The criterion range should tie up with Figure 6.9 at this stage.

(b) Press the (f7/Query) key to see the first record selected. Continue with the 'down' arrow key to look at the other selected records.

(c) Press Escape to return to READY mode.

(iii) A formula as the criterion

Next, employees with 5 or more days absence will be found.

Only the Criterion in cell N4 needs to be altered. It is written as a formula to be applied to the first record of the database, namely as:

+G4>=5

The first absence entry (in cell G4) is checked to see if it is greater than or equal to 5 days. If so, the record is 'selected': if not, the formula is applied to the second record and so on through the database (strictly, the Input range). The above 'formula' is interpreted relatively.

Note: Ignore the value in cell N4—This is the 'logical' value of the formula, i.e. 0 shows because the 'condition' (greater or equal to 5) is untrue for the first record.

The Input and Criterion ranges remain unchanged so need not be specified again. Since the Query operation (Find) is the same as before, simply press the Query key to find the records with 5 or more days absence.

6.4 Extracting records

Often, a list of records meeting certain search criteria is required. It may be in the form of a range of worksheet entries, or more likely, a print-out is required. Suppose for example we are required to make a list of the employees with 5 or more days absence. Although these records were located in the last Find operation, they were not set out in a form suitable for printing.

(i) Listing employees with 5 or more days' absence

Two modifications are required. Firstly, the Output range to receive the list of employees must be specified as an area of the worksheet. Suppose that the records satisfying the search criterion are to be copied into the columns below the Criterion range, say starting in row 10. (If you used datafile RECORD1 in the last section, you will notice that the Output range has already been set up for you, but you will still need to specify it as described in step (b) below. So read on.)

Secondly, the Extract option replaces the Find option previously used. The Input and Criterion ranges do not need any alteration.

(a) Set up the Output range. Copy the field names from range A3.G3 to the first row of the Output range H10.N10 using the Copy command (/ C).

(b) Now issue the Data Query command, so type:

/ D Q	for Data Query
O H10.N10 (↵)	for the Output range
E	to Extract the records of all employees with 5 or more days absence.

The 'extracted' records (for Kent, Lochran, Kettle, Stewart, and Dudson can now be seen set out in cell range H11.N15 of the worksheet. See Figure 6.10.

```
         G         H         I          J          K      L         M        N
                CRITERION RANGE      H3.N4
   ----------------------------------------------------------------------------
 3   ABSENCE  SURNAME   C NAME     SEX          SALARY  DEPT      CONTRACT  ABSENCE
 4         0                                                                    0
 5         0
 6         4                                                           + G4>=5
 7         2
 8         0        Output Range   H10.N10
 9         1
10         0  SURNAME   C NAME     SEX          SALARY  DEPT      CONTRACT  ABSENCE
11         0  Kent      Keith      M              8136  Accts       Jun-82        9
12         0  Lochran   Robert     M              9120  Accts       May-77        7
13         2  Kettle    James      M             11520  Accts       Jun-76        6
14         9  Stewart   Mathew     M             18208  Accts       May-70        5
15         0  Dudson    Jane       F             10104  Accts       Mar-75        5
16         0
```

Figure 6.10 Records 'extracted' from database (5 or more days absence)

(c) To 'browse' through the 'extracted' records, press Q for Quit or press Escape two or three times until you are in READY mode. Then use the 'down' arrow key to look at the records.

The Output (and indeed the Criterion) range does not need to include all the field names. For example in extracting the records in the case just covered, we may only require the employees' names and the number of days absence. The Output range would contain only the field names SURNAME and ABSENCE in cells H10 and I10 in this case.

(ii) More than one criterion: 'And'—two criteria in the same row

Suppose we want to list the female employees who were away 5 or more days. The Criterion must be adjusted by adding the requirements F for Female in cell J4. Pressing the (f7/Query) key puts the records that satisfy both conditions (5 or more days absence and female) into the Output range. Here it is just one record for Jane Dudson.

Notice that we required both conditions to hold 'simultaneously' and so both were entered in the same row of the Criterion range. In contrast, had we required one or other condition to hold, the conditions would have been set out in different rows of the Criterion range. The next example illustrates the 'either/or' case.

(iii) 'Or'—two criteria on different rows

As a final variation, suppose we want to list the Accounts and Staff employees who have more than the average days' absence.

The Criterion needs to be modified in several ways. First, add the entry Accts in L4. Second, the entry in cell N4 becomes:

+G4>@AVG($G$4.$G$53)

On the right hand side of the formula is the special function @AVG which calculates the average of the range of entries G4.G53, the absence entries in column G of the database. The 'absence' range is absolutely addressed (i.e. interspersed with dollar signs) because otherwise the formula will be interpreted relatively in the Query operation.

The above modifications take care of the Accounts employees. However, we also seek employees in Staff Department who have more than the average amount of absence. To cover this condition, an additional row is added to the Criterion range with the above formula in the ABSENCE column and Staff in the DEPT column. This is shown in Figure 6.11.

```
        G          H          I         J             K         L           M           N
                CRITERION  RANGE    H3.N5
                ------------------------------------------------------------------------
 3  ABSENCE  SURNAME    C NAME    SEX           SALARY  DEPT        CONTRACT     ABSENCE
 4        0                                             Accts                          0
 5        0                                             Staff                          0
 6        4
 7        2                                                  +G4>@AVG($G$4.$G$53)
 8        0  OUTPUT     RANGE    H10.N10
 9        1  ------------------
10        0  SURNAME    C NAME    SEX           SALARY  DEPT        CONTRACT     ABSENCE
11        0  Jones      John      M               7056  Accts         Feb-73           4
12        0  Asher      Brian     M               7248  Staff         Apr-71           2
13        2  Kent       Keith     M               8136  Accts         Jun-82           9
14        9  Rodgers    David     M               8856  Accts         Nov-74           4
15        0  Lochran    Robert    M               9120  Accts         May-77           7
16        0  Kettle     James     M              11520  Accts         Jun-76           6
17        2  Franklin   Nick      M              16312  Staff         Apr-69           3
18        4  Stewart    Mathew    M              18208  Accts         May-70           5
19        0  Watson     Norman    M              18976  Accts         Oct-68           4
```

Figure 6.11 Records for employees with more than average absence: accounts and staff departments.

Finally, issue the Data Query command remembering to re-specify the Criterion range (as H3.N5). If the records are Extracted, the results should be as shown in Figure 6.11.

The 1-2-3 Reference Manual explains how criteria for quite complex Data Query selections can be set up.

6.5 Printing records

It is relatively simple to get a print-out of groups of records from the database. To illustrate the steps, we will print out the records extracted in the last section, that is those Accounts and Staff employees with more days' sickness than the average. These records are currently stored in cell range H10/N23.

Before starting the Print command, make sure that you have a printer connected. If you do not, you can save a 'print file' for printing off later.

(a) Type:

/ P	to start the Print command
P	to send the output to the Printer (alternatively F if you want a print File).

The Print menu displayed in the control panel reads:

Range Line Page Options Clear Align Go Quit

We shall use only the options Range, Line, and Go, then Quit to leave the Print menu.

(b) Type:

R	to specify the data Range option
H10.N23 (↵)	to specify the range to be printed
A	to Align
G	to Go.

As explained in the previous chapter, the options Line and Page position the printed output on the printer stationery. Choosing Line advances the printer one line whereas Page moves the printer on to the head of the next page.

Your printer should spring to life at this point (if it is properly configured) and produce output like Figure 6.12.

SURNAME	C NAME	SEX	SALARY	DEPT	CONTRACT	ABSENCE
Jones	John	M	7056	Accts	Feb-73	4
Asher	Brian	M	7248	Staff	Apr-71	2
Kent	Keith	M	8136	Accts	Jun-82	9
Rodgers	David	M	8856	Accts	Nov-74	4
Lochran	Robert	M	9120	Accts	May-77	7
Kettle	James	M	11520	Accts	Jun-76	6
Franklin	Nick	M	16312	Staff	Apr-69	3
Stewart	Mathew	M	18208	Accts	May-70	5
Watson	Norman	M	18976	Accts	Oct-68	4
Beecher	Fay	F	5880	Accts	Jan-71	2

Figure 6.12 Print-out of selected records

(c) To leave the Print menu, type Q to Quit which returns you from MENU to READY mode.

6.6 Date functions

You may have noticed the special @DATE functions used in the CONTRACT column of the database. If not, put the pointer on the cell holding the contract date for say Beattie to explore the entry. What appears as Jan−79 on the screen, has been entered as

@DATE(79,1,2)

That is, the full date '2nd Jan 79' has been entered in a particular format.

1-2-3's special date functions and display formats are worth exploring because they allow calendar 'arithmetic' to be carried out. Of course, dates can always be entered as labels. However, this means that it is not possible to undertake some of the more useful date-related analyses. For example, in searching for a date with the Data Query sequence, it makes no difference whether the date is a label or is in the @DATE format. However, with the @DATE format, you can search for all dates that fall within the next 90 days from today, or all dates that were Saturdays more than 3 years ago, etc. In Section 6.7 we shall apply some simple calendar arithmetic to the personnel records.

The @DATE function allows calendar dates to be turned into serial numbers. The key is shown below:

SERIAL NUMBER	DATE
1	Jan 1, 1900
2	Jan 2, 1900
367	Jan 1, 1901
⋮	⋮
28857	Jan 2, 1979
⋮	⋮
36526	Jan 1, 2000

If a date is written in @DATE format, it will appear on screen as a serial number, for example, @DATE(79,1,2) will be displayed as 28857. However, 1-2-3 has five numeric display formats for dates, so that @DATE(79,1,2) can appear as one of the following:

1. 02–Jan–79   2. 02–Jan   3. Jan–79   4. 02/01/79   5. 02/01

The appropriate display format can be chosen using / Range Format Date. The contract dates in the personnel database have been displayed in the 'Month-Year' format with the sequence:

/R F D 3 — which Data Formats a range of cells with display format number 3.

The abbreviation for the Month-Year display format is D3. Notice that the symbols (D3) appear in the control panel when this format is being used.

The main steps in displaying dates in 1-2-3 are

(a) Enter the date as a serial number, e.g. enter 2nd Jan 1979 as @DATE(79,1,2).
(b) Give the cell a display format, e.g. D3, using / Range Format Date.
(c) Ensure that the column-width is adequate for the display format chosen, e.g. 10 spaces are required for the D1 format, that is, 'Year-Month-Day'. Otherwise, the display will be a row of * symbols meaning 'entry too large'.

In addition to @DATE, there is also a @TODAY function which returns today's serial number (if your computer clock is functioning correctly). There are also three special functions which convert serial numbers into either years, months, or days. For example, if the entry in cell F4 is @DATE(79,1,2), then the function

@MONTH(F4)

will return the value 1 for month January. The other such functions are @YEAR and @DAY.

6.7 Sorting and querying on dates

We will illustrate two uses of calendar arithmetic on the personnel records. Start by Retrieving the File call RECORD1 which you may have used already in Section 6.3 above.

First we will sort records by department and within department by contract date. The steps are:

/ D S A4.G53 (↵) to Data Sort the records in range A4.G53

P E3 (↵) A (↵) to specify DEPT as Primary-Key and the sort order Ascending

S F3 (↵) A (↵ to specify CONTRACT date as Secondary-Key and again the sort order Ascending

G to Go.

The results should tally with Figure 6.13.

	A	B	C	D	E	F	G
1	PERSONNEL	RECORDS	XYZ Co				
2	----------	----------	----------	----------	----------	----------	----------
3	SURNAME	C NAME	SEX	SALARY	DEPT	CONTRACT	ABSENCE
4	Watson	Norman	M	18976	Accts	Oct-68	4
5	Rose	Mary	F	6624	Accts	Apr-70	0
6	Stewart	Mathew	M	18208	Accts	May-70	5
7	Beecher	Fay	F	5880	Accts	Jan-71	2
8	Jones	John	M	7056	Accts	Feb-73	4
9	Rodgers	David	M	8856	Accts	Nov-74	4
10	Dudson	Jane	F	10104	Accts	Mar-75	5
11	Kettle	James	M	11520	Accts	Jun-76	6
12	Harper	Chrissie	F	10272	Accts	Jun-76	2
13	Lochran	Robert	M	9120	Accts	May-77	7
14	Kent	Keith	M	8136	Accts	Jun-82	9
15	Drosser	Martin	M	17560	Admin	Apr-70	3
16	Scarr	Hazel	F	8976	Admin	Jan-71	1
17	Lambert	Eve	F	9816	Admin	Mar-75	3
18	Thwaite	Ossie	M	8976	Admin	Jun-76	0
19	Kingston	Rory	M	8016	Admin	May-77	2
20	Costain	Clodagh	F	8976	Admin	Jun-82	1

Figure 6.13 Sorting records by department then contract date

Next, let us extract the records for employees whose salary review is due, for example, those whose contracts have dates in the range September to December inclusive. We will look at employees in Sales and Marketing. The steps are as follows:

(a) Set up the Criterion. It will consist of a row for each of Sales and Marketing. The condition for contracts falling into the date range September to December can be written as:

@MONTH(F4)> =9

Where F4 holds the contract date for the first record in the database.

Check that your entries for the Criterion range are the same as those shown in Figure 6.14.

```
      H          I           J           K     L           M           N
1   CRITERION RANGE            H3.N5
2   ------------------------------------------------------------------
3   SURNAME    C NAME     SEX               SALARY DEPT       CONTRACT   ABSENCE
4                                                  Sales             1
5                                                  Mktg              1

                                                        @MONTH(F4)>=9
    OUTPUT     RANGE
    ------------------
10  SURNAME    C NAME     SEX               SALARY DEPT       CONTRACT   ABSENCE
11  Turner     Bob        M                   7560 Mktg         Nov-74         0
12  Elliott    Beth       F                  11352 Mktg         Dec-78         1
13  Herbert    Brigid     F                  12984 Mktg         Nov-80         0
14  Sutcliff   Sam        M                  13776 Mktg         Nov-83         1
15  Mantle     Chris      F                   7056 Sales        Sep-78         4
16  Iverson    Steve      M                   7872 Sales        Oct-81         0
```

Figure 6.14 Extracting records with contract date in Sept

(b) Issue the Data Query command, by typing:

/ D Q	for Data Query
I A3.G53 (↵)	for the Input range
C H3.N5 (↵)	for the Criterion range
O H10.N10 (↵)	for the Output range
E	to Extract the records.

The set of records extracted should tally with those shown in Figure 6.14.

CHAPTER 7

Statistical Analysis

This chapter outlines some ways in which 1-2-3 can be employed for statistical analysis. It differs a little from earlier chapters in that it assumes some skills in using 1-2-3 and some acquaintance with statistical methodology. With regard to 1-2-3 the description of procedures will not be as thoroughly detailed as previously. For example, by now you will know when it is appropriate to press Return and how to use commands such as Copy. Therefore, not every 'i' will be dotted and 't' crossed in the ensuing description. As for the statistical knowledge assumed, it may be necessary for the complete 'newcomer' to refer to a standard statistical text.

To analyse a large set of data on salaries of employees, or days absence from work, or weights of packs of butter, you will first need to summarize this data into a few commonly understood measures such as the mean, the standard deviation, the variance, and possibly the maximum and minimum values. 1-2-3 has some useful special functions (like @AVG and @STD) which simplify the task of summarizing data.

Grouping the numbers into value intervals gives the frequency distribution. The distribution can be used to measure the relative frequency of high values (say sales greater than 2000 units) or moderate values (say sales between 1200 and 1500). The Data Fill and Data Distribution commands in 1-2-3 make it easy to calculate frequency distributions. Here the facility to produce a graph of a distribution easily and rapidly is of great value. A graph can show up unexpected features of the data, e.g. much more variability than expected, lack of symmetry, or skewness.

Sometimes it is possible to fit a theoretical model to an empirical distribution. Two of the most common models are the Normal and the Poisson. If a theoretical model is fitted, an effective way of judging the adequacy of the model is to view a graph of 'actuals' against 'fitted' values. Again, 1-2-3 has special functions (and the graphing features) that help in fitting theoretical models to empirical frequencies.

7.1 Summary measures

Figure 7.1 shows the monthly salaries of 27 female employees taken from some company records. The salaries have been entered into the 1-2-3 worksheet from a file called FEMSAL and are set out in column B. We will use this data to illustrate the calculations for the mean, standard deviation, and variance of the salaries. In practice, rather than work through the process of calculating deviation, the special 1-2-3 functions @AVG and @STD would be used, as will be illustrated later in this section.

	A	B
1	WOMENS' SALARIES	
2	Employee	Salary
3	1	1022
4	2	796
5	3	738
6	4	774
7	5	860
8	6	860
9	7	1082
10	8	748
11	9	892
12	10	564
13	11	948
14	12	630
15	13	490
16	14	516
17	15	748
18	16	630
19	17	692
20	18	630
21	19	490
22	20	692
23	21	692
24	22	526
25	23	656
26	24	842
27	25	564
28	26	668
29	27	656

Figure 7.1 Salaries from the file FEMSAL

One extremely useful facility in 1-2-3 is the / Range Name Create command which enables ranges of cells to be named. For example, we can name the data range consisting of cells B3 to B29 FSAL say, by typing:

/ R N C	to Create a Name for a Range
B3.B29	the range in question
FSAL	its name hereafter.

Note: Remember there are two ways of entering commands and specifying ranges. You can type each character or you can use the pointer-movement keys. For example, to enter the range B3.B29, start the command with the pointer on cell B3. When asked for the range to name, 1-2-3 will suggest B3. You respond by 'anchoring' the pointer on B3, i.e. pressing the full stop key, then 'expanding' the pointer to the cell B29 by pressing the End key followed by the down arrow key. The combination of the End key and an arrow key jumps the pointer to the end of an active (or inactive) range of cells in the direction of the chosen arrow key. This helps to speed up range specification when working with large sets of data.

The number of observations, salaries in this case, is easily calculated with the special function:

@COUNT (FSAL)

This has been entered in cell D1 of the sample worksheet set out in Figure 7.2.

	A	B	C	D	E	F	G
1	WOMENS' SALARIES		@COUNT(FSAL) →	27	No of	Employees	
2	Employee	Salary	Deviation	Dev Sqd		Summary	Stats
3	1	1022	303	91966			
4	2	796	↑	↑		Mean	718.7407
5	3	738				Variance	↑
6	4	774	+B3-$G$4	+C3*C3		St Dev	
7	5	860	Salary-mean	$(\text{Deviation})^2$		Max	@SUM(FSAL)/@COUNT(FSAL)
8	6	860				Min	
9	7	1082					
10	8	748					
11	9	892				Sum Dev	
12	10	564				Sum SqDev	
13	11	948					
14	12	630					
15	13	490					
16	14	516					
17	15	748					
18	16	630					
19	17	692					
20	18	630					

Figure 7.2 Calculations for mean and standard deviation of salaries

If you are familiar with the calculation of means and standard deviations, jump to the exercises at the end of this section. Check that the values you obtain using 1-2-3's special functions, @AVG, @VAR and @STD for mean, variance and standard deviation correspond with those in cells H4, H5 and H6 of Figure 7.3. Notice that the @VAR (and hence the @STD) functions use the number of deviations as the divisor (as opposed to the number less 1, the expression favoured by statisticians).

	A	B	C	D	E	F	G	H
1	WOMENS' SALARIES			27	No of	Employees		
2	Employee	Salary	Deviation	Dev Sqd		Summary	Stats	@Function
3	1	1022	303	91966				
4	2	796	77	5969		Mean	718.7407	718.7407
5	3	738	19	371		Variance	23693.08	23693.08
6	4	774	55	3054		St dev	153.9255	153.9255
7	5	860	141	19954		Max		1082
8	6	860	141	19954		Min		490
9	7	1082	363	131957				
10	8	748	29	856				
11	9	892	173	30019		Sum Dev	-5.7E-13	
12	10	564	-155	23945		Sum SqDev	639713.1	
13	11	948	229	52560				
14	12	630	-89	7875				
15	13	490	-229	52322				
16	14	516	-203	41104				
17	15	748	29	856				
18	16	630	-89	7875				
19	17	692	-27	715				
20	18	630	-89	7875				

Figure 7.3 Calculations for mean and standard deviation of salaries

To calculate the mean, which is the sum of all the salary figures divided by the number of salaries, use the formula:

@SUM(FSAL)/@COUNT (FSAL)

where @SUM sums all the salaries and @COUNT counts the number of salaries in the range FSAL. This formula appears in G4. (For this data, the mean salary is £718.7407, which is £719 when rounded to the nearest integer. Normally, this value would be rounded for display purposes by using / Range Format Fixed with the appropriate number of decimal places, perhaps zero in this case. For the moment, we will leave the value unrounded.)

To measure scatter about the mean, the salaries are converted into deviations or differences from the mean salary. The formula for a deviation is shown in Figure 7.2, cell C3. The squared value of this deviation is set out in cell D3. These two values are displayed to the nearest integer using the / Range Format command (Fixed format with 0 decimal places).

The conventional way of measuring scatter consists of averaging the squared deviations to get the variance, i.e.

Variance = (sum of squared deviations)/(number of deviations)

Next, the standard deviation is calculated by taking the square root of the variance, i.e.

Standard deviation $= \sqrt{\text{variance}}$

To calculate these measures, the formulae for the first deviation and its square are copied together down the spreadsheet giving the results shown in Figure 7.3. (That is, Copy FROM C3.D3 TO C4.C29.)

The sum of the deviations and the sum of the squared deviations:

@SUM(C3.C29) and @SUM(D3.D29)

have been entered into cells G11 and G12 respectively. Next, the variance of the salaries:

+G12/27 (or more generally, +G12/D1)

has been put into G5 under the mean. The variance has value 23693 after rounding to the nearest integer.

The standard deviation is obtained by taking the square root of the above quantity, that is, the special function

@SQRT(G5)

and this has been entered below the variance. See Figure 7.3. Thus the standard deviation of salaries is 153.9255 or £154 after rounding.

Sometimes, for reasons of statistical theory, the divisor in the expression for variance is taken as the number of squared deviations minus 1, i.e.

(@COUNT(FSAL) − 1) with value 26 in this example.

Notice that the sum of the deviations (in Cell G11) is displayed as −5.7E−13. This is the standard scientific format for the number −5.7 multiplied by 10 raised to the power −13, i.e. the very small number −0.00000000000057 which is effectively equal to zero. In theory, the sum of the deviations from the mean is zero. Although 1-2-3 can store numbers to 15 decimal places, some slight rounding of the mean and hence the deviations has occurred, which has led to the result displaced. If the results cells are displayed using the Fixed Format with say 2 decimal places, this apparent discrepancy disappears.

In practice, instead of carrying out the mean and variance calculations as displayed in Figure 7.3, 1-2-3 special functions similar to the familiar @SUM function would normally be used. For example, @AVG (list) gives the mean or average of all the active cell values in a list. By list, we mean a range of cells or a list of individual cells: by active, cells containing entries (which could include the character 0) but not empty (or blank) cells. So @AVG(FSAL) or @AVG(B3.B29) gives the mean salary for the 27 employees. Similarly @VAR (list) and @STD (list) give the variance and standard deviation of a list of entries.

Exercise

(i) Check the values obtained in the spreadsheet calculations and set out in column G of Figure 7.3, with those obtained using the appropriate 1-2-3 special functions, namely, @AVG(FSAL), @VAR(FSAL), and @STD(FSAL). (The @ function values are displayed in column H).

(ii) Is the divisor used in the special function @VAR the number of squared deviations or 1 less?

(iii) Find the maximum and minimum salaries using @MAX(FSAL) and @MIN(FSAL). (See cells H7 and H8 of Figure 7.3).

Figure 7.3 shows how the values calculated by the special @ functions compare with those calculated from first principles.

7.2 Distributions

With sizeable sets of numbers (say more than 30), we summarize the pattern of variation by grouping the numbers into 'value' intervals and counting the frequency with which numbers fall into each interval. The result is called the frequency distribution. With 1-2-3, the Data Distribution and Data Fill commands allow you to obtain frequency distributions very easily. If the frequency distributions are displayed graphically via the Graph commands, further insights about the nature of the variation in the data can be gained.

The sequence of steps to obtain and display frequency distributions is described below, using the Butter pack data, i.e. readings of the weight of supposed one-pound (16 ounce) packs of butter. The complete data set (120 readings of the weight of butter packs) is contained in a 1-2-3 file called PACKS. The first 18 weights are shown in column A of the spreadsheet in Figure 7.4.

Once again, keying in can be minimized by naming the range of cells containing the weights. That is, with the Range Name Create command, name the range of entries (A3.A122) containing the weights PAC. In fact, this range has already been named PAC and the name saved when the PACKS file was saved. You can explore this by issuing the Range Name Create command and pressing Return to confirm that PAC does indeed refer to the highlit range A3.A122.

	A	B	C	D	E	F	G
1	BUTTER PACKS		@COUNT(PAC)→120		Weights		
2	Weight		Summary	Statistics		Weight	Distribution
3	15.54					Interval	Freq
4	16.41		Max	17.30←@MAX(PAC)		14.50	
5	16.05		Min	14.68		14.75	
6	17.03		Mean	16.05		15.00	
7	14.95		St Dev	0.52←@STD(PAC)		15.25	
8	16.37					15.50	
9	16.62					15.75	
10	15.91				Bin range	16.00	
11	16.97				F4.F16	16.25	
12	16.89					16.50	
13	15.99		A3.A122			16.75	
14	15.42		contains 120 weights			17.00	
15	15.88		This range 'named' PAC			17.25	
16	16.49					17.50	
17	16.15						
18	16.3						
19	15.77						
20	15.7						

Figure 7.4 Butter pack data with summary statistics

In passing, it is worth pointing out that it is not necessary to store the set of readings in one column of the spreadsheet as shown in Figure 7.4. The butter packs data could occupy say the first twelve rows and the first ten columns of the spreadsheet. This range of cells would be 'named' PAC and thereafter the analysis would be unaltered. Here, the observations have been laid out in a single column to enable the summary calculations to be displayed alongside the data. The only other advantage of the layout is the possibility of sorting the weights by size using the Data Sort command.

The data can be summarized by calculating the maximum and minimum pack weights and also the mean and standard deviation of the set of pack weights. For example, the maximum weight is given by formula:

@MAX(PAC)

the resultant value being 17.30 ounces.

The other 1-2-3 special functions, @MIN, @AVG, and @STD have been used to calculate these values. In Figure 7.4, they are displayed with 2 decimal places (/ Range Format Fixed 2, etc.).

At this point, if you have not done so already, Retrieve the file called PACKS and calculate the summary statistics shown in columns C and D of Figure 7.4. Try to keep the same layout as shown in the figure.

Before using the Data Distribution command, the Bin range must be prepared. This consists of a column of values increasing from top to bottom. These values form the 'bins' or class intervals for the distribution. In deciding the position of the column to be designated the Bin range, there must be an empty column to the right in which the resulting distribution frequencies will be stored. The cell below the 'frequencies' column must also be empty (to capture any readings that fall above the last value of the Bin range).

The summary measures are most useful in deciding the intervals (or 'Bins') for the frequency distribution. The maximum and minimum statistics in Figure 7.4 suggest that a range of Bin values from 14.5 to 17.5 oz. will be appropriate. To get about a dozen classes for the distribution the width of each bin should be about .25 oz. Column F contains the Bin range (cells F4 to F16) and column G (cells G4 to G17) will receive the resulting frequencies.

To set up the Bin range and get the frequency distribution as shown in Figure 7.5, do the following:

(i) With the cell pointer on F4, type:

/ D F	to start the Data Fill command
F4.F16	for the Fill range (i.e. about 12 cells—see below)
14.5	for the Start value
.25	for the Step
17.5	for the Stop value.

Notice that 1-2-3 fills in values until either the range is filled or the stop value is encountered.

At this stage the Bin range should appear like cells F4 to F16 in Figure 7.4.

(ii) To get the distribution, type:

/ D D	to start the Data Distribution
PAC	to specify the Values range
F4.F16	to specify the Bin range.

A frequency distribution similar to that in cells G4 to G17 in Figure 7.5 should be visible at this stage. To complete the layout add a Total line in row 18.

The interpretation of the frequencies is as follows: there were no weights less than 14.5 ounces, one weight was between 14.5 and 14.75 ounces, two weights were between 14.75 and 15.0 ounces, etc. . . . and no weights were greater than 17.5 ounces.

To compare the distributions in several sets of data, it is conventional to turn the frequencies into relative frequencies or percentages. To do this, each frequency is divided by the total frequency and the results either left as decimals or converted to percentages. For example, into cell H4, enter the formula:

+G4/G$18

and display the resulting proportion as a percentage with the Range Format Percentage sequence (in say P0 format). Then Copy the formula in H4 down column H as far as

	A	B	C	D	E	F	G	H	I
1	BUTTER PACKS			120	Weights			+G4/G$18	+I4+H5
2	Weight		Summary	Statistics		Weight	Distribution		
3	15.54					Interval	Freq	Freq %	Cum Freq
4	16.41		Max	17.30		14.50	0	0%	0%
5	16.05		Min	14.68		14.75	1	1%	1%
6	17.03		Mean	16.05		15.00	2	2%	3%
7	14.95		St Dev	0.52		15.25	6	5%	8%
8	16.37					15.50	10	8%	16%
9	16.62			Frequencies		15.75	14	12%	28%
10	15.91			from the		16.00	20	17%	44%
11	16.97			Data Distribution		16.25	22	18%	63%
12	16.89			command		16.50	22	18%	81%
13	15.99					16.75	16	13%	94%
14	15.42					17.00	4	3%	98%
15	15.88					17.25	2	2%	99%
16	16.49					17.50	1	1%	100%
17	16.15						0	0%	100%
18	16.3					Total	120	100%	
19	15.77								
20	15.7						@SUM(G4.G17)		

Figure 7.5 Frequency distributions for Butter pack data

row 18. The resulting relative frequency distribution for butter packs is shown rounded to the nearest per cent in Figure 7.5. Thus we see that 12 per cent of the packs were between 15.75 and 16 ounces.

As well as looking at the relative frequency distribution, it is often useful to calculate the cumulative relative frequency distribution. This tells us the relative frequency with which pack weights fall below a certain value, e.g. how frequently weights fall below 16 ounces. To calculate cumulative relative frequencies for a value in the Bin range, you add the frequencies in all cells to the right hand side and above the value in question. The formulae to obtain cumulative relative frequencies in column I are as follows:

+H4 in cell I4

+I4 +H5 in cell I5

and then copy the formula I5 down to I17. Now use the Range Format Percentage sequence to display the resulting relative frequencies in the range I4.I17 in the form of percentages.

The cumulative relative frequency distribution should look like that in column I of the spreadsheet in Figure 7.5. In fact, for this data, 44 per cent of packs were actually below 16 ounces. After adding suitable headings, you may wish to print the results at this stage. (See Chapter 5 for details.)

It is worth displaying these distributions graphically. A full account of using the Graph commands is given in Chapter 5, but a brief résumé appropriate in the context of frequency distributions is given below.

Let us suppose that we wish to display the distributions in the form of Line graphs (the main option being Bar graphs).

(i) Type / G to start the Graph command.

The Graph menu has the following options:

Type X A B C D E F Reset View Save Options Name Quit

(ii) Choose Type from this menu, and choose Line as the graph type.

The Graph menu returns.

(iii) Choose X and specify the X range of data as cells F4.F17, i.e. the 'bin' values.

(iv) Choose to specify the A range of data as G4.G17, i.e. the frequencies.

(v) Select View to see the graph of the frequency distribution.

You can improve the graph by adding titles at the top and on the axes of the graph (use the / Graph Options Titles command). Once again keystroking can be reduced by naming the various ranges to be graphed in advance (using the Range Name Create command). Figures 7.6 and 7.7 show the kind of graphs you can get for the Butter pack data.

Press any key to return from the graph to the spreadsheet again, and choose the option Quit to leave the Graph menu.

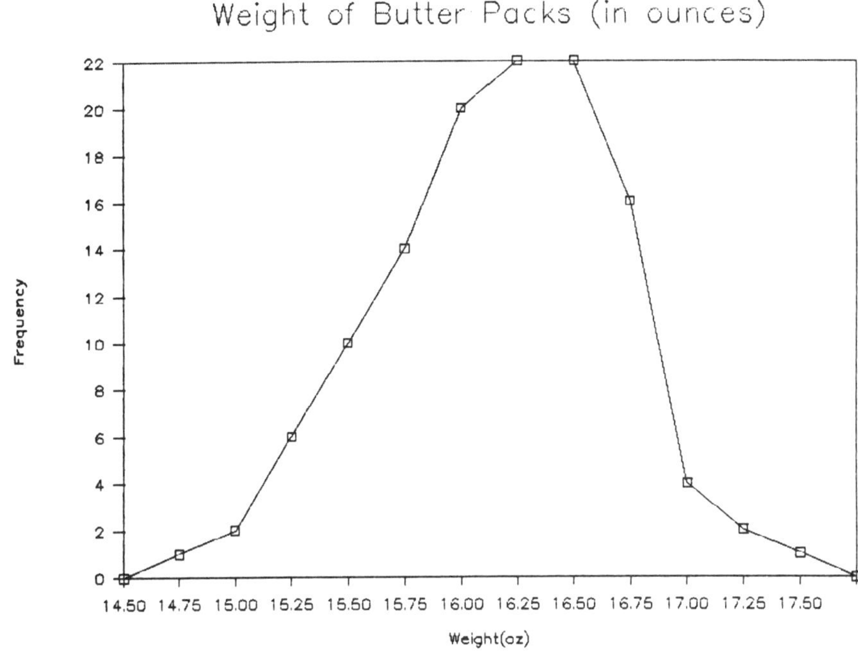

Figure 7.6 Frequency distribution for Butter pack data

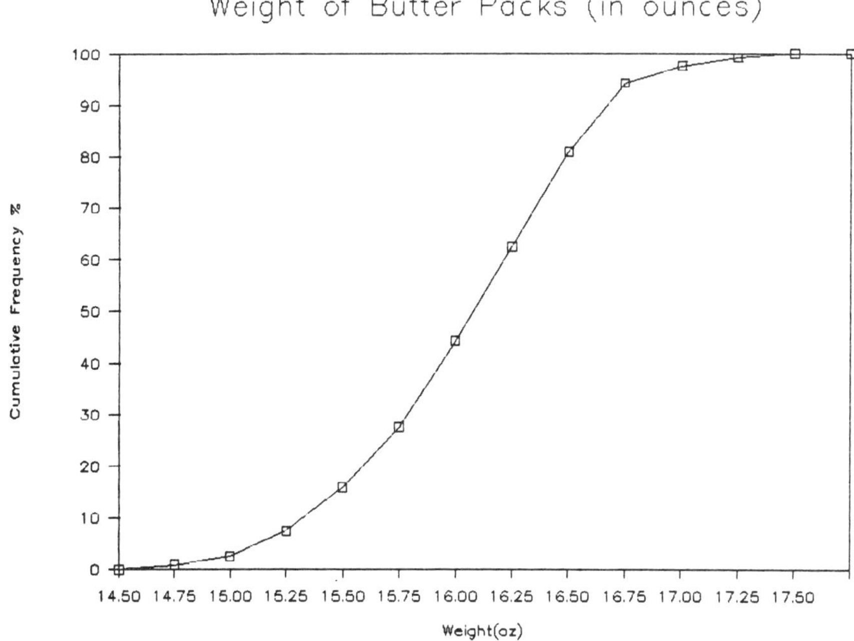

Figure 7.7 Cumulative distribution for Butter pack data

7.3 Fitting theoretical models—Normal distribution

The humpbacked symmetrical form of the frequency distribution and the sigmoid (or S) shape of the cumulative frequency distribution for the Butter pack data suggest a particular model, the Normal distribution, for this data. Figure 7.8(a) illustrates the shape of the Normal distribution—for more details consult any statistics textbook. The Normal distribution has two defining parameters, its mean value and its standard deviation. Given these values, the percentages of values falling in different intervals can be read off from Normal tables. In particular, the percentages of values lying within 1, 2, and 3 standard deviations of the mean value are as shown in Figure 7.8(b).

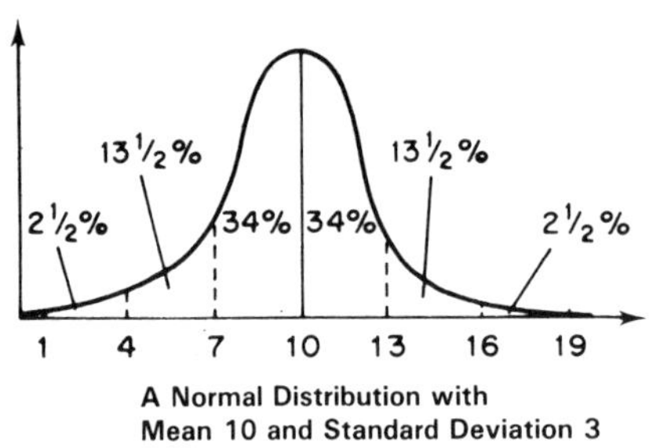

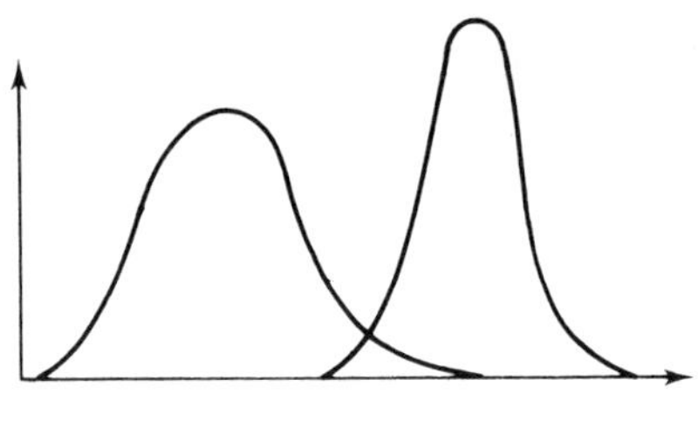

Figure 7.8(a) The Normal distribution

% of readings Within or Outside the stated limits	± distance from the mean (where σ is the standard deviation)								
	.5σ	.8σ	1σ	1.6σ	2σ	2.6σ	3σ	3.3σ	3.9σ
	%	%	%	%	%	%	%	%	%
Within:	40	58	68	90	95	99	99.7	99.9	99.99
Outside:	60	42	32	10	5	1	.3	.1	.01

Figure 7.8(b) Descriptive properties of the Normal distribution

A quick check of the adequacy of the Normal model for the Butter pack data is to compare the actual percentages of weights falling in intervals around the mean with those expected under a Normal model using rounded values for the mean and standard deviation of weight of 16 and .5 ounces respectively. To carry out this check, set up a new Bin range in column J (see Figure 7.9). Use the Data Fill command starting with 14.5 ounces (3 standard deviations below the mean), the intervals (step) being .5 ounces to finish with the value 17.5 ounces (3 standard deviations above the mean). The resulting relative frequencies are then compared with the expected frequencies derived from Figure 7.8(b). The comparison for the Butter pack data is shown in Figure 7.9. The actual frequencies and the expected frequencies (i.e. those expected assuming a normal distribution with mean 16 and standard deviation .5 ounces) correspond quite closely.

	E	F	G	H	I	J	K	L	M
1	BUTTER PACKS								
2	Weight Distribution					Weight Distribution			Normal
3	Interval	Freq		Freq %	Cum Freq	Interval	Freq	Freq %	Exp Freq
4	14.50	0		0%	0%	14.50	0	0.0%	0.1%
5	14.75	1		1%	1%	15.00	3	2.5%	2.1%
6	15.00	2		2%	3%	15.50	16	13.3%	13.6%
7	15.25	6		5%	8%	16.00	34	28.3%	34.1%
8	15.50	10		8%	16%	16.50	44	36.7%	34.1%
9	15.75	14		12%	28%	17.00	20	16.7%	13.6%
10	16.00	20		17%	44%	17.50	3	2.5%	2.1%
11	16.25	22		18%	63%		0	0.0%	0.1%
12	16.50	22		18%	81%	Total	120	100.0%	100.0%
13	16.75	16		13%	94%				
14	17.00	4		3%	98%				
15	17.25	2		2%	99%				
16	17.50	1		1%	100%				
17		0		0%	100%				
18	Total	120		100%					

Figure 7.9 Comparison of Butter pack distribution with Normal

7.4 Fitting the Poisson model

We now turn to a different set of data, the telephone call data contained in the file CALLS. As we shall see, this data cannot be modelled by fitting a normal distribution. Another theoretical model called the Poisson distribution turns out to be appropriate and in this section we shall go through the steps of fitting the distribution.

The data consists of readings of the number of telephone calls arriving minute by minute at a switchboard. Sometimes no calls arrive, sometimes 2, sometimes (but rarely) as many as 5 calls arrive in a minute. 250 readings have been stored in a file with the name CALLS.

Figure 7.10 shows the first 18 readings in the cells of column A of the spreadsheet. It also shows the results of summarizing the data and obtaining the distribution. The procedure for doing this is the same as that used on the Butter pack data. In brief the main steps are as follows:

(i) Name the data range CALL for convenience, i.e. use / Range Name Create to name the range A3.A252 containing all the observations, CALL.

(ii) Calculate summary statistics (maximum, minimum, mean, and standard deviation of the number of calls per minute) using the special functions @MAX(CALL), @MIN(CALL), @AVG(CALL), @STD(CALL).

(iii) To improve presentation, round the summary statistics to say 2 decimal places, i.e. use / Range Format Fixed to format the cells containing the summary statistics.

(iv) Get the frequency distribution of the number of calls.

Use / Data Fill to set up the intervals (Bin range) on the basis of the observed maximum and minimum number of calls.

Use / Data Distribution to obtain the frequency distribution. Check that @COUNT(CALL) in cell D1 equals the Total frequency for the distribution.

The spreadsheet should look similar to that of Figure 7.10 at this stage. Inspection of the frequencies shows that this data is far from being 'symmetrical humpbacked'. This is shown even more dramatically by graphing the frequencies.

	A	B	C	D	E	F	G
1	TELEPHONE	CALLS	@COUNT(CALL)→250 readings				
2	Calls per	Minute	Summary	Statistics	Calls		Distribution
3		2			Interval		Freq
4		3	Max	5		0	51
5		0	Min	0		1	94
6		4	Mean	1.46←@AVG(CALL)		2	65
7		1	St Dev	1.17		3	24
8		0			Bin range	4	10
9		1				5	6
10		2	A3.A252			6	0
11		1	contains 250 readings			7	0
12		2	of calls per minute.				0
13		1			Total		250
14		0	This range is 'named' CALL				
15		3					
16		2					
17		0					
18		1					
19		1					
20		0					

Figure 7.10 Distribution of number of telephone calls

Using the Graph command, choose the Line graph as the Type, specify the X range as the Bin range and the A range as the frequencies and then View the graph. 1-2-3 should produce a graph of the frequency distribution that is similar to Figure 7.11.

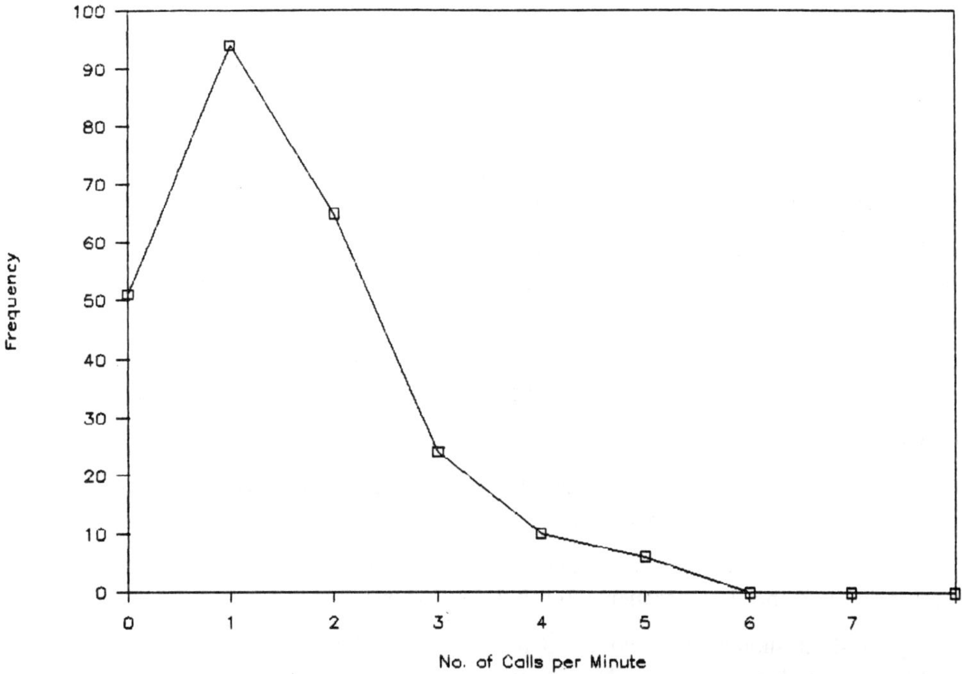

Figure 7.11 Graph of telephone call data

Statistical theory suggests that a suitable theoretical model for this type of distribution is the so-called Poisson distribution. This distribution describes the proportion of times we shall get 0, 1, 2, 3, or more events occurring in a fixed time interval when we know that

(a) events occur as if 'at random'

(b) the average number of occurrences in the fixed time interval is *M* say.

Here for example the value of *M*, the mean call rate, is 1.46 calls per minute (approximately 3 calls every 2 minutes).

The mathematical form of the distribution is:

proportion of time 0 events occur = $P(0)$ = EXP($-M$)
proportion of time 1 event occurs = $P(1)$ = M*EXP($-M$)
proportion of time 2 events occur = $P(2)$ = M*M*EXP($-M$)/2, etc.

Inspection of these expressions shows their recursive nature.

In fact, $P(1) = M*P(0)$, $P(2) = (M/2)*(P(1)$,. . . , and in general,

$P(r) = (M/r)*P(r-1)$

EXP($-M$) is a mathematical function which has a unique value for each value of *M*. There is a special function, @EXP(), which gives its value.

To go from proportions to frequencies (out of a total frequency of 250 readings), each proportion is multiplied by the total frequency.

For the calls data, the average number of calls per minute, *M*, is given by @AVG(CALL) currently stored in cell D6. This value, shown as 1.46, is used in calculating EXP($-M$) and hence the Poisson proportions, each then being subsequently multiplied by 250.

Figure 7.12 shows the formulae to obtain the expected Poisson frequencies for the telephone call data. Thus @EXP(−D6), which is approximately the same as @EXP(−1.46) evaluates as 0.231309. This is $P(0)$, the expected proportion of minutes with 0 cells assuming the Poisson model (23% approximately). Our data set consists of 250 minutes, hence the expected number of minutes with 0 calls is 250*0.231309 = 57.8 after rounding, as shown in cell H4. Using the simple relationship between successive terms of the Poisson distribution, the expected number of minutes with 1 call is 57.8*M, which evaluates as 84.7.

The fit of the Poisson frequencies to the actual frequencies is shown graphically in Figure 7.13. Again, the correspondence of the theoretical model and empirical data is quite close.

	A	B	C	D	E	F	G	H	
1	TELEPHONE	CALLS		250	readings			250*EXP(-D6)	
2	Calls per	Minute	Summary	Statistics		Calls	Distribution	Poisson	
3	2					Interval	Freq	Exp Freq	
4	3		Max	5		0	51	57.8	←
5	0		Min	0		1	94	84.7	← +H4*D6
6	4		Mean	1.46 ←	Use for	2	65	62.0	← +H5*D6/2
7	1		St Dev	1.17	Poisson	3	24	30.2	← +H6*D6/3
8	0				frequencies	4	10	11.1	
9	1					5	6	3.2	
10	2					6	0	0.8	
11	1					7	0	0.2	
12	2						0	0.0	
13	1					Total	250	250.0	
14	0								
15	3								
16	2								
17	0								
18	1								
19	1								
20	0								

Figure 7.12 Actual frequencies and Poisson frequencies

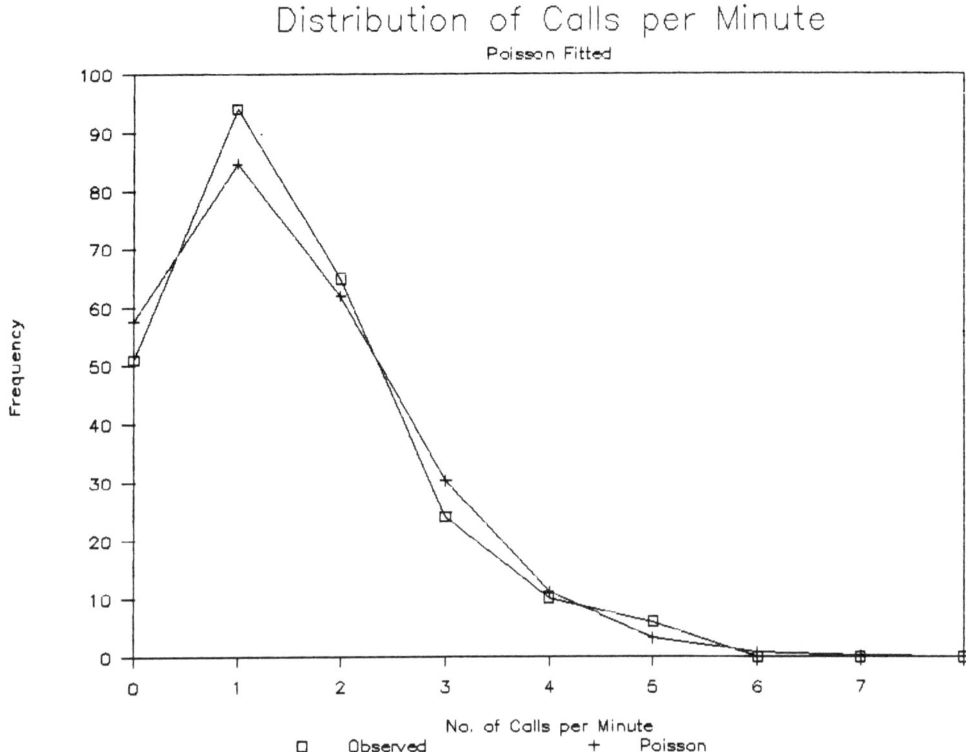

Figure 7.13 Graph showing actual and Poisson frequencies

CHAPTER 8

Survey Data

In this chapter, we discuss ways in which 1-2-3 can produce results from surveys, for example from small market research surveys, or attitude surveys. The ideas will be illustrated by analysing the findings in one such survey. It must be emphasized that using 1-2-3 as described here would only be appropriate for small surveys involving a small number of variables. The variables would need to be quantitative or easily coded from their original qualitative form. These limitations result from the size, nature, and purpose of the 1-2-3 package: at present, this form of software is not intended to be a substitute for the full statistical analysis package. However, for small surveys much useful analysis can be undertaken with 1-2-3.

The survey we shall discuss in this chapter concerned attitudes towards unionization on the part of a random sample of employees in a non-unionized company. In the survey, data was collected on salary, length of service with the company and a measure of attitude to unionization for each employee in the sample.

The sets of information collected for each employee, the 'cases', can be regarded as records in a database. So information from the survey can be entered into the 1-2-3 worksheet, using rows as 'cases' and columns as fields. As we saw in Chapter 6, 1-2-3 has some special Data commands for database tasks such as sorting and searching or 'querying' records. For example, / Data Sort allows the order of the records to be changed allowing, for example, records for male employees to be sorted out from those of female employees.

We have already used / Data Distribution in Chapter 7. An important task in survey analysis is to get distributions of survey variables or 'hole counts' as they are colloquially known. Therefore it is a straightforward matter to get distributions of salaries and years service, etc. for the employees. However, distributions of subgroups are also of interest. For example, how do the distributions of salary compare for employees for and against the union? With judicious sorting of records, we can use the Data Distribution command to get distributions of subgroups of interest such as these.

In Chapter 6, we used the Data Query command to select records satisfying certain conditions or criteria. The cells of the Criterion range specify exactly what conditions the different fields of the record have to satisfy. The Data Query command allows particular subgroups of records satisfying specified conditions to be found or 'extracted'.

Associated with Data Query are some special functions (@D) which calculate summary statistics for the subgroups of records sorted out by the data query operation. Thus, counts, averages, standard deviations, etc., can be calculated for subgroups of records of interest.

Name	Sex of employee	Monthly salary (f)	Number of years service	Attitude to Union	Name	Sex of employee	Monthly salary (f)	Number of years service	Attitude to Union
Cornell	Male	796	8	U	Bull	Male	692	8	F
Dyer	Female	516	3	F	Bunn	Male	490	2	F
Day	Female	892	33	A	Britain	Male	818	24	A
Westwood	Male	986	18	U	Wensley	Female	738	21	A
Smith	Male	716	9	A	Ball	Female	630	7	F
Boyd	Male	692	12	A	Old	Male	656	4	F
Kirk	Female	656	12	U	Truelove	Female	748	16	A
Jackson	Male	1148	21	U	Sloan	Male	856	22	A
Beaumont	Female	668	2	U	Masters	Male	588	3	F
Miller	Male	760	6	F	Jones	Female	1080	17	A
Oldfield	Male	892	19	A	Stoll	Male	704	2	F
Sagawa	Female	860	20	A	Narnia	Male	604	5	A
Senior	Female	490	1	F	March	Male	630	6	U
Simpson	Male	748	12	A	Lloyd	Male	946	29	A
Boice	Male	748	11	U	Angelo	Female	692	14	U
Burgess	Male	774	3	F	Hill	Male	856	9	U
Carlson	Female	526	8	U	Thirtle	Female	796	13	A
Ingrams	Male	774	10	F	Walker	Female	1022	25	A
Wood	Male	1184	35	A	Wilson	Male	678	10	F
McCleod	Male	552	2	F	Spriggs	Male	830	18	F
Martin	Female	630	4	F	Rivett	Female	564	7	U
Largely	Female	692	13	U	Lambert	Male	678	10	F
Packard	Male	678	7	A	King	Male	892	15	A
Plessey	Female	860	20	A	Hunt	Male	1050	30	A
Pope	Female	490	4	U	Hartley	Female	948	18	F
White	Male	716	13	F	Foster	Male	796	19	A
Rumbold	Male	588	1	F	Edgerley	Male	630	9	U
Harris	Female	656	6	U	Enders	Male	704	1	U
Goldhill	Female	842	9	U	Ash	Female	774	12	A
Freeman	Male	960	24	A	Allen	Male	830	17	F
Higson	Female	564	1	F	Carter	Male	716	7	U
Jennings	Female	748	10	F	Reagan	Female	692	14	F
Eaton	Male	774	11	A	Mondale	Male	716	9	F
Targett	Female	630	5	U					

Figure 8.1 Results for 67 employees

We have already met the Data Table command for helping with sensitivity analysis in the spreadsheet modelling of Chapter 4. This command can also be used to organize the calculation of the subgroup statistics needed in analysing the survey results, i.e. for the calculation of summary statistics for subgroups.

With data on a variety of variables, one of the main objectives with a survey is to get cross tabulations, that is, counts of the number and characteristics of employees classified on two or more dimensions of the survey. One particularly useful special function is @DCOUNT which together with the Data Table command can give cross tabulations.

Finally, 1-2-3 graphics can be brought to bear on the many distributions and tables that emerge from a survey.

In the following sections, these ideas will be explored using the survey results. Some 67 cases or records from the survey are set out in full in Figure 8.1. The data is stored in the UNION datafile.

8.1 Setting up the database

The tabular layout and data in Figure 8.1 can be copied into the 1-2-3 worksheet much as they are. All the data for an individual employee can be set out on one row of the worksheet—this is a record. All the entries for a particular variable, say 'salary' can be arranged in one column, under the field name SALARY.

Try entering the field names (headings) and the first two records (i.e. data for employees Cornell and Dyer) as shown in Figure 8.2.

```
     A        B            C             D         E
1  ATTITUDE SURVEY  -  UNIONISATION
2  -----------------------------------------------------
3  NAME      SEX       ATTITUDE      SALARY   SERVICE
4  Cornell   M         U                796         8
5  Dyer      F         F                516         3
```

Figure 8.2 Entering the first two records

Notice that some simple coding has been introduced—M, F for Male, Female and F, A, U for For, Against, Undecided respectively. This reduces both the amount of keying in and the memory requirements of the worksheet. Also, the variables have been reordered so that the qualitative variables come first (NAME, SEX, ATTITUDE) followed by the quantitative ones (SALARY, SERVICE). The file UNION contains all the records shown in Figure 8.1, of which you have entered the first two. So, type:

/ F R UNION   to File Retrieve the file called UNION.

Figure 8.3 shows the first 'page' of the worksheet: to look at other rows use the 'Pg Dn' and 'Pg Up' keys to jump the pointer in 'pages' down and up the worksheet.

	A	B	C	D	E
1	ATTITUDE	SURVEY	- UNIONISATION		
2	-----------	-----------	-----------	-----------	-----------
3	NAME	SEX	ATTITUDE	SALARY	SERVICE
4	Cornell	M	U	796	8
5	Dyer	F	F	516	3
6	Day	F	A	892	33
7	Westwood	M	U	986	18
8	Smith	M	A	716	9
9	Boyd	M	A	692	12
10	Kirk	F	U	656	12
11	Jackson	M	U	1148	21
12	Beaumont	F	U	668	2
13	Miller	M	F	760	6
14	Oldfield	M	A	892	19
15	Sagawa	F	A	860	20
16	Senoir	F	F	490	1
17	Simpson	M	A	748	12
18	Boice	M	U	748	11
19	Burgess	M	F	774	3
20	Carlson	F	U	526	8

Figure 8.3 First 17 records in the UNION database

8.2 Data summary and distribution

Suppose management wants a summary of salaries from this survey and also wants to look separately at salaries for Male and Female employees. This involves calculating a few summary statistics such as averages, and possibly the maximum and minimum values. In addition, grouping salaries into 'value intervals' gives the frequency distribution of salaries.

The special functions @AVG, @MAX and @MIN, introduced in the last chapter, are used to calculate averages, and maximum and minimum values quickly. Also, the Data Distribution command gives the frequency distribution of the salaries for all employees. Further insights come from using the Graph command to produce the graph of the salary distribution. To get out the distributions for male and female employees separately, the database must be reordered by sex of employee initially. (In the steps below, we shall Data Sort on sex then salary as it allows us to check some of the emerging results visually.)

The main steps are:

(a) Sort the records first (Primary sort) in sex order (Male then Female) then next (Secondary sort) in ascending salary order. That is, type:

/ D S — to Data Sort records

D A4.E70 — for the Data-Range to be rows 4 to 70

P B3 D — for the Primary key to be SEX in Male-Female order

S D3 A — for SALARY to be the Secondary key and the sort order to be Ascending

G — to Go.

Figure 8.4 shows the first 20 rows of the worksheet at this stage. The records for Male employees should be in rows 4 to 43 and records for Females in rows 44 to 70.

(b) Salaries are in cell range D4.D70, the salaries for Males being in range D4.D43, whilst those for Females are in D44.D70. It helps to Name these Ranges at the outset, say, SAL, MSAL, and FSAL using the Range Name Create command. So type:

/ R N C D4.70 SAL to Name the salary cell range

/ R N C D4.D43 MSAL to Name the mens' salary range

/ R N C D44.D70 FSAL to Name the womens' salary range.

	A	B	C	D	F
1	ATTITUDE SURVEY - UNIONISATION				
2	-----------	----------	----------	----------	----------
3	NAME	SEX	ATTITUDE	SALARY	SERVICE
4	Bunn	M	F	490	2
5	Mcleod	M	F	552	2
6	Masters	M	F	588	3
7	Rumbold	M	F	588	1
8	Narnia	M	A	604	5
9	Edgerley	M	U	630	9
10	March	M	U	630	6
11	Old	M	F	656	4
12	Packard	M	A	678	7
13	Wilson	M	F	678	10
14	Lambert	M	F	678	10
15	Boyd	M	A	692	12
16	Bull	M	F	692	8
17	Stoll	M	F	704	2
18	Enders	M	U	704	1
19	White	M	F	716	13
20	Carter	M	U	716	7

Figure 8.4 Union records after sorting on Sex and Salary

(c) Study Figure 8.5 and enter the labels shown in columns F, G, and H.

Get summary statistics for all salaries in column G as shown in Figure 8.6 by entering 1-2-3 special functions such as:

@AVG(SAL) in cell G4

@MAX(SAL) in cell G5

@MIN(SAL) in cell G6

formatting the average salary to the nearest integer (/ R F F etc.).

(d) Before issuing the Data Distribution command, the 'Bin range' must be prepared. This consists of a column of values increasing from top to bottom. These values form the 'Bins' or value intervals for the distribution. In deciding the position of the column to be used as the Bin range, there must be an empty column to the right in which the resulting distribution frequencies will be stored.

Since salaries go from a minimum of 490 (G6) to a maximum of 1184 (G5), the Bin range can be set up in column F using the Data Fill command as follows. With the pointer on F11, type:

/ D F for Data Fill

F11.F18 for the Fill range

```
      A        B          C              D          E        F          G         H
 1  ATTITUDE SURVEY - UNIONISATION                         Summary  Statistics          1
 2  ----------------------------------------------------------------------------------  2
 3  NAME      SEX       ATTITUDE      SALARY  SERVICE Salaries All                      3
 4  Bunn      M         F                490        2 Ave                               4
 5  Mcleod    M         F                552        2 Max                               5
 6  Masters   M         F                588        3 Min                               6
 7  Rumbold   M         F                588        1                                   7
 8  Narnia    M         A                604        5 Salary    Distrib   SAL            8
 9  Edgerley  M         U                630        9 --------------------------       9
10  March     M         U                630        6 Interval     Freq      % Freq    10
11  Old       M         F                656        4                                  11
12  Packard   M         A                678        7
13  Wilson    M         F                678       10
14  Lambert   M         F                678       10
15  Boyd      M         A                692       12
16  Bull      M         F                692        8
17  Stoll     M         F                704        2
18  Enders    M         U                704        1
19  White     M         F                716       13
20  Carter    M         U                716        7
```

Figure 8.5 Setting up the worksheet for Salary Distribution

```
      A        B          C              D          E        F          G          H
 1  ATTITUDE SURVEY - UNIONISATION                         Summary  Statistics
 2  ---------------------------------------------------------------------------------
 3  NAME      SEX       ATTITUDE      SALARY  SERVICE Salaries All
 4  Bunn      M         F                490        2 Ave                750 <-- @AVG(SAL)
 5  Mcleod    M         F                552        2 Max               1184 <-- @MAX(SAL)
 6  Masters   M         F                588        3 Min                490 <-- @MIN(SAL)
 7  Rumbold   M         F                588        1
 8  Narnia    M         A                604        5 Salary    Distrib   SAL
 9  Edgerley  M         U                630        9 --------------------------
10  March     M         U                630        6 Interval     Freq      % Freq
11  Old       M         F                656        4       500
12  Packard   M         A                678        7       600
13  Wilson    M         F                678       10       700
14  Lambert   M         F                678       10       800                leave
15  Boyd      M         A                692       12 Bins  900 <--           blank
16  Bull      M         F                692        8      1000
17  Stoll     M         F                704        2      1100
18  Enders    M         U                704        1      1200
19  White     M         F                716       13            Bin range
20  Carter    M         U                716        7            F11.F18
```

Figure 8.6 Adding Summary Statistics and Distribution Intervals

500	for the Start
100	for the Step
(↵)	to confirm the Stop of 2047.

The worksheet should now tie up with Figure 8.6. Add the label Total as shown in F20.

(e) Since we require distributions for male and female employees as well, we can prepare a suitable template at this stage for the results. We need to copy the distribution segment in columns F, G, and H across to columns I, J, and K for male salaries and L, M, and N, for female salaries. The layout is shown in Figure 8.7. So, with the pointer on F8, type:

/ C F8.H20	to Copy FROM range F8.H20 TO
I8	so that I8 is the top left hand location of the copied range.

Repeat the copying operation to L8 as well. You will need to change the labels for the distributions for male and female employees to MSAL and FSAL.

(f) Now the salary distributions can be obtained. First, for all salaries, with the pointer on F11, the first bin, type:

/ D D	for Data Distribution
SAL	for the Values range to be the salary range SAL
F11.F18	for the Bin range.

The resulting salary distribution is shown in column G of Figure 8.8. The frequencies can be interpreted as follows: 3 employees have salaries below 500, 7 have salaries in the range 500–600, etc.

To compare the distributions, for example, for male employees versus all employees, the different numbers of cases must be allowed for. The frequencies must be converted to percentage frequencies. This is done as follows:

Enter the formula for total frequency (@SUM(G11.G19)) in G20, then enter the first expression for relative frequency. That is, in H11, type:

+G11/G$20

(The 'mixed' addressing of G20 means that, when copied, the column label G will change relative to position, whereas the row will always be row 20, irrespective of column. If you feel happier, put $G$20 in the formula instead.)

Put the percentage format on this cell:

/ R F P 0	to Format H11 to the nearest whole percentage.

Then Copy the contents of H11 downwards to H20. The necessary formulae and results are shown in Figure 8.8.

(g) The distributions of salary for male and female employees are obtained in the same manner. The only differences are the Value ranges (MSAL and FSAL) and the location of the Bin ranges (I11.I18 and L11.L18). (You will also need to copy the formula for Total frequency (in G20) to J20 and M20. Similarly, copy the first relative frequency formula from H11 to K11 and N11 for completeness. After copying, check that the denominators in

	F	G	H	I	J	K	L	M	N
1	Summary	Statistics							
2	----------	----------	----------						
3	Salaries	All							
4	Ave	750							
5	Max	1184							
6	Min	490							
7									
8	Salary	Distrib	SAL	Salary	Distrib	MSAL	Salary	Distrib	FSAL
9	----------	----------	----------	----------	----------	----------	----------	----------	----------
10	Interval	Freq	% Freq	Interval	Freq	%Freq	Interval	Freq	%Freq
11	500			500			500		
12	600			600			600		
13	700			700			700		
14	800			800			800		
15	900			900			900		
16	1000			1000			1000		
17	1100			1100			1100		
18	1200			1200			1200		
19									
20	Total			Total			Total		

Figure 8.7 Template for Salary Distributions—all, male and female employees

	A	B	C	D	E	F	G	H
1	ATTITUDE SURVEY - UNIONISATION					Summary	Statistics	
2	------------	------------	------------	------------	------------	------------	------------	------------
3	NAME	SEX	ATTITUDE	SALARY	SERVICE	Salaries	All	
4	Bunn	M	F	490	2	Ave	750	
5	Mcleod	M	F	552	2	Max	1184	
6	Masters	M	F	588	3	Min	490	
7	Rumbold	M	F	588	1			+G11/G$20
8	Narnia	M	A	604	5	Salary	Distrib	SAL
9	Edgerley	M	U	630	9	------------	------------	------------
10	March	M	U	630	6	Interval	Freq	% Freq
11	Old	M	F	656	4	500	3	4%
12	Packard	M	A	678	7	600	7	10%
13	Wilson	M	F	678	10	700	18	27%
14	Lambert	M	F	678	10	800	19	28%
15	Boyd	M	A	692	12	900	11	16%
16	Bull	M	F	692	8	1000	4	6%
17	Stoll	M	F	704	2	1100	3	4%
18	Enders	M	U	704	1	1200	2	3%
19	White	M	F	716	13		0	0%
20	Carter	M	U	716	7	Total	67	100%
							@SUM(G11.G19)	

Figure 8.8 Salary Distribution for all employees

the relative frequency formulae are the appropriate Total frequencies.) Figure 8.9 shows the results. The relative frequency distributions suggest that the female employees tend to earn less than the male employees. For example, whereas 34 per cent of men earn less than 700 pounds per month, the comparable percentage for women is 55 per cent.

8.3 Graphs of distributions

To get a quick graph of the salary distributions, use the Graph command to draw some Bar charts. The sequence of choices from the Graph menu is circular: you are continually returned to the Graph menu from which you Escape or Quit.

(a) Start with the pointer or F11 and then type:

/G to start the Graph command.

This gives the Graph menu with the following options:

	F	G	H	I	J	K	L	M	N	
1	Summary	Statistics								
2	------------	------------	------------							
3	Salaries	All								
4	Ave	750								
5	Max	1184								
6	Min	490	All employees			Male employees			Female employees	
7										
8	Salary	Distrib	SAL	Salary	Distrib	MSAL	Salary	Distrib	FSAL	8
9	------------	------------	------------	------------	------------	------------	------------	------------	------------	9
10	Interval	Freq	% Freq	Interval	Freq	%Freq	Interval	Freq	% Freq	10
11	500	3	4%	500	1	3%	500	2	7%	11
12	600	7	10%	600	3	8%	600	4	15%	12
13	700	18	27%	700	9	23%	700	9	33%	13
14	800	19	28%	800	14	35%	800	5	19%	14
15	900	11	16%	900	7	18%	900	4	15%	15
16	1000	4	6%	1000	3	8%	1000	1	4%	16
17	1100	3	4%	1100	1	3%	1100	2	7%	17
18	1200	2	3%	1200	2	5%	1200	0	0%	18
19		0	0%		0	0%		0	0%	19
20	Total	67	100%	Total	40	100%	Total	27	100%	20

Figure 8.9 Salary Distributions for all, male and female employees

Type X A B C D E F Reset View Save Options Name Quit

(b) Choose the option Type which leads to a menu of graph Types from which you choose Bar.

(c) From the Graph menu, choose X, the horizontal axis, and specify the X range as the Bin range, i.e. F11.F18.

(d) From the Graph menu, choose A, the first data series to be plotted and specify the range as H11.H18 (the relative frequencies for all salaries).

(e) From the Graph menu, choose View to go to the graph. Press any key to return.

(f) Optional. Improve the graph by adding titles and legends. To do this, choose Options and then Titles to add suitable text to your graph. To display the vertical relative frequency scale as percentages, choose Options then Scale Y-axis Format Percentage 0 decimal places. Use Quit twice to return to the main Graph menu and View. From the Graph menu, Name the graph GRAPH1 using Name Create.

Your graph should be something like Figure 8.10. As is commonly the case, the salary distribution is somewhat skewed to the right, that is, the mean salary is to the right of the median. (One other difference is the adjusted numbers on the horizontal axis. Strictly speaking in bar charts of this type, the bar should 'stand on' a value that represents the

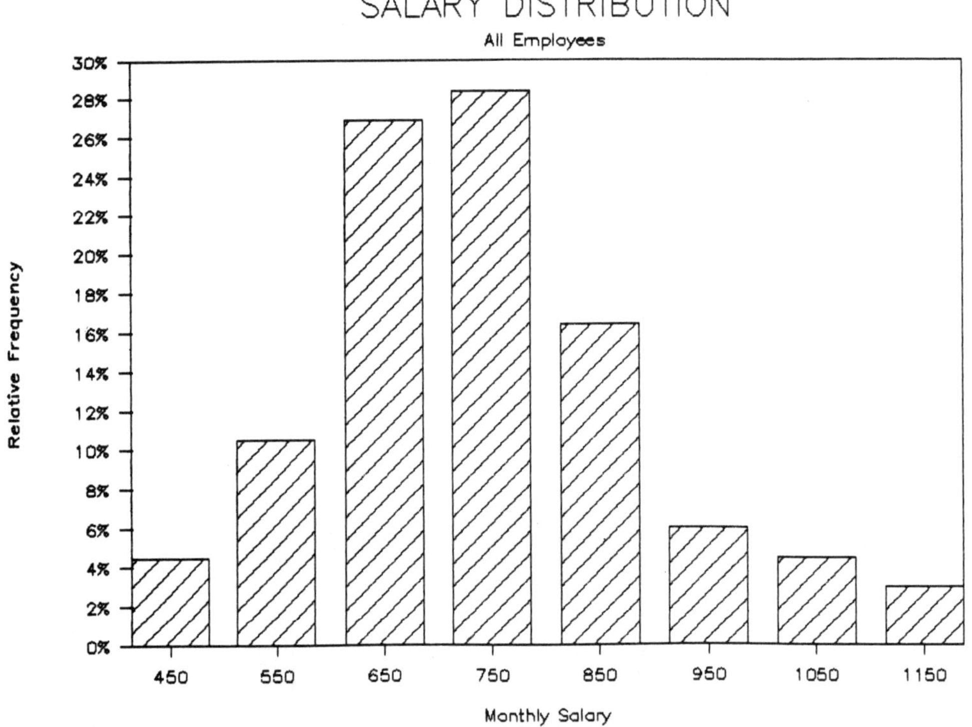

Figure 8.10 Bar chart showing the Salary Distribution for all employees

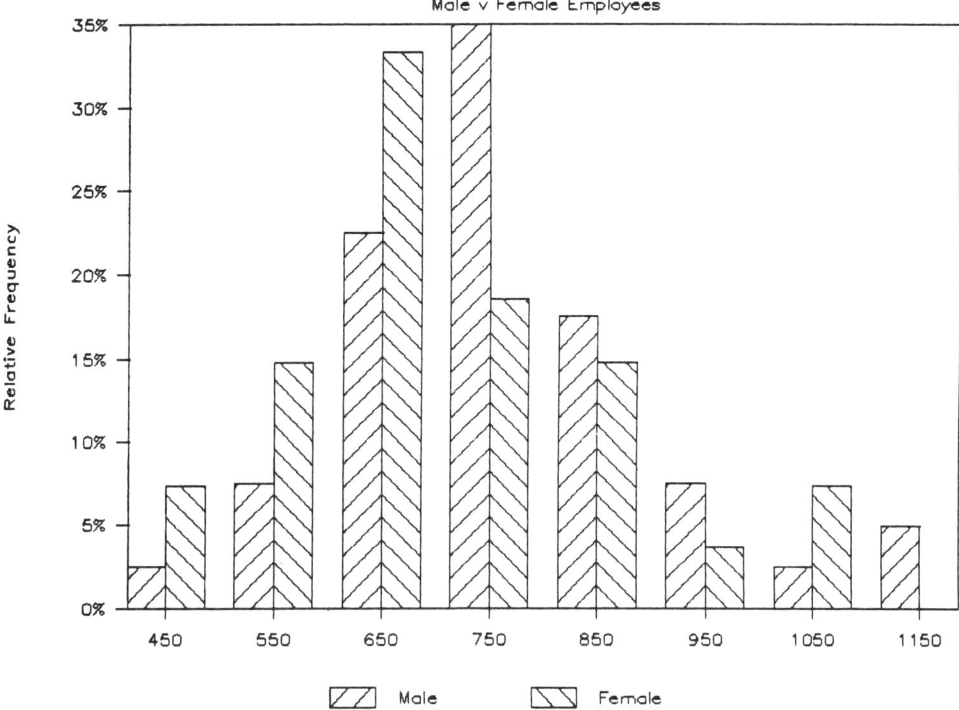

Figure 8.11 Salary Distributions for male v. female employees

midpoint of the interval. A column of midpoints has been used for the X range of data, not F11.F18 as stated in the text.)

For a second graph, compare the salary distributions of male and female employees by specifying the relative frequencies for male salaries, K11.K18, as the A range of data in the graph and for the female employees, N11.N18, as the B range. (See Figure 8.11.) Once again, this graph demonstrates the tendency for female salaries to be lower than those for males.

Distributions for other variables can be obtained in a similar manner. For example, if the records are sorted by ATTITUDE, and the ranges noted for those Against, For, and Undecided about unionization, we can get distributions for these three subgroups in the same manner as for the two sex subgroups. Before trying to do this, you may wish to save your file, calling it say SURVEY so that you can use the same layout for other distributions. Your CM disc contains a datafile called UNION1 which shows the analysis and graphs obtained so far.

8.4 Database statistical functions

As well as getting distributions of variables in the survey, we can also get statistics for subgroups of records. For example, differences in the average salary for Male employees who are Against as opposed to For unionization may be of interest. We can also get cross tabulations, e.g. how many employees fall into each sex-attitude group.

The special 1-2-3 functions such as @SUM, @AVG, etc., which are useful in numerical analysis have their database counterparts. These database functions, denoted @DSUM, @DAVG, etc., are used 'on the back of' Data Query operations. A subgroup of records is selected by Data Query and the @D special functions perform calculations on one field of the selected records (e.g. on the SALARY field).

The form of the @D special functions is illustrated by the average, namely:

@DAVG (Input range, offset, Criterion range)

where the Input and Criterion ranges are those specified in the Data Query operation. That is, the Input range defines the set of records to be queried. The Criterion range contains the conditions a record must satisfy to be selected by the data query. The 'offset' specifies the field (column) on which calculations are to be carried out. The notation for the offset is 0 for the first column, 1 for the second, etc. Thus the offset for salary is 3 and for service 4.

To use the database functions, we need to set up the worksheet for Data Query. This involves clearing out the distributions. The procedure is:

(i) Type:

/ R E F1.N20	to Range Erase the 9 columns of summary statistics and distributions.

(ii) Shrink column F to 1 character width. With the pointer on column F, type:

/ W C S 1	to Set the Column-width to 1 character.

This makes a border between the records and the ensuing calculations.

For Data Query, a Criterion range must be set up. Figure 8.12 shows this set up adjacent to the records in columns G across to K. The main steps are:

(a) Copy the field names from range A3.E3 to G3.K3 using the Copy command.

(b) Specify the Criterion to select only those records with M (for Male) in the SEX field and A for Against in the ATTITUDE field.

(c) If you dislike typing cell ranges, you can 'name' the Input and Criterion ranges with the Range Name Create command. Suppose we wish to call the Input range DB for (DataBase) and the Criterion range CRIT, type:

/ R N C DB	A3.E70 and
/ R N C CRIT	G3.K4

to name the ranges. Of course, if you change either of the cell ranges, you will need to 'create' the names again.

(d) To calculate the average salary for Male employees who are Against unionization, enter the formula for average salary, namely:

	D	E	F	G	H	I	J	K
1				CRITERION RANGE				
2	----------------	-----		----------	----------	----------	----------	----------
3	SALARY	SERVICE		NAME	SEX	ATTITUDE	SALARY	SERVICE
4	490	2			M	A		
5	552	2						
6	588	3						
7	588	1						
8	604	5						
9	630	9						
10	630	6						

Figure 8.12 Criterion range to select records of males against unionization

@DAVG(DB,3,CRIT) in cell H8

as shown in the worksheet of Figure 8.13. (Some additional labels are required and the average salary has been rounded.)

The value for the average salary, 840, has been entered into the Average Salary Table below (i.e. into I14) as a value using Range Value, which converts a formula cell into its current numeric value.

To do this, point at H8 and type:

/ R V (↵) I14 (↵)

to put the current numeric value of cell H8 into cell I14.

To get the corresponding results for Male employees who are For unionization, change A to F in the Criterion. The value in the formula cell (H8) changes to 689. It is keyed into the Average Salary Table as before.

8.5 Data tables

A more systematic approach to repeated calculation of the average salary for each subgroup is provided by the Data Table command. In Chapter 4, this command was used to carry out sensitivity analysis on the spreadsheet model. Two 'inputs', Growth rate and Price, were varied and the effect on profits was set out in a Data Table. The command was / D T 2, the 2 standing for two 'Input cells'. When Growth only was varied, the command was / D T 1.

You can use / Data Table 2 with H4 (Sex) and I4 (Attitude) as the two Input cells for the Data Table. The layout prior to issuing the / D T 2 command is shown in Figure 8.14 and can be loaded from disc by retrieving file UNION2 from your CM disc. The top left hand cell (G13) of the Data Table contains the formula for average salary which is identical to that in cell H8.

Start the Data Table 2 command, specify the Table range as G13.J15, the 1st Input cell as H4 and the 2nd as I4. The results can be seen in Figure 8.15. There is not much difference between the two rows of salary figures in the Data Table, except for the undecided group. The salaries for undecided male employees look significantly higher than those for females. (As an exercise, see whether average service length differs for these six groups. Note that it is only necessary to change the offset number in the @DAVG in cell G13 to achieve this. Then press the (f8/Table) key.)

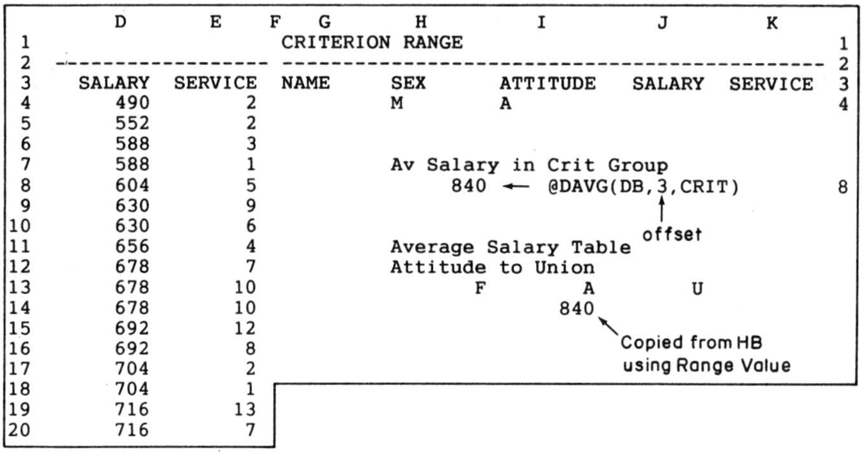

```
            D        E     F   G          H            I            J          K
 1                         CRITERION RANGE                                          1
 2   -----------------  -------------------------------------------------------   2
 3     SALARY  SERVICE  NAME        SEX        ATTITUDE    SALARY   SERVICE        3
 4        490        2              M          A                                    4
 5        552        2
 6        588        3
 7        588        1              Av Salary in Crit Group
 8        604        5                   840 <-- @DAVG(DB,3,CRIT)                   8
 9        630        9                                    ^
10        630        6                                 offset
11        656        4              Average Salary Table
12        678        7              Attitude to Union
13        678       10                    F          A          U
14        678       10                             840
15        692       12                                \Copied from H8
16        692        8                                 using Range Value
17        704        2
18        704        1
19        716       13
20        716        7
```

Figure 8.13 Average salary calculations for different sex-attitude groups

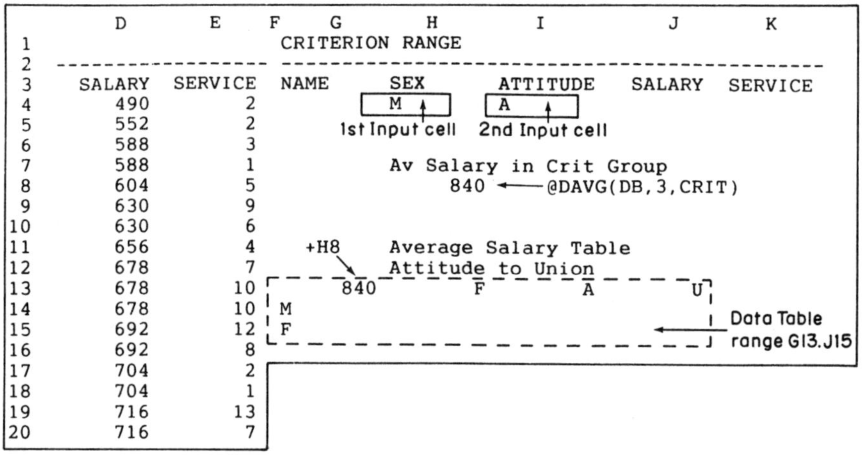

```
            D        E     F   G          H            I            J          K
 1                         CRITERION RANGE
 2   -----------------  -------------------------------------------------------
 3     SALARY  SERVICE  NAME        SEX        ATTITUDE    SALARY   SERVICE
 4        490        2            [ M  ^ ]    [ A   ^ ]
 5        552        2         1st Input cell  2nd Input cell
 6        588        3
 7        588        1             Av Salary in Crit Group
 8        604        5                  840 <---- @DAVG(DB,3,CRIT)
 9        630        9
10        630        6
11        656        4        +H8  Average Salary Table
12        678        7           \ Attitude to Union
13        678       10  ---- 840 ---------- F ------- A ----------- U
14        678       10  | M                                          |
15        692       12  | F                                 <--------| Data Table
16        692        8  ------------------------------------------------ range G13.J15
17        704        2
18        704        1
19        716       13
20        716        7
```

Figure 8.14 Layout for Data Table 2

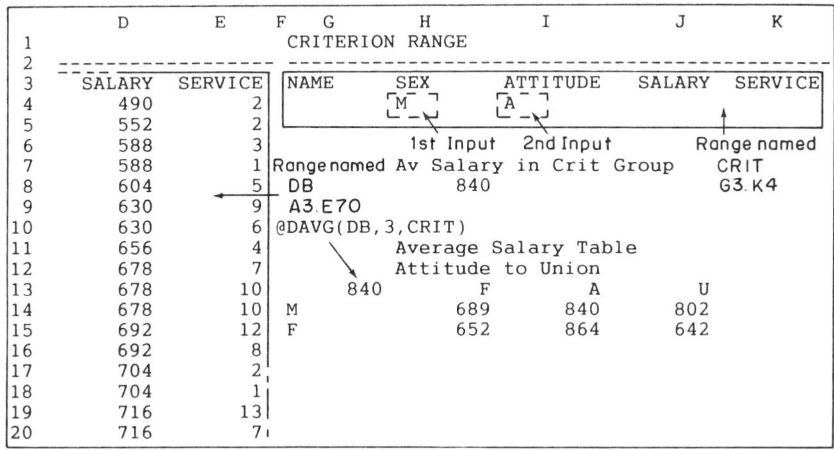

Figure 8.15 Results for Data Table with Sex and Attitude as 'inputs'

There are several other statistical functions for use with database selection criteria, for example @DMAX, @DMIN and @DSTD (for standard deviations). One further statistical function should be mentioned, namely:

@DCOUNT

which counts the non-blank cells in the offset field of the selected records.

@DCOUNT can be used to get cross tabulations. For example, if we want to know the number of employees who fall into each sex-attitude category:

Change the formula in cell G13 of the Data Table to

@DCOUNT(DB,3,CRIT)

and press the (f8/Table) key.

The results are set out in Figure 8.16 and illustrated in a pie-chart in Figure 8.17. There appear to be proportionately fewer men than women who are undecided about unionization. The proportions for and against the union look much the same for men and women.

One further type of analysis concerns the existence or otherwise of relationships between variables such as salary and years' service for the employees. In the next chapter, we look at ways of measuring the correlation between sets of variables and of fitting equations to underlying relationships.

	D	E	F	G	H	I	J	K
1			CRITERION RANGE					
2								
3	SALARY	SERVICE	NAME		SEX	ATTITUDE	SALARY	SERVICE
4	490	2			M	A		
5	552	2						
6	588	3						
7	588	1			Employees in Crit Group			
8	604	5			15			
9	630	9						
10	630	6	@DCOUNT(DB,3,CRIT)					
11	656	4			Number of Employees			
12	678	7			Attitude to Union			
13	678	10		15	F	A	U	
14	678	10	M		16	15	9	
15	692	12	F		8	9	10	
16	692	8						
17	704	2						
18	704	1						
19	716	13						
20	716	7						

Figure 8.16 Results for Data Table on Number of Employees—sex by attitude

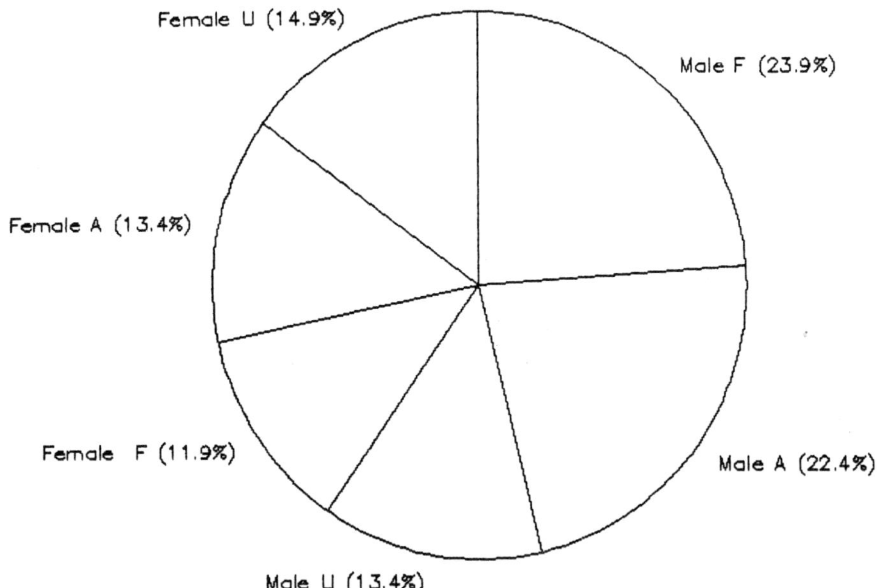

Figure 8.17 Pie chart showing percentages of employees in each sex-attitude group

CHAPTER 9

Analysis of Relationships

In the previous chapter, we showed how small surveys can be analysed with 1-2-3. For example, the salary distributions of male and female employees were determined. However, apart from comparing the salaries of those employees for as opposed to against unionization, we stopped short of analysing any of the potential relationships in the data. For example, is there a tendency for employees with long service records to have higher salaries than those who have just joined?

In this chapter, we will look at some special routines for analysing relationships, in particular, how we can measure correlation and regression using 1-2-3. Again, 1-2-3 graphics are useful for checking assumptions and gauging the adequacy of models fitted.

The techniques are explained in non-technical terms as far as is possible. However, the interested reader is advised to consolidate on the assumptions and the uses (and abuses) of regression in any standard statistics textbook.

9.1 Scatter plots

To begin, we will examine the records of female employees in the survey data of Chapter 8. The purpose is to see whether there is a tendency for salaries to be higher for those employees who have served with the company for many years. The starting point in analysing the relationship between two variables, like salary and service, is to get a scatter plot. This is easily obtained with 1-2-3: the graph Type is the so-called XY graph. Both axes of the XY graph are numerically scaled, in contrast to the Line graph for which only the vertical axis is truly numeric.

(i) Start by entering the data for the 27 female employees into the 1-2-3 worksheet as shown in Figure 9.1. The simplest way is to retrieve the file called FSALSER which contains this information. If you key the data in yourself, keep the layout identical to Figure 9.1, i.e. start the readings in column B row 3 and leave cell D1 empty.

(ii) To simplify keystroking, the range of salary readings will be named Y and the range of service readings X, i.e. use

/ Range Name Create Y B3.B29

to attach name Y to cell range B3.B29 and similarly

/ Range Name Create X C3.C29

(Remember that if you start with the pointer on cell B3 say and 'anchor' it by typing in a 'full stop', the End key followed by the down arrow will expand the pointer down

	A	B	C
1		SURVEY RESULTS	
2	Employee	Salary	Service
3	1	1022	25
4	2	796	13
5	3	738	21
6	4	774	12
7	5	860	20
8	6	860	20
9	7	1082	17
10	8	748	16
11	9	892	33
12	10	564	1
13	11	948	18
14	12	630	7
15	13	490	1
16	14	516	3
17	15	748	10
18	16	630	4
19	17	692	14
20	18	630	5
21	19	490	4
22	20	692	13
23	21	692	14
24	22	526	8
25	23	656	6
26	24	842	9
27	25	564	7
28	26	668	2
29	27	656	12

Figure 9.1 Monthly salary and length of service for 27 employees

to B29. Also if the pointer appears to be anchored already, press Backspace to allow it to move freely.)

(iii) With the Graph commands, choose the XY type of graph specifying the X range as X and the A range as Y. Then View the graph.

It will almost certainly be necessary to go into the Options menu to alter the Format of the Graph to Symbols only to get a scatter plot like Figure 9.2. If your graph looks like an untidy cobweb with lines joining up the data points in seemingly random fashion, choose:

Options, then Format, choose A then Symbols.

Return to the Graph menu to View the resulting scatter plot.

Notice that with an XY graph, the position of a data point is fixed by both its horizontal distance along the years' service scale as well as by its vertical distance up the salary scale. In contrast, with a Line graph, although the readings are scaled vertically, they are spaced out at regular intervals along the horizontal axis with the years' service readings attached as labels. You can demonstrate the difference for yourself by changing the graph type from the XY type to the Line type and back.

Once again, suitable titles and axis labels such as those in Figure 9.2 can be added via the Options menu. When the graph is considered 'satisfactory', it can be named and the datafile saved to disc.

The graph shows that salary does appear to be related to years' service. However, there is a lot of variation in salary levels for employees with roughly the same service level, although there is a tendency for high salary to be coupled with long service. One approach is to calculate the correlation of salary and service, that is, the strength of the 'straight line' association between the two.

However, suppose that we want to be able to predict an employee's salary, given that we know how long she has been with the company. In this case, the aim is to find a simple equation that best fits the data. As a starting point, the best fitting straight line would allow us to make rough predictions of salary given that we know an employee's service. With a scatter plot like Figure 9.2, it is not obvious what line should be fitted. The standard statistical approach is to determine mathematically the line with least scatter of points about it. Using this criterion (called the least-squares criterion) the slope and intercept of the best fitting linear equation can be calculated. The resulting line is called the regression line, more particularly, the regression of salary (Y) on service (X). It is conventional to call X the 'independent' or 'explanatory' variable and Y the 'dependent' variable, since the Y values 'depend' on the X values, at least as far as the equation is concerned.

Unlike the first version, Release 2 of 1-2-3 has a built-in regression facility, which comes under the Data part of the menu. The following section shows how this can be used to carry out regression on the salary–service data.

9.2 Regression and Correlation

To calculate the measures of correlation and regression for two variables such as salary and service, we use the Data Regression sequence. In this section, we perform regression

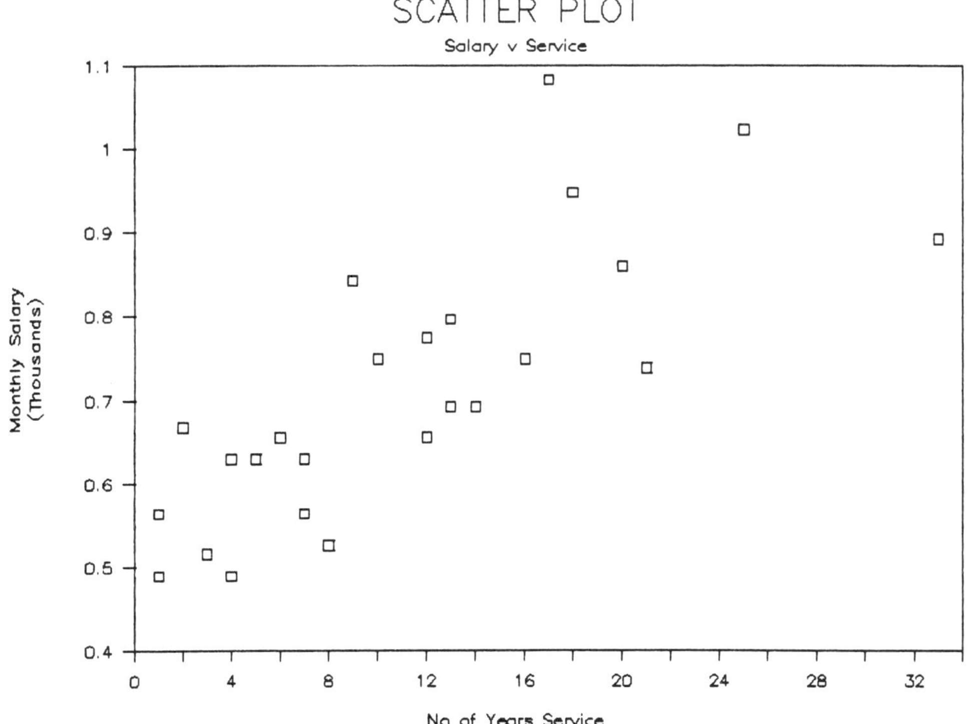

Figure 9.2 Plot of salary v. service for 27 employees

on the data in the FSALSER file containing the salary and service data. The objective is to estimate the relationship between salary and service for the female employees. As part of this analysis, we shall calculate the correlation between salary and service for this data.

The data on salary (Y) and service (X) occupy columns B and C, respectively, starting in row 3, and they have been 'named' Y and X as described in Section 9.1.

To carry out the calculations to obtain a regression line, it is merely necessary to tell 1-2-3 the cell ranges containing the 'dependent' and 'independent' variables and where the 'output' of the regression calculations is to be put in the worksheet. The steps are as follows:

(i) type:

/ D R for Data Regression

(ii) choose the X range and specify it as X (or C3.C29),

(iii) choose the Y range and specify it as Y (or B3.B29),

(iv) choose the Output range and specify it as I3 (i.e. one page to the right of the data),

(v) choose Go to execute the regression of Salary on Service

The results of the regression analysis are displayed starting in column I. After rounding the entries in cell ranges L4.L6 and K10.K11 to 2 decimal places (with / Range Format Fixed 2), the screen display should tally with that shown in the inset part of Figure 9.3.

	A	B	C
1		SURVEY RESULTS	
2	Employee	Salary	Service
3	1	1022	25
4	2	796	13
5	3	738	21
6	4	774	12
7	5	860	20
8	6	860	20
9	7	1082	17
10	8	748	16
11	9	892	33
12	10	564	1
13	11	948	18
14	12	630	7
15	13	490	1
16	14	516	3
17	15	748	10
18	16	630	4
19	17	692	14
20	18	630	5
21	19	490	4
22	20	692	13
23	21	692	14
24	22	526	8
25	23	656	6
26	24	842	9
27	25	564	7
28	26	668	2
29	27	656	12

I	J	K	L	
	Regression Output:			3
Constant		Intercept =	539.09	4
Std Err of Y Est			101.21	5
R Squared			0.60	6
No. of Observations			27	7
Degrees of Freedom			25	8
				9
X Coefficient(s)		15.40 = Slope		10
Std Err of Coef.		2.52		11

Figure 9.3 Regression output for the data on salary and service

The regression output gives us the coefficients for the regression line together with various measures that summarize how well the line fits the data. The equation of the regression line can be constructed from the 'Constant' or intercept (539.09 in cell L4) and the 'X Coefficient' or slope (15.40 in cell K10).

Thus the best fitting line given by regression for predicting salary from years' service has the equation:

Predicted Salary = 539 + 15.4 * (years' service)

One 'global' measure of the goodness of fit of the equation to the data is given by 'R Squared' in cell L6. This quantity takes a value between 0 and 1. Provided there is plenty of data, high values close to 1 occur when the relationship between variables is more or less a straight line relationship: values near 0 suggest no relationship at all. The value of 0.60 in cell L6 for this data suggests that goodness of fit is moderate, that is, as we anticipated the fitted line has considerable scatter about it.

To illustrate this point visually, it is worth superimposing the fitted line on the original data. To do this, we must first evaluate the 'fitted values', that is, the salary values given by the regression equation for each employee based on her observed service (her X value). These fitted values will be displayed in column D. The discrepancy between the actual salary value in column B and the fitted value in column D is called the 'residual'. It is important to calculate the residuals when undertaking regression analysis for a variety of reasons.

The formulae for the Fitted and Residual values for the first employee are shown in D3 and E3 in Figure 9.4. So the next step is to enter the formulae for the first employee and then copy them down for each row corresponding to an employee. The steps are:

	A	B	C	D	E
1		SURVEY RESULTS			
2	Employee	Salary	Service	Fitted	Residual
3	1	1022	25	924	98
4	2	796	13	739	57
5	3	738	21	862	-124
6	4	774	12	724	50
7	5	860	20	847	13
8	6	860	20	847	13
9	7	1082	17	801	281
10	8	748	16	785	-37
11	9	892	33	1047	-155
12	10	564	1	554	10
13	11	948	18	816	132
14	12	630	7	647	-17
15	13	490	1	554	-64
16	14	516	3	585	-69
17	15	748	10	693	55
18	16	630	4	601	29
19	17	692	14	755	-63
20	18	630	5	616	14
21	19	490	4	601	-111
22	20	692	13	739	-47
23	21	692	14	755	-63
24	22	526	8	662	-136
25	23	656	6	631	25
26	24	842	9	678	164
27	25	564	7	647	-83
28	26	668	2	570	98
29	27	656	12	724	-68

D3: +$L$4+$K$10*C3
E3: +B3-D3

Figure 9.4 Calculations for Fitted and Residual values

(vi) In cell D3, enter the formula:

+$L$4+$K$10*C3

and in cell E3, enter the formula for the Residual value:

+B3−D3

Display these two entries to the nearest integer value using / Range Format Fixed 0 decimal places.

(vii) Next, copy the formulae for the Fitted and Residual values in cells D3 and E3, respectively, into the data rows below.

That is, with the pointer on D3, type:

/ C D3.E3 D4.D29 to Copy From range D3.E3 To range D4.D29

(viii) To see how well the regression line fits the data, reproduce the scatter plot of salaries against service and superimpose the fitted values (in D3 to D29) on to the graph. That is, type:

/ G V to View the scatter plot again.

From the Graph menu, specify the B range as D3.D29, then View.

Ideally, the salary−service observations should be Symbols unconnected by lines and the fitted values should be Lines or both Symbols and Lines. With the commands on the Options menu, you can Format the A range of data to be Symbols only, and the B range to be Lines: also, suitable Titles can be added. When you View the graph, the effect should be like Figure 9.5.

The scatter plot shows that although the fitted line captures the general trend for higher salaries to be associated with longer service with the company, the observations vary quite widely about the line.

We can measure this 'residual' variation by calculating its standard deviation. (In fact, the regression line is the line for which this residual standard deviation is least: the standard deviation is the square root of the 'variance' and the criterion we used, 'least squares', means least variance about the line). Before doing this calculation though, you should scan the residuals to ensure that they appear to be irregular, both in size and sign. It is not sensible to summarize the residual variation into a measure, such as the standard deviation, if the residuals display a systematic pattern. The presence of such a pattern is not obvious when the residuals are in an arbitrary order, such as is the case here. There is more information to be gleaned from the scatter plot in Figure 9.5. In the graph, the residuals (vertical differences of points from the line) on the left hand side are for 'low' fitted values, whereas on the right hand side they correspond to 'high' values. The scatter of points about the line should tend to be roughly the same size along the line: it should not get significantly larger (or smaller) moving from left to right along the line.

The residuals appear to be satisfactorily random in size and sign for the salary−service data. There is no marked tendency for them to be larger for high fitted values than for low values. It would be easy to apply the special function @STD() to the residuals in column E to

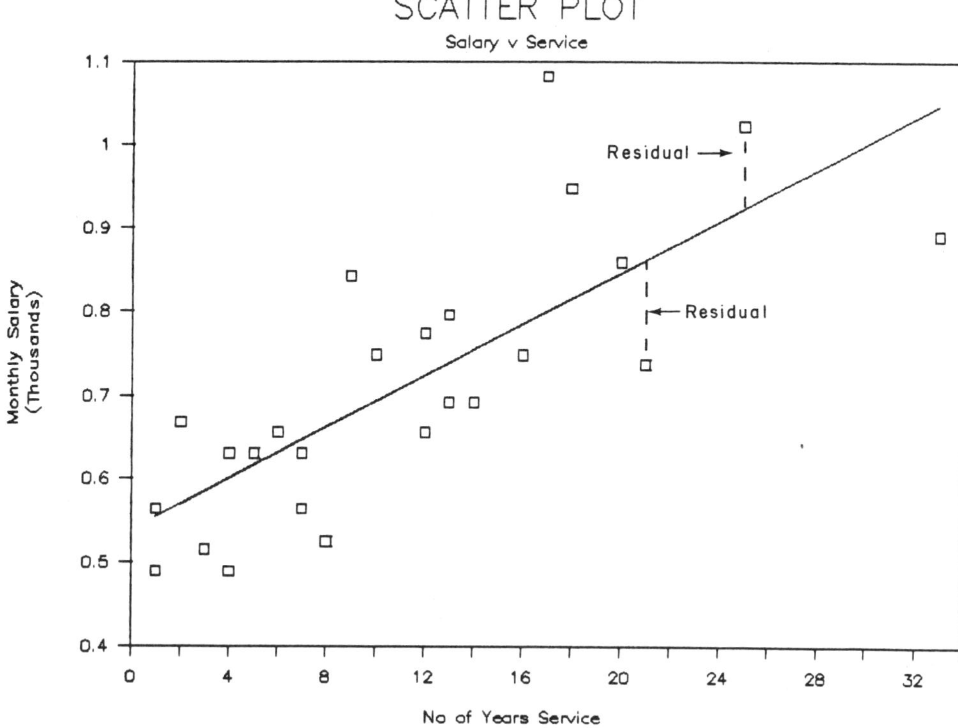

Figure 9.5 Regression line superimposed on Figure 9.2

calculate their standard deviation. In practice, a slightly more efficient estimation procedure is used. The result of this is given in the regression output shown in Figure 9.3. Cell L5, labelled as 'Std Err of Y Est', contains the value 101.21 for estimated residual standard deviation. The size of the residual scatter about the line tells us how well the line fits the data, particularly when we judge its size relative to say the mean value or standard deviation of the salary figures (Y). (You may wish to evaluate the standard deviation of the salary figures using @STD(Y), where Y is the name given to the range of salary values (B3.B29). The units are salary units, namely pounds.)

For this data, the residual standard deviation is relatively high, 101, as compared with 154, the standard deviation of the salary readings. In other words, even when we make an allowance for the tendency for salaries to rise as length of service rises, there is still much 'unexplained' variability in the salary figures.

Thus the two summary measures, the residual standard deviation and R Squared described earlier, tell us how well the line fits the data. R Squared is in fact the square of the correlation coefficient. Hence taking its square root using @SQRT(L6), we can estimate the correlation coefficient as 0.77 after rounding. This measure is interpreted as the strength of straight line (or linear) association between the salary variable and the service variable in this set of 27 readings. Correlation is measured on a scale from -1 to $+1$, the sign indicating whether the two variables increase together (positive correlation) or whether one variable increases as the other decreases (negative correlation). Here, the graph shows that salary increases with years' service, so we have observed a moderately positive correlation coefficient between salary and length of service.

Therefore, recapping the results, the correlation between salary and service is positive and moderately strong (0.77): the best fitting equation for predicting the salary of an employee from her length of service is

Predicted Salary = 539 + 15.4*(years' service)

This has an R Squared value of 0.60 or 60 per cent, which indicates considerable variation in salaries not 'explained' by differing service, the standard deviation of this unexplained variation being 101 pounds.

Datafile FSALSER1 on your CM disc contains the correlation and regression analysis described in this section and includes named graphs for the scatter plot and fitted regression line.

9.3 Multiple regression

The same approach can be used to fit an equation when the observations consist of readings on three or more variables. The data in Figure 9.6 concern the number of car trips undertaken daily by households in different areas. The variables are Y, the average number of daily car trips per household for the area, X(1) the average household size and X(2), the average number of cars per household in the area. The aim is to find an equation relating the number of car trips daily (Y) to the two explanatory variables, household size (X(1)) and the number of cars per household (X(2)).

	A	B	C	D
1		CAR TRIPS		
2	Area No	Trips	Size	Cars
3	1	3.8	2.2	0.3
4	2	5	2.8	0.6
5	3	5.1	3	0.2
6	4	5.7	3	0.8
7	5	7.3	3.7	0.7
8	6	7.4	3.4	1.3
9	7	7.7	3.4	1.4
10	8	7.9	4	1
11	9	8.5	4.6	0.2

Figure 9.6 Area averages for daily car trips, household size and number of cars

Figure 9.7 shows visually how the number of car trips (Y) relates to one of these variables, average household size (X(1)) and suggests that a straight line can be fitted to the data. The scatter plot and the following analysis can be carried out as described in the previous section. (The data can be keyed into the worksheet or retrieved from a datafile called TRIPS on the CM disc.)

The regression output in Figure 9.8 results from taking the number of car trips as the Y variable and household size as the X variable. That is, in carrying out the regression calculations, the Y range has been specified as B3.B11 and the X range as C3.C11. The Output range has been taken as cell I3. The calculations to obtain the fitted and residual values are illustrated in Figure 9.9.

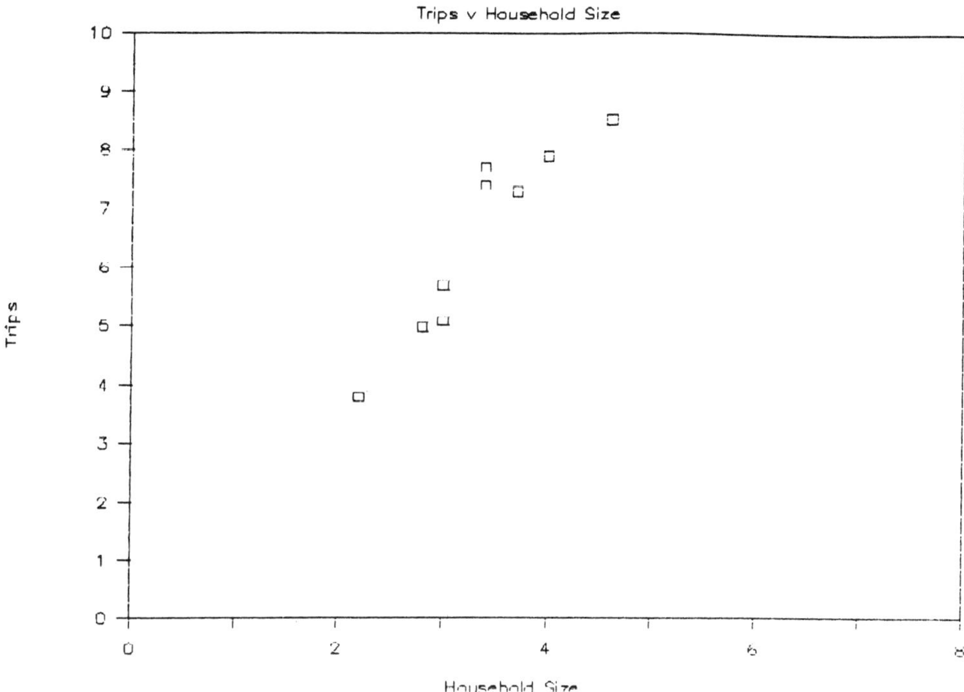

Figure 9.7 Daily car trips v. household size

The best fitting line turns out to have an intercept of −0.65 (cell L4) and a slope of 2.13 (cell K10). Simplifying and rounding, the result of the analysis is that the best fitting line has the equation:

Predicted number of trips per household = −0.6 + 2.1∗(average household size)

The fit of the regression line is quite good as can be seen in Figure 9.10, where the fitted values have been superimposed over the scatter plot. The statistical measures of the fit of the line, namely the residual standard deviation of 0.64 trips (in cell L5) and the R Squared value of 0.86 (in L6) confirm what we can see in the graph, that is, a reasonably good fit.

In passing, it is worth mentioning that 1-2-3's regression algorithm does allow the estimation of the best fitting line through the origin, that is, the line with 'zero intercept'. Intuitively, it may seem more sensible to fit a line through the origin so that 'zero household size' will result in zero (rather than −0.6) trips per household. In practice, statisticians prefer the best fitting relationship overall without constraining the line to pass through the origin. Their preference is based on much practical experience, which shows that many relationships, which are satisfactory over normally observed data values, often change in structure as variables approach zero.

Returning to the equation explaining variation in number of car trips in terms of variation in average household size, data is also available on the average number of cars per household. Therefore, it is worth seeing if this variable accounts for any of the residual

	A	B	C	D	I	J	K	L	
1		CAR TRIPS							1
2	Area No	Trips	Size	Cars					2
3	1	3.8	2.2	0.3		Regression Output:			3
4	2	5	2.8	0.6	Constant			-0.65	4
5	3	5.1	3	0.2	Std Err of Y Est			0.64	5
6	4	5.7	3	0.8	R Squared			0.86	6
7	5	7.3	3.7	0.7	No. of Observations			9	7
8	6	7.4	3.4	1.3	Degrees of Freedom			7	8
9	7	7.7	3.4	1.4					9
10	8	7.9	4	1	X Coefficient(s)		2.13		10
11	9	8.5	4.6	0.2	Std Err of Coef.		0.32		11

Figure 9.8 Linear regression of car trips on household size

	A	B	C	D	E	F	I	J	K	L	
1		CAR TRIPS			Model 1	+$L$4+$K$10*C3	Model 1:	Trips on Size			1
2	Area No	Trips	Size	Cars	Fitted	Residual					2
3	1	3.8	2.2	0.3	4.05	-0.25 ← +B3-E3		Regression Output:			3
4	2	5	2.8	0.6	5.33	-0.33	Constant		Intercept=	-0.65	4
5	3	5.1	3	0.2	5.75	-0.65	Std Err of Y Est			0.64	5
6	4	5.7	3	0.8	5.75	-0.05	R Squared			0.86	6
7	5	7.3	3.7	0.7	7.25	0.05	No. of Observations			9	7
8	6	7.4	3.4	1.3	6.61	0.79	Degrees of Freedom			7	8
9	7	7.7	3.4	1.4	6.61	1.09					9
10	8	7.9	4	1	7.89	0.01	X Coefficient(s)		2.13 = Slope		10
11	9	8.5	4.6	0.2	9.17	-0.67	Std Err of Coef.		0.32		11

Figure 9.9 Calculations for fitted and residual values

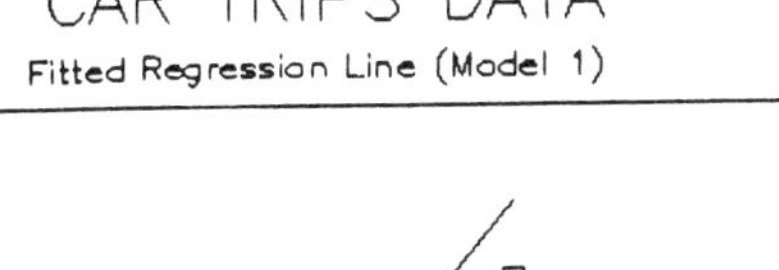

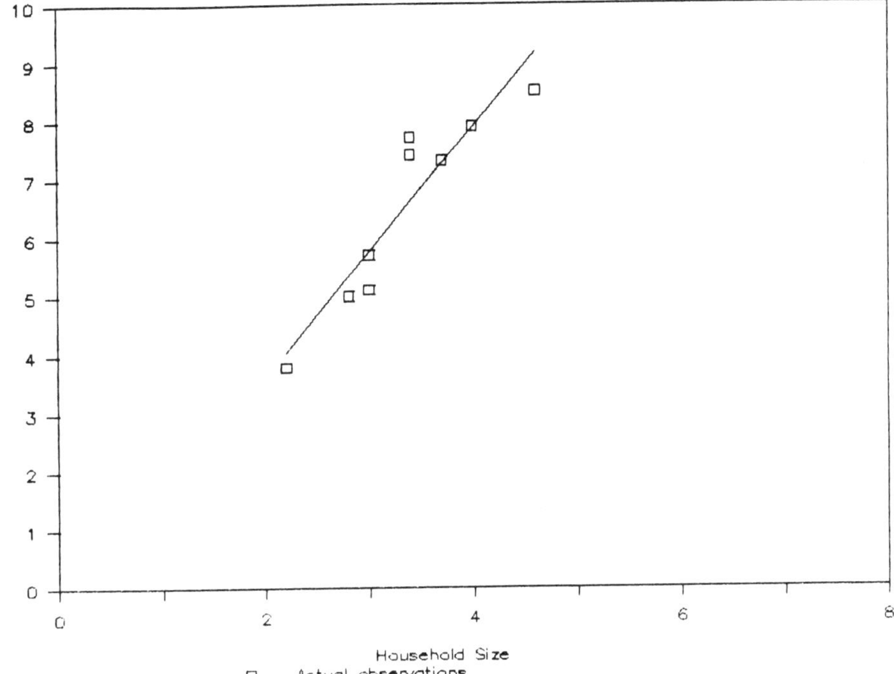

Figure 9.10 Regression of car trips on household size

variation in trips per household. We obtain the best fitting linear relationship relating trips to size and cars by an extension of simple linear regression, namely, multiple regression. Working in three dimensions with the observations on three variables, the problem is to find the best fitting plane. The 'least squares' principle is used to determine the plane about which residual scatter (measured by standard deviation) is least.

Returning to the menu for Data Regression, it is merely necessary to respecify the X range and also say where the Output range is to be located. In particular, the X range must now be defined as the column of Size values and the adjacent column of Cars values, that is, the cell range C3.D11. Suppose that the Output range for this regression of Trips on Size and Cars is to be located two pages across the spreadsheet, namely starting in cell Q3.

The main steps in carrying out the multiple regression analysis are therefore:

(i) choose / Data Regression,
(ii) check that the Y range is specified as B3.B11,
(iii) specify the X range as C3.D11,
(iv) specify the Output range as Q3,
(v) choose Go to regress Trips on Size and Cars and get the results output in cell Q3 and beyond,
(vi) round the regression results, for example use / Range Format Fixed with 2 decimal places on the cell ranges T4.T6 and S10.T11.

The results should tally with the regression output part of Figure 9.11. Interpreting the output values, the best fitting linear equation is:

Predicted number of trips per household = −1.25 + 2.04*(average size per household) + 1.27*(average number cars per household)

where the constant (−1.25) comes from cell T4 and the 'slope' coefficients come from cells S10 and T10 in the worksheet. These latter coefficients show the 'partial' or incremental effect of the variables. Thus for areas with much the same level of household size, an increase of 1 in the average number of cars per household will give rise to an additional 1.27 trips per day.

Next, the Fitted values for Trips using the second regression equation are calculated.

(vii) Applying the best fitting linear equation relating Trips to Size and Cars, the formula for the Fitted value for Area 1 to enter in cell G3 is:

+$T$4+$S$10*C3+$T$10*D3

and the formula for the corresponding Residual value in cell H3 is:

+B3−G3

(viii) To improve the legibility of these values, use / Range Format Fixed to 2 decimal places on the formula cells.

(ix) Lastly, copy the formulae in G3 and H3 down to the data rows below.

The Fitted and Residual values should tie up with those in Figure 9.11.

It is important to check down column H to ensure that the residuals look reasonably irregular and random. A more rigorous approach would be to plot Residual values against Fitted values using the Graph commands.

(x) Plot actual trips (column B) and fitted trips (column G) area by area. That is, type:

/ Graph Type Line to choose a Line Type of Graph.

Specify the X range as the area numbers, that is, A3.A11, the A range as actual Trips, B3.B11, and the B range as Fitted values, G3.G11. Then View the graph.

Figure 9.12 shows the resulting graph. The fitted values are exceedingly close to the actual values. (You may need to use the Format option to display the A range (actual trips) as a line rather than points to get an exact replica of Figure 9.12.)

The numerical results of the regression analysis are shown in Figure 9.11. The fitted values have been calculated from the linear equation:

Predicted number of trips per household = −1.25 + 2.04* (average size per household) + 1.27* (average number cars per household)

where the coefficients come from cells T4, S10, and T10 in the worksheet.

The visual impression of the graph in Figure 9.12 is confirmed by the statistical measures conventionally used to judge the 'goodness of fit' of the fitted equation. R Squared is high (0.99 in T6) and the residual standard deviation is 0.22 trips (in T5).

	A	B	C	D	E	F	G	H
1		CAR TRIPS			Model 1		Model 2	
2	Area No	Trips	Size	Cars	Fitted	Residual	Fitted	Residual
3	1	3.8	2.2	0.3	4.05	-0.25	3.62	0.18
4	2	5	2.8	0.6	5.33	-0.33	5.22	-0.22
5	3	5.1	3	0.2	5.75	-0.65	5.12	-0.02
6	4	5.7	3	0.8	5.75	-0.05	5.89	-0.19
7	5	7.3	3.7	0.7	7.25	0.05	7.19	0.11
8	6	7.4	3.4	1.3	6.61	0.79	7.34	0.06
9	7	7.7	3.4	1.4	6.61	1.09	7.47	0.23
10	8	7.9	4	1	7.89	0.01	8.18	-0.28
11	9	8.5	4.6	0.2	9.17	-0.67	8.38	0.12
12								

Q	R	S	T	
Model 2: Trips on Size & Cars				1
				2
Regression Output:				3
Constant			-1.25	4
Std Err of Y Est			0.22	5
R Squared			0.99	6
No. of Observations			9	7
Degrees of Freedom			6	8
				9
X Coefficient(s)		2.04	1.27	10
Std Err of Coef.		0.11	0.17	11

+B3-G3

$T$4+$S$10*C3+$T$10*D3

Constant 'Size slope' 'Cars slope'

Figure 9.11 Multiple regression results

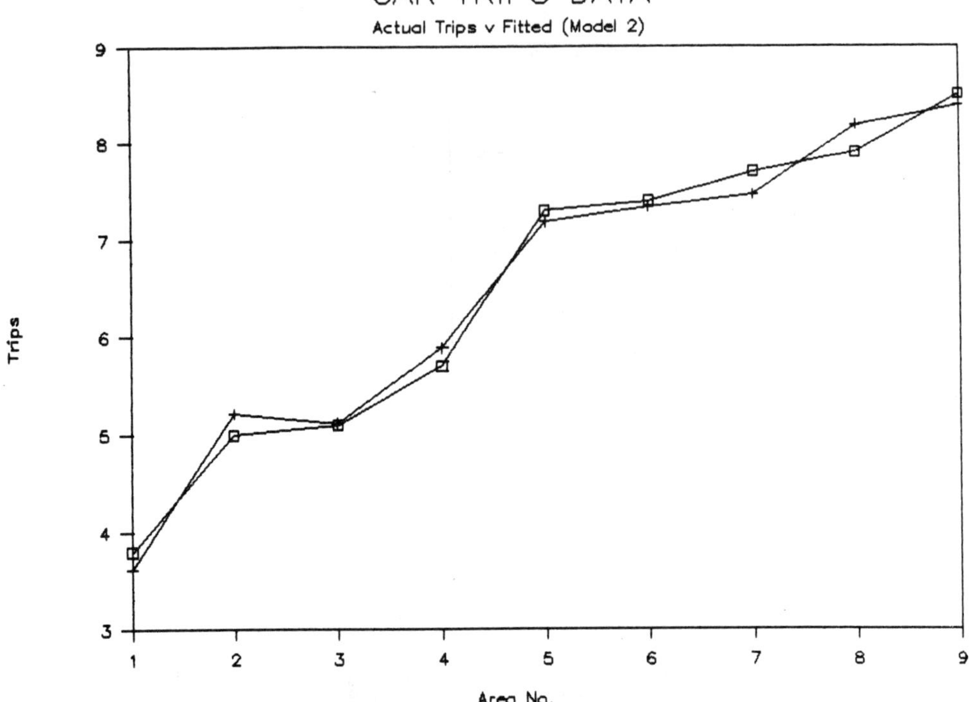

Figure 9.12 The fit of the equation

The regression coefficients (or X Coefficients as Lotus calls them) are set out in cells S10 and T10. Underneath in row 11 are their standard errors. Taking the ratio of each regression coefficient to its standard error (X Coefficient/Standard Err of Coef.) we get the so-called T-values. You need to refer to a statistics book to understand the 'significance' of these values. Basically, the T-values help in deciding whether the individual variables are 'contributing' to the model. A very rough and ready test is to say that a variable is worth including in the model if its T-value is 2 or more: otherwise, the variable is best excluded and the analysis rerun without it. Here, both variables have T-values that exceed 2. (The values are 2.04/0.11 and 1.27/0.17.) We conclude that the addition of the cars as another explanatory variable is an improvement.

To summarize, the model with size of household and cars per household (denoted Model 2) has a higher R Squared value compared with the earlier model including only household size (0.99 versus 0.86). The 'unexplained' variation, measured in terms of the residual standard deviation has been reduced from 0.64 trips to 0.22 trips by including cars in the equation.

Regression analysis is used again in the next chapter on sales forecasting. In addition, it is explained further and employed in several applications in *Advanced Spreadsheet Modelling*.

CHAPTER 10

Sales Forecasting

Much routine sales forecasting depends on analysing past sales readings, identifying the patterns in past sales and projecting these forward into the future as sales forecasts. The methods are those of time series analysis. 1-2-3 can assist the process in a variety of ways. Graphs of sales readings suggest the way a particular sales series should be modelled. 1-2-3 commands enable 'smoothing' and estimation of 'seasonal effects' to be carried out with ease. The regression facility allows trends to be estimated quickly.

In this chapter, after an opening discussion of the main features of sales data, some sample sales readings are smoothed firstly using moving averages. Next, forecasting with exponential smoothing is illustrated. Then, we work through a method for estimating the seasonal factors. Lastly, trend estimation is illustrated for different types of sales growth. Linear regression (explained in some detail in the previous chapter) is employed to help fit a variety of trend equations.

10.1 Trend seasonal and random components in a time series

In analysing past sales data, it is important to pinpoint the different movements in the data. Most sales readings will vary from period to period reflecting random fluctuations in the level of sales. In addition, some sales readings show an overall upward (or downward) trend in the mean level of sales. Many sales are seasonal causing a regular seasonal fluctuation in the level of sales. Finally, some time series display a cyclical fluctuation, usually longer than a year in period, perhaps related to the business cycle. The forecasting method must take account of the constituent movements of a time series in order to produce sensible projections for the future. In addition, assumptions must be made about how the different components of a time series combine together. Is the model for the time series multiplicative or additive? This in turn gives rise to different ways of estimating the seasonal effects.

Figure 10.1 shows quarterly sales of a seasonal item, swimwear. Data for 24 quarters (or periods) is displayed graphically. The seasonal nature of sales is immediately apparent with high sales repeatedly in the third quarter and a drop in sales in the fourth quarter. There is also a strong upward trend in sales and some further random fluctuation from quarter to quarter. These components, trend, seasonal and random variation, represent the main patterns in the series. There is little evidence of a cyclical movement. In fact, the cyclical factor is usually ignored in routine short term forecasting, the impact of any cycle being long rather than short term. Therefore, in the following discussion, we shall consider

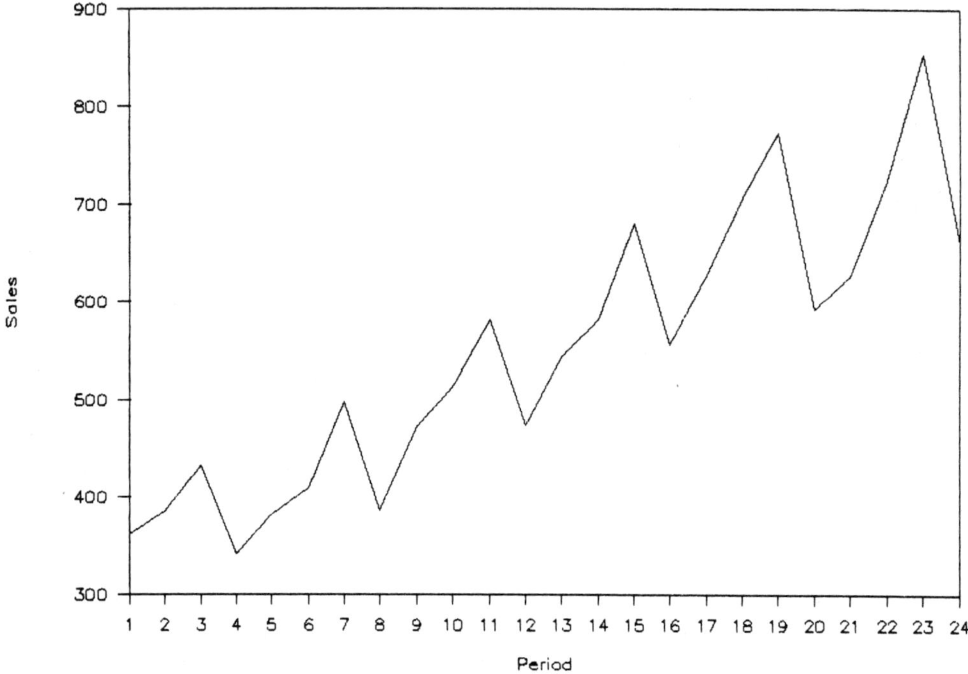

Figure 10.1 Sales series with trend and seasonal pattern

a sales series (Y) to be made up simply of trend, seasonal, and random components, denoted T, S, and R respectively.

Looking further at Figure 10.1, the amplitude of the seasonal fluctuations appears to be larger at higher sales levels than at lower levels. This suggests that the underlying model for sales is a multiplicative one, that is:

$$Y = T \times S \times R$$

For example, the level of sales in the second quarter say is obtained by multiplying the trend component by the seasonal factor for the second quarter.

Where there is trend in a series, the seasonal variation is frequently found to be greater at higher levels of sales than at lower levels, implying that the multiplicative model is the appropriate one. However, there are cases where the seasonal pattern is of much the same amplitude from year to year. In these cases, the seasonal pattern can be regarded as 'adding on' to any trend. The underlying model is assumed to be additive therefore with equation:

$$Y = T + S + R$$

Another series showing the monthly demand for percolators from January (period 1) to November (Period 11) is plotted in Figure 10.2. This series displays a lot of random fluctuation from month to month but no seasonal pattern (as far as is known) and no trend.

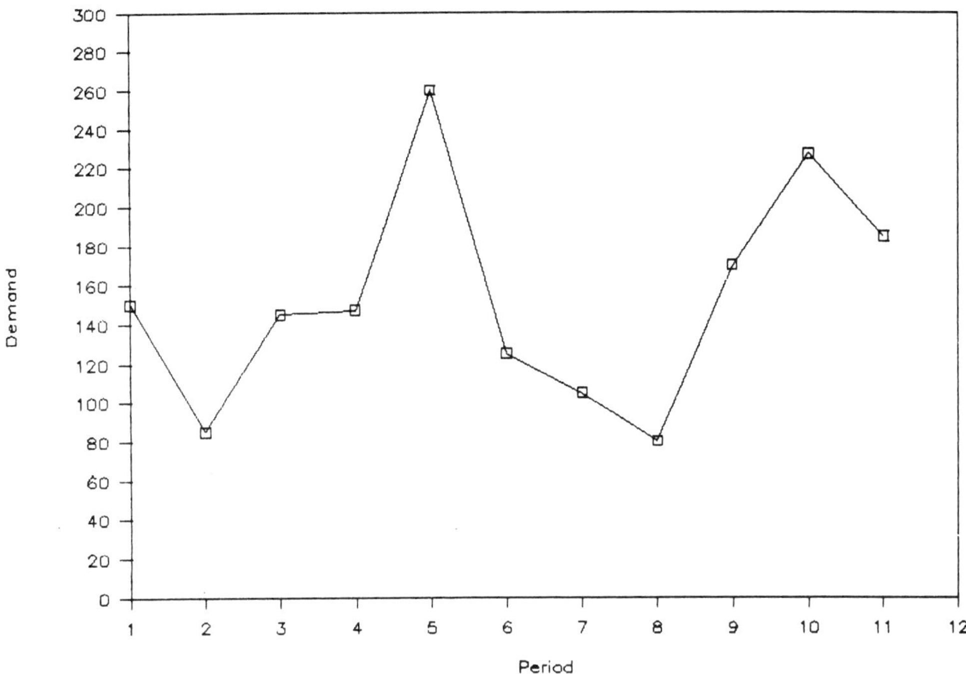

Figure 10.2 Sales series with random variation

Suppose a forecast is required for December (period 12). How should we use the past sales history to produce the forecast?

What is needed is a method of smoothing out the random variations in demand from period to period which will reveal the underlying average level of demand. If possible, the method of smoothing must also be more responsive to new rather than old data since sales forecasting must be responsive to recent trends.

10.2 Moving averages

The simplest form of smoothing consists of calculating arithmetic averages of past sales readings and 'rolling' the averaging forwards as more readings become available. For example, the forecast for period 12 could be obtained by averaging the demand for periods 9, 10, and 11. When a demand reading becomes available for period 12, this can be included in the average and the oldest reading (for period 9) dropped from the average. The moving average calculations will be illustrated in full for the percolator data already shown in Figure 10.2.

Key the percolator demand data into the 1-2-3 worksheet as shown in Figure 10.3, with the demand readings in range B3.B13, putting headings '3 Period moving averages' and '5 Period moving averages' abbreviated as indicated. Alternatively, retrieve the file PERC from your CM disc.

	A	B	C	D
1	MOVING AVERAGES		3 Period	5 Period
2	Period	Demand	Mov Ave	Mov Ave
3	1	150		
4	2	85		
5	3	145		
6	4	147		
7	5	260	Monthly	
8	6	125	← demand	
9	7	105	for	
10	8	80	percolators	
11	9	170		
12	10	227		
13	11	185		
14	12	NA	← @NA	

Figure 10.3 Layout of worksheet for moving averages

(Notice the use of the special function @NA in Cell B14. This has been used to indicate that the demand reading for period 12 is (as yet) Not Available. It is a useful safeguard when formulae are copied. The value of any formula that inadvertently references cell B14 will also be displayed as Not Available (NA). As soon as a value is entered in B14, the formula in question will be evaluated correctly.)

The 3 Period moving average based on periods 1, 2, and 3 is given by:

@AVG(B3.B5)

This average is positioned at the centre of the range of data it refers to, i.e. alongside period 2 in cell C4. (Use / Range Format Fixed to display the moving average to the nearest whole number (F0) so that the actual value shows as 127.)

Moving the 3 Period average forwards one period, the demand reading for period 1 is dropped and the reading for period 4 included instead, so that the 3 Period moving average is given by

@AVG(B4.B6)

However, instead of keying this formula into cell C5, the first moving average formula (in C4) can be copied down column C. So with the pointer on cell C4, type:

/ C C 4   to Copy the formula FROM C4 to cell range C5.C12.

The moving averages should look similar to the values in column C of Figure 10.4. The 5 Period moving averages shown in Column D of the figure are calculated in the same way, starting with formula:

@AVG(B3.B7)   in cell D5.

Once again round these averages to the nearest integer (F0) using / Range Format Fixed as before.

If the last (i.e. most recent) moving average values are used for forecasting, the 3 Period average suggests 194 for demand in period 12 and the 5 Period average 153—(in cells C12 and D11 respectively). Which forecasting scheme is preferable and hence which forecast should be used?

To answer this, it is instructive to look at these moving averages plotted against the actual demand for percolators. Using the Graph commands, specifying as the A range the demand

	A	B	C	D	
1	MOVING AVERAGES		3 Period	5 Period	
2	Period	Demand	Mov Ave	Mov Ave	
3	1	150	↙@AVG(B3.B5) and Copy		
4	2	85	127		
5	3	145	126	157	← @AVG(B3.B7)
6	4	147	184	152	and Copy
7	5	260	177	156	
8	6	125	163	143	
9	7	105	103	148	
10	8	80	118	141	
11	9	170	159	153	
12	10	227	194		
13	11	185			
14	12	NA			

Figure 10.4 Formulae for 3 and 5 period moving averages

data (i.e. range B3.B14), and as the B and C ranges the two sets of moving averages (C3.C14 and D3.D14 respectively), a graph similar to Figure 10.5 can be obtained.

(The graph you first obtain will have different scaling which will tend to make demand look even more variable on the limited scale than it truly is. In Figure 10.5, the scaling of demand from 0 to 300 has been done 'manually' using Scale on the Options Menu of the Graph commands. That is, having specified the data ranges for the graph and its type (Line), from the Graph menu choose Options then Scale then specify:

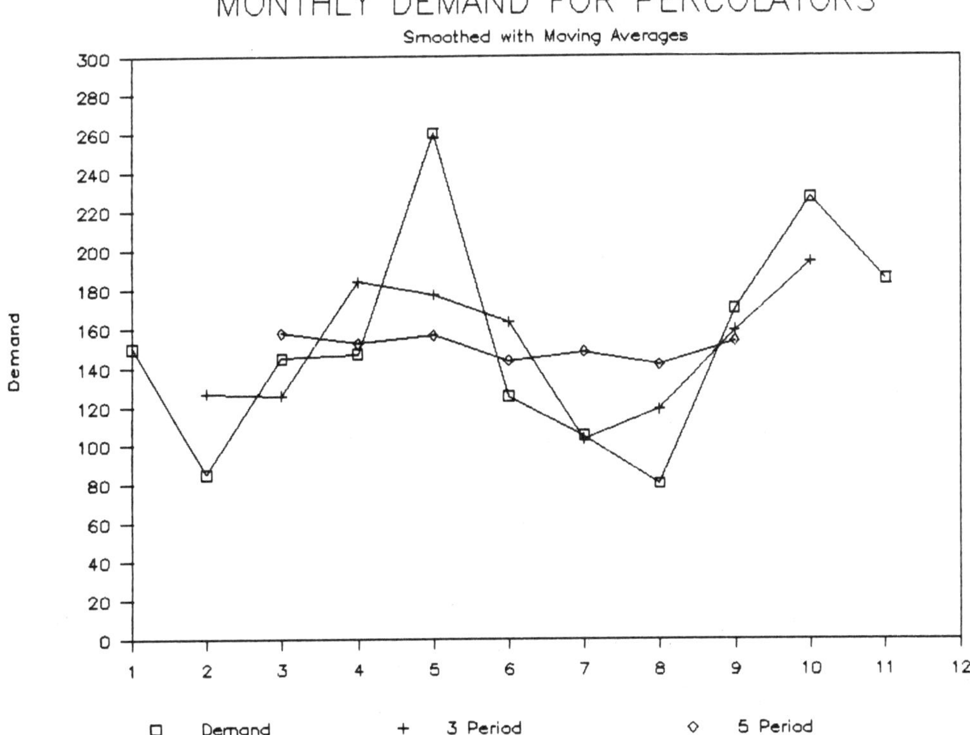

Figure 10.5 Percolator demand smoothed by 3 and 5 period moving averages

and put the Lower and Upper Limits equal to 0 and 300 respectively.)

As can be seen in Figure 10.5, the moving average 'smoothes' out the fluctuations in the monthly demand figures. The longer average (5 Period) smoothes more effectively than the shorter one which tends to follow the fluctuations in demand. This suggests that the 5 Period forecast of 153 for period 12 is preferred to the 3 Period forecast. Notice also that if forecasts for period 13 and beyond were required at this stage, the same forecast, namely 153 units per period, would be used for these future periods.

In general, if many observations are included in the average, all movements in the series other than marked linear trends tend to get smoothed out. The moving average also becomes rather unresponsive to changes in demand which is undesirable in the context of forecasting. On the other hand, if too few readings are included, very little smoothing is achieved and the moving average tends to follow the original series. Usually 5 to 7 periods' data are used, although on monthly data a 12 month moving average is common because it will remove the seasonal pattern as well as the random fluctuation.

10.3 Exponential smoothing

In calculating moving averages, all the readings included in the average are given the same weight. For example, in the 5 Period moving average, when any reading forms part of the average, it is given the weight 1/5. Thus relatively old data has the same influence on the average as recent, relatively new data. It could be argued that a more sensible form of weighting would put more emphasis on recent as opposed to ancient data.

One widely used method called exponential smoothing in effect gives most weight to the most recent data and decreasing weight to data as it recedes into the past. Although this sounds complex, the basic equation for producing a new average each time a new reading is available, is intuitively sensible:

new average = old average + A*(forecasting error)

or since the 'average' is used as the forecast for sales in the next period

new forecast = old forecast + A*(forecasting error)

The 'forecasting error' is the actual demand minus the forecast demand for the period. A, the so-called smoothing constant, has a value between 0 and 1.

For example, suppose that the forecast demand for May is 150 and that actual demand in May turns out to be 185. The forecast for June needs to be revised upwards because the previous forecast was too low, the 'forecasting error' being (185 − 150) or 35. One way of achieving this revision is to add on some fraction of the forecasting error. If the forecasting error is large, it causes a more major adjustment to the forecast than does a smaller forecasting error. Also, in this case, the forecast underestimates demand. The forecasting error is positive which results in an upward adjustment to the forecast for June. (If the forecasting error for May were negative, the equation would give a reduced forecast for June.) For this data, new forecast = 150 old forecast + A*(185−150) forecasting error

If A is large (say .5), the new forecast will be revised upwards from 150 to 167.5: if A is small (say .1), the updating is less volatile changing the forecast upwards from 150 to 153.5.

It can be shown that the forecast given by the exponential smoothing equation discussed above is in effect a weighted average of past demand values, the weights forming an exponentially decreasing series of the form:

$A, A(1-A), A(1-A)^2, A(1-A)^3, \ldots$

For example, if A = .5, the weights given to past demand values making up the exponentially smoothed average, starting with the newest reading, would be:

.5, .25, .125, .0625, . . .

The weights can be seen to decrease very rapidly, the most recent demand value having a weight of .5 in the average.

For A =.1, the weights would be:

.1, .09, .081, .0729, . . .

that is, they decline more gradually, the most recent reading having a weight of .1.

These ideas are illustrated by exponentially smoothing the percolator data used in the previous section. Start by keying in the data from scratch or modify your existing worksheet, so that your screen display looks like Figure 10.6. Column C will contain the Exponentially Smoothed Averages, column D the Forecasts and E the Forecasting Errors. Initially, the smoothing constant A (in D1) has been given the low value, .1.

	A	B	C	D	E	F
1	EXPONENTIAL	SMOOTHING		0.01	Smoothing	Constant
2	Period	Demand Ex	Sm Av	Forecast	Error	
3	1	150				
4	2	85		150	-65	
5	3	145		↑	↖	
6	4	147		Starting Value		(+B4-D4)
7	5	260		for Forecast		
8	6	125				
9	7	105				
10	8	80				
11	9	170				
12	10	227				
13	11	185				
14	12	NA				

Figure 10.6 Layout of worksheet for exponential smoothing

Although data for 11 periods has been entered, assume at the start that only the reading for period 1 is known (150). We use this as a starting Forecast for period 2 (hence the value 150 in cell D4). The formula for Forecasting Error in E4 is:

+B4−D4

that is, Demand in period 2 − Forecast for period 2.

Using the equation for exponential smoothing, enter the following expression in cell C4 for the Exponentially Smoothed Average:

+D4+$D$1*E4

that is, old forecast +.1*(forecasting error).

The smoothing constant is absolutely addressed ($D$1) because we shall shortly need to Copy the formula in C4.

With a smoothing constant *A* of .1 in D1, this expression evaluates to 143.5. To ensure that the exponentially smooth values do not have too many decimal places, display this to the nearest integer (F0 format).

Since the value in C4 is the new forecast for period 3, with the pointer on D5, enter the formula:

+C4

to make the forecast for period 3 equal to the last exponentially smoothed value.

Now copy the formula in C4 down column C, the formula in D5 down column D and the expression for Error in E4 down column E. The worksheet should look like Figure 10.7 at this stage. The forecast for period 12 is given as 155 (close to that given by the 5 Period moving average).

	A	B	C	D	E	F
1	EXPONENTIAL	SMOOTHING		0.1	Smoothing	Constant
2	Period	Demand	Ex Sm Av	Forecast	Error	
3	1	150	+D4+$D$1*E4 ↙			
4	2	85	144	150	-65	← (+B4-D4)
5	3	145	144	144 ← +C4	2	
6	4	147	144	144	3	
7	5	260	156	144	116	
8	6	125	153	156	-31	
9	7	105	148	153	-48	
10	8	80	141	148	-68	
11	9	170	144	141	29	
12	10	227	152	144	83	
13	11	185	155	152	33	
14	12	NA		155		

Figure 10.7 Exponentially smoothed values with $A = .1$ used as forecasts

Once again, a graph of results is instructive. Use the previous graph settings, in particular, keep the A range as specified with the demand data. Choosing a Line graph from the Graph menu, and specifying as the B range the forecasts in column D, a graph similar to that shown in Figure 10.8 can be obtained. The exponentially smoothed values carve a central path through all the fluctuations in demand.

The effect on smoothing of changing the smoothing constant can be easily seen once the graph of Figure 10.8 has been set up. With the pointer on cell D1, change to a high value for the smoothing constant, say .5, and view the graph by merely pressing the Graph key (f10). If the forecasts in cell range D4.D14 are retained for each selected value of the smoothing constant (using the Range Value command), it is possible to superimpose forecasts with different values of smoothing constant on the same graph. For example, Figure 10.9 shows the difference in smoothing when using high (.5) and low (.1) values for the smoothing constant.

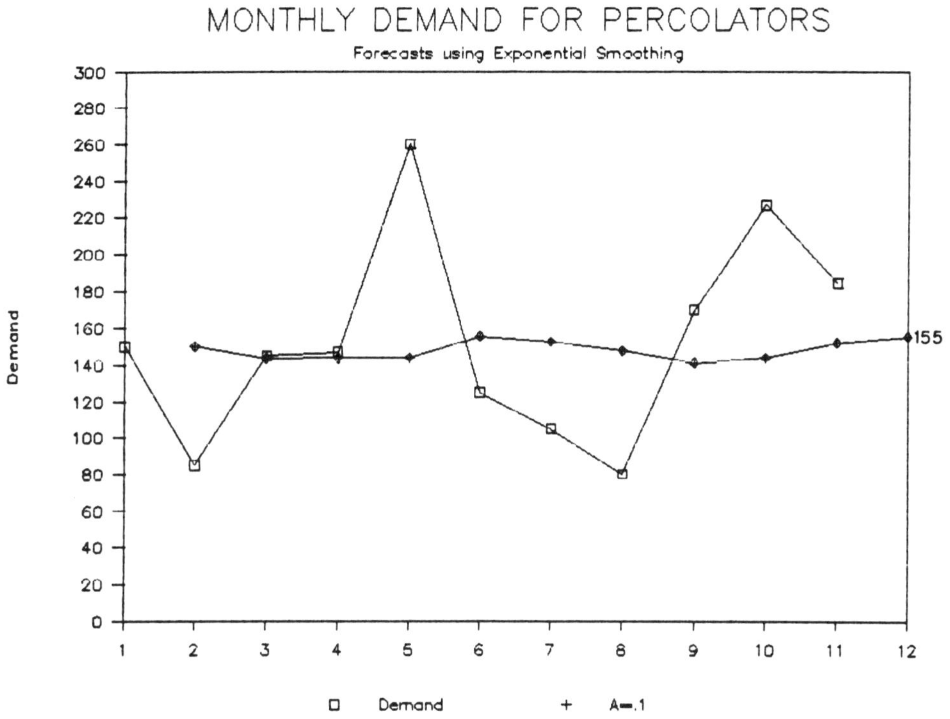

Figure 10.8 Exponentially smoothed demand with $A = .1$

The percolator data contains a lot of random variation but no significant change in mean level, i.e. no trend. For this type of data, smoothing rather than responsiveness is required. For this reason, low values of the smoothing constant appear to give better forecasts than higher values.

We look next at some methods for estimating trend and seasonal factors in sales forecasting. Exponential smoothing can be extended to cover sales series displaying trend and seasonal patterns but the details take us beyond the scope of this introductory chapter.

10.4 Trend and seasonal variation

As discussed earlier, there are two main models which are assumed to underly the relationships between the components of a time series: the multiplicative and the additive models. If Y represents the actual sales say, then these models can be written as:

$$Y = T \times S \times R \qquad \text{and } Y = T + S + R$$

where T, S, and R denote the trend, seasonal, and random components of the sales series.

Clearly, the method of 'decomposing' a sales series in order to isolate the seasonal factors will differ according to whether the model is multiplicative or additive. The steps

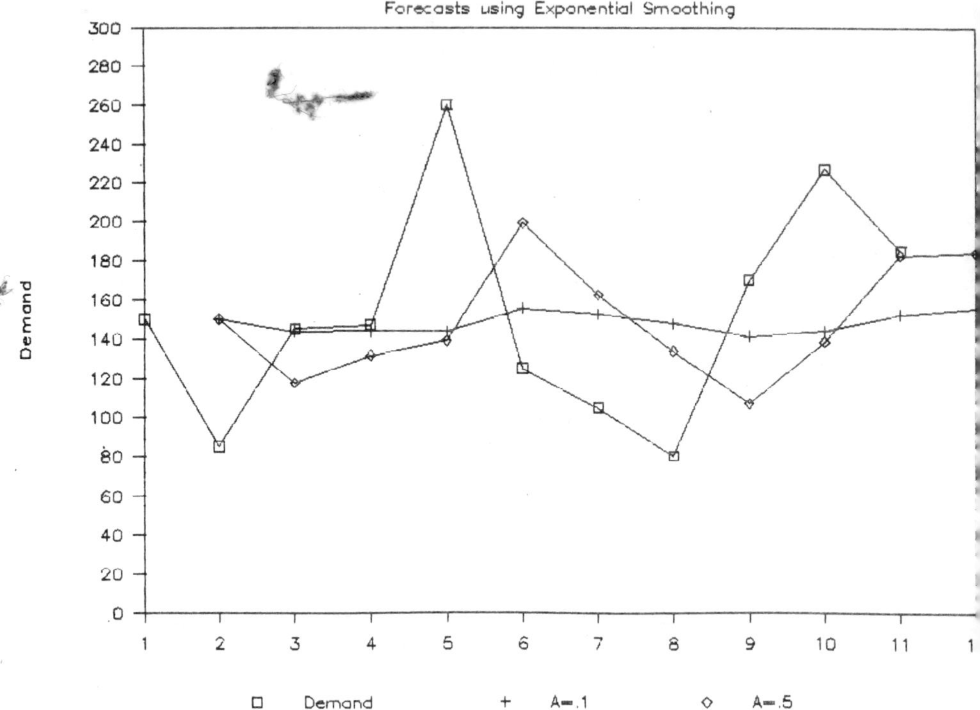

Figure 10.9 Exponentially smoothed demand with (a) $A = .1$, (b) $A = .5$

in the process are similar however. First, the trend is estimated and then removed period by period from the data (either by division or subtraction). The resulting 'detrended' series shows the seasonal and random variation:

$$Y/T = S \times R \qquad \text{or } Y - T = S + R$$

Next, the seasonal component is estimated by averaging the detrended series month by month or quarter by quarter. If desired, the sales series can be seasonally adjusted or 'deseasonalized':

$$Y/S = T \times R \qquad \text{or } Y - S = T + R$$

Deseasonalizing sales readings is often important because changes in the trend of sales become more apparent when not masked by seasonal variation.

Finally, if required, the random component can be isolated by eliminating the seasonal effect from the detrended series:

$$Y/(T \times S) = R \qquad \text{or } Y - T - S = R$$

This 'decomposition' will be applied to the swimwear data illustrated in Figure 10.1 with the primary objective of estimating the seasonal factors. Since the plot suggests that seasonal variation is more marked at high as opposed to low levels of sales, we shall assume the multiplicative model applies.

There are two main ways of estimating the trend: plotting moving averages (and fitting the trend curve by eye) and using regression analysis to determine the trend equation. We shall examine each in turn. So the steps in the analysis will consist of:

(i) fitting the trend by moving averages or regression,

(ii) estimating seasonal effects by dividing sales by moving averages,

(iii) projecting the trend and multiplying by the seasonal effects to obtain forecasts.

Figure 10.10 shows the quarterly sales of swimwear (column B in range B3.B26). This data can be entered by Retrieving the File called SWIM. Alternatively, the data can be keyed in from scratch. In this case, set up the spreadsheet to look exactly like Figure 10.10. Remember the /Data Fill sequence for entering the periods. Key in the sales data starting in B3.

	A	B	C	
1	SWIMWEAR	(QUARTERLY	SALES)	
2	Period	Sales	Mov Av	
3	1	362		
4	2	385		
5	3	432	380	← @AVG(B3.B6)
6	4	341	385	and Copy
7	5	382	391	
8	6	409	408	
	7	498	419	
	8	387	442	
	9	473	468	
	10	513	489	
	11	582	511	
	12	474	528	
	13	544	546	
	14	582	570	
	15	681	591	
	16	557	612	
	17	628	643	
	18	707	666	
	19	773	675	
	20	592	675	
	21	627	679	
24	22	725	700	
25	23	854	717	
26	24	661	NA	
27	25	NA ↖ @NA		

Figure 10.10 Swimwear data with moving averages

Lastly, enter the formula for the 4 Quarters moving average. The expression for the first four quarters is:

@AVG(B3.B6)

which has been entered on the row for period 3, in cell C5. Display this value to the nearest integer (F0 format). To obtain the sequence of moving averages, put the pointer on C5 and Copy the formula from C5 to range C6.C23.

We must digress slightly to deal with a problem that crops up when moving averages are based on an even number of observations. We made the point in Section 10.2 that the moving average is located at the midpoint of the datapoints in the average, i.e. midway between periods 2 and 3, and not strictly speaking adjacent to period 3. To correct for the fact that the moving averages are out of kilter with the sales readings, we average adjacent moving averages. The resulting averages are called 'centred' moving averages. Figure 10.11 shows how the 'centred' moving averages are obtained. The first centred average in D5 is located adjacent to the sales reading for period 3 and is entered in D5 by the formula:

@AVG(C5.C6)

	A	B	C	D	
1	SWIMWEAR	(QUARTERLY	SALES)	Centred	
2	Period	Sales	Mov Av	Mov Av	
3	1	362			
4	2	385			
5	3	432	380	383	← @AVG(C5.C6)
6	4	341	385	388	and Copy
7	5	382	391	399	
	6	409	408	413	
	7	498	419	430	
	8	387	442	455	
	9	473	468	478	
	10	513	489	500	
	11	582	511	519	
	12	474	528	537	
	13	544	546	558	
	14	582	570	581	
	15	681	591	602	
	16	557	612	628	
	17	628	643	655	
	18	707	666	671	
	19	773	675	675	
	20	592	675	677	
	21	627	679	689	
24	22	725	700	708	
25	23	854	717	NA	
26	24	661	NA		
27	25	NA			

Figure 10.11 Swimwear data with centred moving averages

Once again format this to the nearest integer (F0) and Copy the formula down column **D** to range D6.D24.

Figure 10.12 shows these centred moving averages superimposed on the original plot of the swimwear data (Figure 10.1). This is achieved by choosing a Line type of graph; specifying as the X range the periods 1 to 25 (range A3.A27); as the A range the sales data (range B3.B27) and as the B range the centred moving averages (D3.D27).

As can be seen, the 4 Quarters moving average has both smoothed out random variation and removed the seasonal pattern from the sales series. The averages show the remaining upward trend in sales. In fact, since the trend curve is approximately linear, it would be sensible to fit a straight line to the moving average and extend this to forecast the future level of sales. Using the last four values of the moving average a trend of about 9.38 units per quarter can be estimated (see F22 in the next worksheet, Figure 10.13).

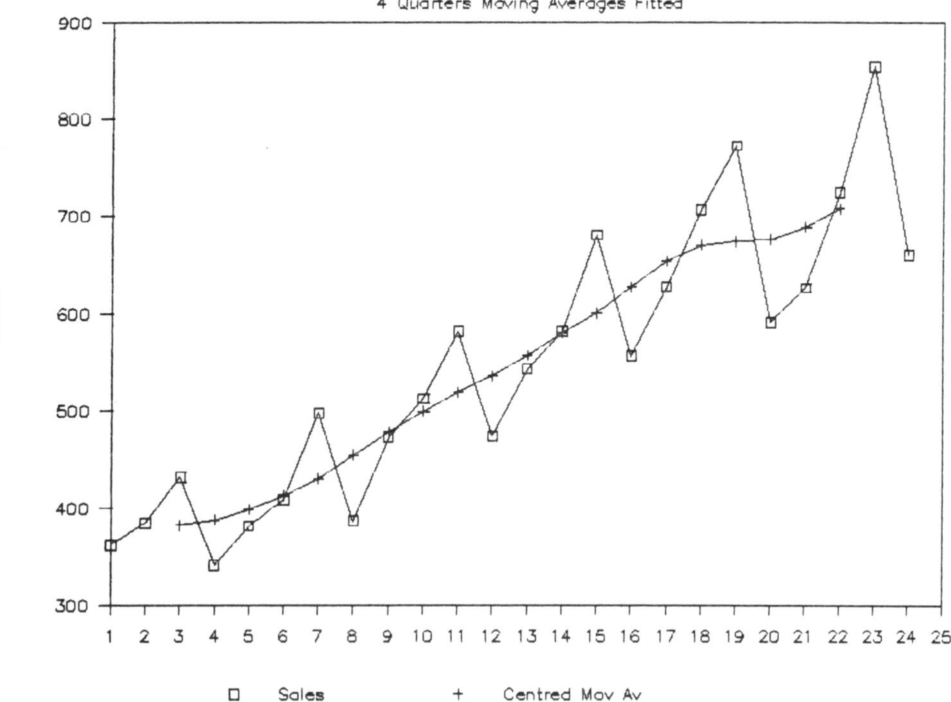

Figure 10.12 Four quarters moving averages for swimwear data

The seasonal factors can now be estimated by calculating the ratio of actual sales to the corresponding moving average. The steps are shown in Figure 10.13. The ratios in column E are obtained by dividing the sales readings (column B) by the moving averages (column D). So in cell E5 enter the formula:

+B5/D5

round it to the nearest integer (F0) and Copy the formula to range E6.E22.

Finally, all the ratios for the first quarter are averaged to give the first seasonal factor and similarly for the other quarters. For example, the ratios in E5, E9, E13, E17, and E21 all refer to the third quarter, and the average of these values:

@AVG(E5,E9,E13,E17,E21)

is the estimated seasonal factor for the third quarter (see F5).

Thus for the swimwear data, the average level of sales needs to be multiplied by 1.14 to bring sales up to the correct level for the third quarter and similarly multiplied by .87 to obtain the fourth quarter sales.

At the foot of Figure 10.13, tentative forecasts have been calculated for periods 25, 26, 27, and 28. To get the trend value for period 25, three multiples of the estimated trend per quarter had been added to the last available moving average (708 evaluated for period 22). The resulting level of sales, 736 (in cell D28) must be multiplied by the first quarter seasonal

	A	B	C	D	E	F	
1	SWIMWEAR	(QUARTERLY	SALES)	Centred		Seasonal	
2	Period	Sales	Mov Av	Mov Av	Sales/M Av	Factors	
3	1	362			+B5/D5	@AVG(E5,E9,E13,E17,E21)	
4	2	385			and Copy ↘	↙ and Copy	
5	3	432	380	383	1.13	1.14	
6	4	341	385	388	0.88	0.87	
7	5	382	391	399	0.96	0.96	← 1st quarter
8	6	409	408	413	0.99	1.02	← 2nd quarter
	7	498	419	430	1.16		
	8	387	442	455	0.85		
	9	473	468	478	0.99		
	10	513	489	500	1.03		
	11	582	511	519	1.12		
	12	474	528	537	0.88		
	13	544	546	558	0.98		
	14	582	570	581	1.00		
	15	681	591	602	1.13		
	16	557	612	628	0.89		
	17	628	643	655	0.96		
	18	707	666	671	1.05	Estimated	
	19	773	675	675	1.15	Trend	
	20	592	675	677	0.87	9.38	
	21	627	679	689	0.91		↖ (D22-D18)/4
	22	725	700	708	1.02		
	23	854	717				
26	24	661					
	Forecasts			Trend(T)	T x S		
28	25		+D24+3*F22 →	736	705	← +D28*F7	
29	26		+D28+F22 →	746	760	← +D29*F8	
30	27			755	858	← +D30*F5	
31	28			764	669	← +D31*F6	

Figure 10.13 Calculating seasonal factors and forecasts for swimwear sales

factor, .96 (in F7) to give the forecast 705 (in E28). Similarly, the forecasts for periods 26, 27, and 28 are obtained.

The almost linear appearance of the moving averages in Figure 10.12 suggest that a more rigorous approach to trend estimation might be to obtain the regression of Sales on Period. The regression line can then easily be extended to give forecasts for future periods. This approach has been carried out using the Data Regression command to compute the regression of Sales (Y) on period (t). Specify the Y range as B3.B26, the X range as A3.A26 and the Output range as H3. The results are set out in Figure 10.14. The inset panel shows the regression calculations from which the best fitting line can be deduced, namely:

$$\text{Sales} = 326 + 17.8t \qquad \text{where } t = \text{Period} = 1,2,3, \ldots$$

where the intercept and slope (cells K4 and J10 respectively) have been rounded using Range Format. The equation above is taken as the trend line. It is shown graphically in Figure 10.15. The fitted line is graphed from the fitted Sales values obtained by substituting $t = 1, 2, 3, \ldots$ into the trend equation. This involves entering the formula for the trend in Sales in period 1 in cell C3, namely:

$K$4 + $J$10*A3

This formula is then copied down column C to get the Trend values shown in Figure 10.16.

Forecasts can be obtained by extrapolating the trend line and multiplying by the seasonal factors. However, the seasonal factors were evaluated assuming that the moving averages

	A	B
1	SWIMWEAR	(QUARTERLY SALES)
2	Period	Sales
3	1	362
4	2	385
5	3	432
6	4	341
7	5	382
8	6	409
9	7	498
10	8	387
11	9	473
12	10	513
13	11	582
14	12	474
15	13	544
16	14	582
17	15	681
18	16	557
19	17	628
20	18	707
21	19	773
22	20	592
23	21	627
24	22	725
25	23	854
26	24	661

	H	I	J	K
1	Regression of Sales on period			
2				
3		Regression Output:		
4	Constant			326
5	Std Err of Y Est			63
6	R Squared			0.81
7	No. of Observations			24
8	Degrees of Freedom			22
9				
10	X Coefficient(s)		17.8	
11	Std Err of Coef.		1.9	

Figure 10.14 Regression of sales on period for swimwear data (regression results inset)

encapsulated the trend. It is preferable to re-do the analysis as shown in Figure 10.16. Thus trend figures in column C come from the regression line in Figure 10.14, the ratios in column D come from dividing Sales (column B) by Trend (column C) and the Seasonal Factors in column E come from averaging ratios for like quarters. Finally, forecasts are obtained for periods 25 to 28 in cells E29 to E32.

10.5 Trend curves

A linear trend implies that on average the mean level of sales changes by roughly the same amount period by period. The deseasonalized swimwear data was of this form but unfortunately not all trend curves are simply straight lines. In this section we look at two other commonly occurring forms of trend: exponential growth curves and S curves. We illustrate the steps necessary to fit them to data. Fortunately, with suitable modifications, linear regression can be used to estimate the equations.

Exponential curves

The file VCR contains sales of one company's cassette recorders over 24 periods. Figure 10.17 shows the data in column B. To analyse the trend in sales, Retrieve the File and use the Graph commands to produce a Line graph of sales (B3.B26) against time (A3.A26). Figure 10.18 shows that the trend in sales is not linear but more like an 'exponential' curve.

The exponential curve arises when the sales of a product (or company) increase not by the same amount period by period but by roughly the same proportion, say 5 per cent per period. For the VCR data, the increase in sales is relatively small at low levels of sales, but at higher levels the increase is much greater. However, if the percentage increase per

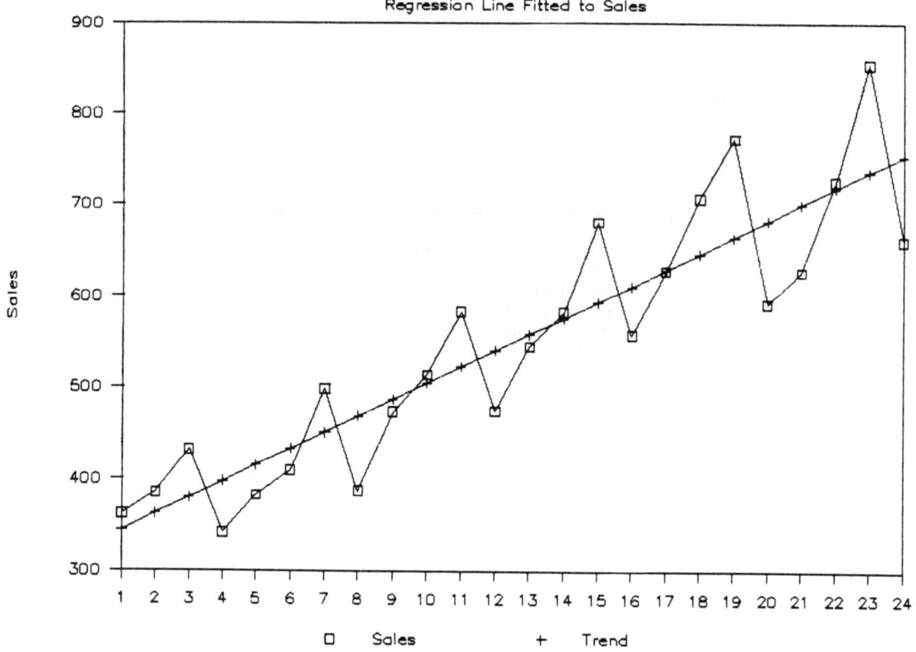

Figure 10.15 Trend line fitted by regression

	A	B	C	D	E
1	SWIMWEAR	(QUARTERLY	SALES)		Seasonal
2	Period	Sales	Trend	Sales/Tr	Factors
3	1	362	344	1.05	0.97
4	2	385	362	1.06	1.02
5	3	432	379	1.14	1.14
6	4	341	397	0.86	0.87
7	5	382	415	0.92	
8	6	409	433	0.94	
	7	498	451	1.11	
	8	387	468	0.83	
	9	473	486	0.97	
	10	513	504	1.02	
	11	582	522	1.12	
	12	474	540	0.88	
	13	544	558	0.98	
	14	582	575	1.01	
	15	681	593	1.15	
	16	557	611	0.91	
	17	628	629	1.00	
	18	707	647	1.09	
	19	773	665	1.16	
	20	592	682	0.87	
	21	627	700	0.90	
	22	725	718	1.01	
	23	854	736	1.16	
	24	661	754	0.88	
	FORECAST	SALES			
28	Period		Trend(T)	Seas F	TxS
29	25		772	0.97	748
30	26		789	1.02	808
31	27		807	1.14	919
32	28		825	0.87	718

Figure 10.16 Seasonal factors and forecast using regression to fit trend

period is evaluated it is found to vary around 12 per cent. (You can check this for yourself by calculating the percentage increase in each period (for example 100* (B26−B25)/B25) and using @AVG to average the percentages.)

The general equation for an exponential trend curve is:

Sales = EXP($a + bt$) where t = Period = 1, 2, 3, . . .

Taking natural (or base e) logarithms, this equation transforms to:

Log (Sales) = $a + bt$ where t = 1,2,3, . . .

The approach we used for trend estimation with the swimwear sales, linear regression, can only be used for data which is linear. However, if the Logs of sales readings rather than Sales are plotted against time, the points will lie roughly on a straight line if the trend is truly exponential.

Figure 10.17 shows the procedure for getting logs of readings. With the pointer on C3, key in the 1-2-3 special function for natural logarithms:

@LN(B3)

which with suitable rounding, (F2), gives the value 5.25 for the natural log of Sales in period 1. Finally, Copy the formula for logs down column C.

Use the Graph commands to plot Log (Sales) against Time. The resulting graph should show a near linear relationship (see Figure 10.19) which will permit regression to be used to estimate the trend of the transformed relationship.

To carry out regression, using Data Regression, specify:

Y range C3.C26

X range A3.A26

	A	B	C	
1	VCR SALES			
2	Period	Sales	Log(Sales)	
3	1	190	5.25	←@LN(B3)
4	2	182	5.20	and
5	3	246	5.51	Copy
6	4	258	5.55	
7	5	270	5.60	
8	6	345	5.84	
	7	355	5.87	
	8	412	6.02	
	9	431	6.07	
	10	489	6.19	
	11	573	6.35	
	12	644	6.47	
	13	746	6.61	
	14	793	6.68	
	15	923	6.83	
	16	1028	6.94	
	17	1125	7.03	
	18	1267	7.14	
	19	1491	7.31	
	20	1637	7.40	
	21	1814	7.50	
24	22	2083	7.64	
25	23	2315	7.75	
26	24	2585	7.86	

Figure 10.17 VCR sales together with Log (Sales) data

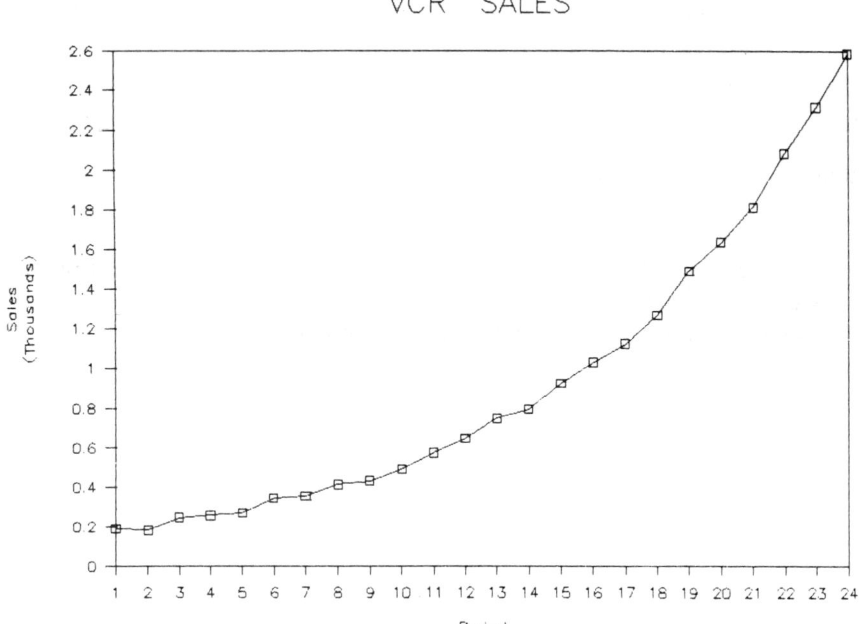

Figure 10.18 Plot of video cassette recorder sales against time

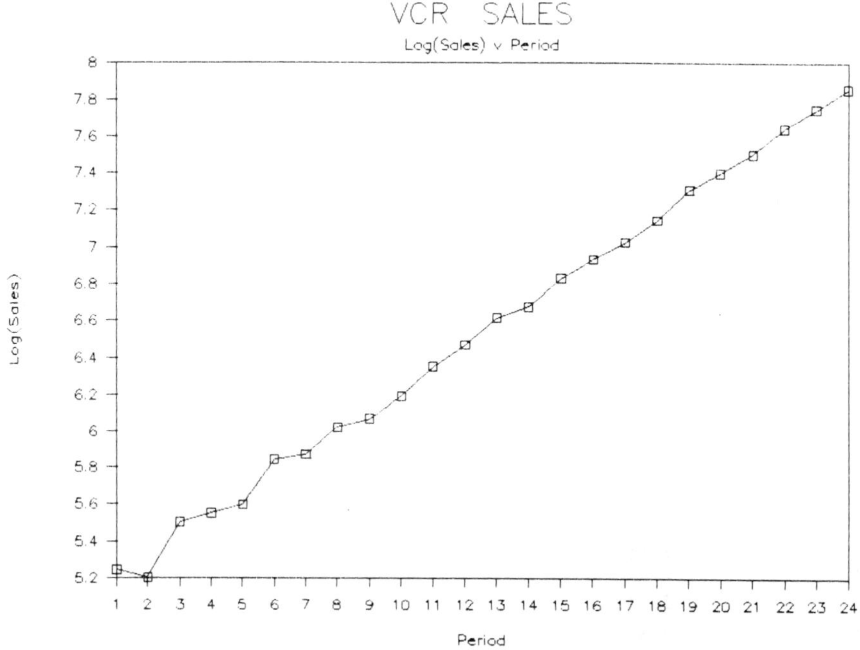

Figure 10.19 Log(Sales) plotted against time

Output range H3

The results are displayed in Figure 10.20. From the regression results shown inset the equation for the trend is:

Log (Sales) = 5.08 + .12t where t = 1,2,3, . . .

or Sales = EXP(5.08 + .12t) where t = 1,2,3, . . .

The Fitted Log (Sales) values and the corresponding Fitted Sales values are shown in columns D and E of Figure 10.20. The first Fitted value in cell D3 is obtained from the regression line, the formula being:

+$K$4 + $J$10 * A3

The corresponding Fitted Sales value in cell E3 is obtained by 'antilogging' the value in cell D3 using the formula:

@EXP(D3)

Where @EXP is the special exponential function introduced in Chapter 7. The formulae in cells D3 and E3 are copied down for periods 2 to 24. If required, they can be extrapolated for a few future periods by adding the values 25, 26, 27, etc. at the bottom of column A.

The fit of the trend equation can be judged by superimposing the Fitted Logs (Sales) values on the graph of Log (Sales)—Figure 10.19, or by adding Fitted Sales to the original graph of Sales—Figure 10.18. The actual equation for the trend curve can be obtained as follows:

As was shown, Sales = EXP(5.08 +.12 t) = EXP(5.08) + EXP(.12 t)

Use the special function @EXP to evaluate EXP(5.08) and EXP(.12). The results are approximately 160 and 1.12 respectively. So the fitted trend curve has equation:

Sales = $160 * 1.12^t$ where t = 1,2,3, . . .

Notice that the coefficient 1.12 implies a 12 per cent increase in sales each period. Had this regression estimate been less than 1 in value, say .90, the model would have been one of sales decay rather than growth. This would have been evident from the initial sales graph. The exponential model includes both sales growth and sales decay, the percentage change being roughly constant from period to period.

S Curves

If sales statistics cover a period long enough to encompass most of the life cycle of a product, the trend curve often looks roughly S-shaped in form. One famous series based on sales of colour television sets led to the study of this form of curve. Sales growth is slow at first, then increases dramatically and finally tails off as saturation level is reached. Intuitively, this model should be appropriate for many innovative products which after an initial delay in acceptance sell in ever increasing volumes until the market is flooded.

One mathematical form for the S curve is:

	A	B	C	D	E
1	VCR SALES			Fitted	Fitted
2	Period	Sales	Log(Sales)	Log(Sales)	Sales
3	1	190	5.25	5.19	180
4	2	182	5.20	5.31	202
5	3	246	5.51	5.42	227
6	4	258	5.55	5.54	255
7	5	270	5.60	5.66	286
8	6	345	5.84	5.77	321
9	7	355	5.87	5.89	360
10	8	412	6.02	6.00	405
11	9	431	6.07	6.12	455
12	10	489	6.19	6.24	510
13	11	573	6.35	6.35	573
14	12	644	6.47	6.47	644
15	13	746	6.61	6.58	723
16	14	793	6.68	6.70	812
17	15	923	6.83	6.81	911
18	16	1028	6.94	6.93	1023
19	17	1125	7.03	7.05	1149
20	18	1267	7.14	7.16	1291
21	19	1491	7.31	7.28	1449
22	20	1637	7.40	7.39	1627
23	21	1814	7.50	7.51	1827
24	22	2083	7.64	7.63	2052
25	23	2315	7.75	7.74	2304
26	24	2585	7.86	7.86	2587

	H	I	J	K
1	Regression of Log(Sales) on period			
2				
3		Regression Output:		
4	Constant			5.08
5	Std Err of Y Est			0.04
6	R Squared			1.00
7	No. of Observations			24
8	Degrees of Freedom			22
9				
10	X Coefficient(s)		0.12	
11	Std Err of Coef.		0.00	

Figure 10.20 Fitting trend curve to VCR data (regression results inset)

Sales = EXP($a - b/t$) where t = Period = 1, 2, 3, . . .

Taking natural logs of both sides, this becomes:

Log (Sales) = $a - b/t$ where t = 1, 2, 3, . . .

So if the S curve is appropriate, we would expect a plot of Log (Sales) against (1/Period) to be linear.

The file CTV contains sales figures (in millions of dollars) for colour television sets (see the first two columns of Figure 10.21). Retrieve File CTV and use the Graph commands to plot a Line graph of Sales (column B) against Period (column A). Your graph should correspond to Figure 10.22 showing an S-shaped trend.

Next, take natural logs of Sales and evaluate (1/Period) by setting up the appropriate formulae in cells C3 and D3 as shown in Figure 10.21. Then construct a graph of Log (Sales) against (1/Period). Figure 10.23 shows an XY scatter plot of this transformed data. It is reasonably linear, so the equation of the best fitting line can be estimated by linear regression.

The results of using Data Regression as in the previous example are shown in Figure 10.24. (You can easily check these by specifying the Y range as C3.C26, the X range as D3.D26 and the Output range as H3. Your results should correspond to those shown in the inset of Figure 10.24.) The best fitting line has equation:

Log (Sales) = 1.48 − 5.79/t where t = 1, 2, 3, . . .

taking the coefficients from cells K4 and J10 of Figure 10.24. Transforming the equation to the original scale, we have:

Sales = EXP(1.48 − 5.79/t) where t = 1, 2, 3, . . .

	A	B	C	D	
1	COLOUR TV	SALES			@LN(B3)and Copy
2	Period	Sales	Log(Sales)	1/Period	
3	1	0.02	-3.77	1.00	← 1/A3 and Copy
	2	0.16	-1.85	0.50	
	3	0.33	-1.11	0.33	
	4	0.48	-0.73	0.25	
	5	1.20	0.18	0.20	
	6	1.75	0.56	0.17	
	7	2.00	0.69	0.14	
	8	2.51	0.92	0.13	
	9	2.37	0.86	0.11	
	10	2.94	1.08	0.10	
	11	2.87	1.05	0.09	
	12	2.94	1.08	0.08	
	13	3.13	1.14	0.08	
	14	3.24	1.18	0.07	
	15	3.15	1.15	0.07	
	16	3.52	1.26	0.06	
	17	3.54	1.26	0.06	
	18	3.31	1.20	0.06	
	19	3.55	1.27	0.05	
	20	3.37	1.21	0.05	
	21	3.37	1.21	0.05	
24	22	3.40	1.22	0.05	
25	23	3.70	1.31	0.04	
26	24	3.49	1.25	0.04	

Figure 10.21 Colour TV data with transformed variables

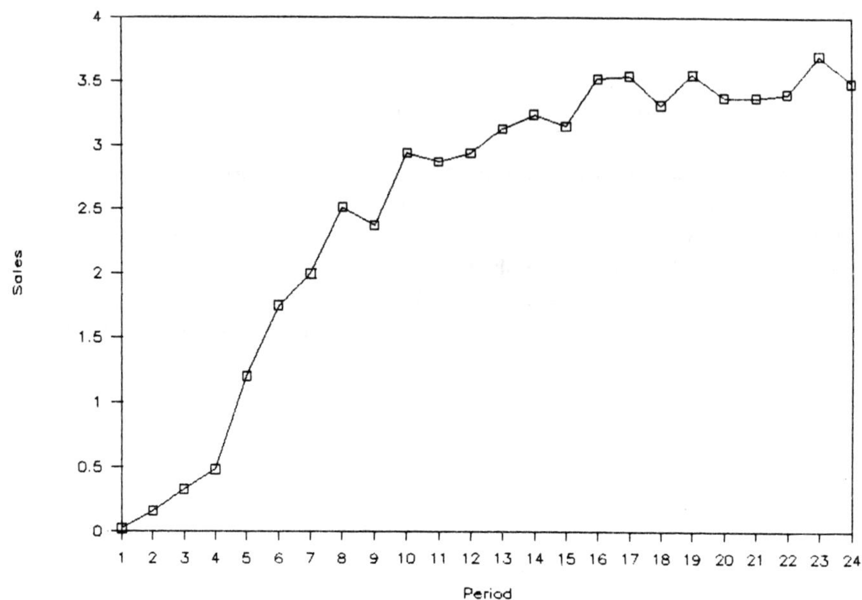

Figure 10.22 S-shaped trend for CTV data

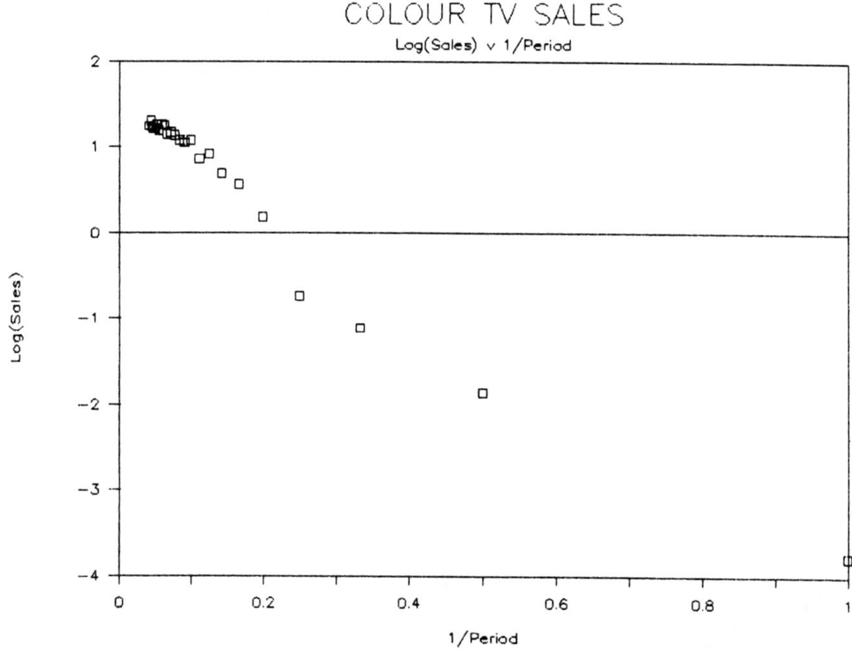

Figure 10.23 Scatter plot of Log(Sales) against 1/time

	A	B	C	D	E	F
1	COLOUR TV SALES				Fitted	Fitted
2	Period	Sales	Log(Sales)	1/Period	Log(Sales)	Sales
3	1	0.02	-3.77	1.00	-4.31	0.01
4	2	0.16	-1.85	0.50	-1.42	0.24
	3	0.33	-1.11	0.33	-0.45	0.64
	4	0.48	-0.73	0.25	0.03	1.03
	5	1.20	0.18	0.20	0.32	1.38
	6	1.75	0.56	0.17	0.51	1.67
	7	2.00	0.69	0.14	0.65	1.92
	8	2.51	0.92	0.13	0.75	2.13
	9	2.37	0.86	0.11	0.84	2.30
	10	2.94	1.08	0.10	0.90	2.46
	11	2.87	1.05	0.09	0.95	2.59
	12	2.94	1.08	0.08	1.00	2.71
	13	3.13	1.14	0.08	1.03	2.81
	14	3.24	1.18	0.07	1.06	2.90
	15	3.15	1.15	0.07	1.09	2.98
	16	3.52	1.26	0.06	1.12	3.05
	17	3.54	1.26	0.06	1.14	3.12
	18	3.31	1.20	0.06	1.16	3.18
	19	3.55	1.27	0.05	1.17	3.23
	20	3.37	1.21	0.05	1.19	3.28
	21	3.37	1.21	0.05	1.20	3.33
	22	3.40	1.22	0.05	1.21	3.37
	23	3.70	1.31	0.04	1.23	3.41
	24	3.49	1.25	0.04	1.24	3.44

Regression of Log(Sales) on 1/Period		
Regression Output:		
Constant		1.48
Std Err of Y Est		0.28
R Squared		0.95
No. of Observations		24
Degrees of Freedom		22
X Coefficients	-5.79	
Std Err of Coef.	0.28	

Figure 10.24 Fitting trend curve to colour TV data

Many other curves can be transformed to linear relationships and their equations estimated using linear regression. From the equations of these trend curves, forecasts for future periods can be evaluated and combined with seasonal effects, if relevant, as was done for the swimwear sales series.

CHAPTER 11

Financial Planning Models

Probably, the most common application of 1-2-3 is in financial planning or budgeting. The earlier chapters used a very simple example of profit planning to introduce the 1-2-3 spreadsheet and commands. This chapter discusses another example of profit planning, a two product example, and describes how to build more generalized spreadsheets.

The second half of the chapter is devoted to explaining and developing the Budget Worksheet approach. This approach to planning is instructive particularly to non-accountants as it provides a unified way of producing the various financial statements required in planning.

11.1 Profit planning for Orbit

'Spreadsheeting' with 1-2-3 was developed in Chapters 2, 3, and 4 in the context of a firm manufacturing one product for sale. We will now produce a model for quarterly profits for two products, treating the price, cost, and growth rates as planning values. The object is to forecast profits over the next two years given various assumptions about sales volumes and growth, prices, variable and fixed costs. First, some details about the firm and its products are given.

Orbit Electronics manufactures calculators and digital watches. Over the last few months, quarterly sales volumes have averaged at roughly 3500 units for calculators and 5300 units for watches. These values can be used as initial values for the first quarter of 1986. Management expect sales of calculators to grow at a rate of about 2 per cent per quarter. However, sales of digital watches look likely to decline at 10 per cent per quarter unless some action is taken.

Currently the variable cost of a calculator is 10 pounds and it can be sold for 15 pounds. The comparable cost and price for a digital watch are 6 and 12 pounds respectively. In making profit projections, these costs and prices can be assumed to hold initially (as a base case) for the next two years. Part of the planning will involve looking at the effect on profit of changing the prices and costs.

As well as variable costs, there are quarterly fixed costs of 9000 pounds for staff, 6000 for transport, and 5400 for 'miscellaneous' expenses. These total to quarterly fixed costs of 20,400 pounds. In addition, there are promotional expenses. Currently 6000 pounds per quarter is spent on promoting the two products.

As mentioned, the objective is to produce projections of contribution and profit (before tax and interest) for the next two years. Figure 11.1 shows a suitably structured 1-2-3 template for Orbit's planning exercise. Most of the worksheet is devoted to calculating the

```
              A                  B          C         D         E          F          G
 1  ORBIT ELECTRONICS                   QUARTERLY PROFIT  FORECASTS
                                     1         2          3          4          5          6
 3  CALCULATORS
 4  Sales Volume
 5  Sales Revenue
 6  Variable Costs
 7  Contribution
 8  WATCHES
 9  Sales Volume
10  Sales Revenue
11  Variable Costs
12  Contribution

14  PROFIT & LOSS
15  Total Sales
16  Variable Costs
17  Total Contributn
18  Fixed Costs
19  Promotion

21  Profit (PBIT)

23  %Contribn/Sales
24  %Profit/Sales

26  Planning         Values
    --------------------------
28  Calculator Price
29  Calculator Cost
30  CalculatorGrowth
31  Watch Price
32  Watch Cost
33  Watch Growth
```

Figure 11.1 Structure of worksheet for Orbit

contribution from the sales of calculators and watches and then the overall profit before tax and interest (row 21). The assumptions about price, cost and growth for each product are set out in the form of 'planning values' from row 28 onwards.

The main steps are to enter the assumptions (such as the calculator price of 15), to set up the formulae for the first quarter, to model the growth (or decline) of sales of calculators and watches, to copy the formulae across to other quarters and add the appropriate expressions for the annual totals in columns J and K.

11.2 Modelling for Orbit

First of all load the ORBIT datafile, i.e. type

/ F R ORBIT

to get the spreadsheet layout shown in Figure 11.1.

Numerical entries

Next enter the planning values from B28 down to B33. The sales growth rates are input as decimals (i.e. .02 in B30 for the rate of growth of calculators, and −.10 in B33 for the rate of decline in watches). They can be displayed as percentages with the Range Format Percentage command if required.

Then, enter the first quarter's fixed costs (20400 in B18) and the quarterly promotional expense (6000 in B19).

Next, enter the starting sales volumes for calculators (3500 in B4) and for watches (5300 in B9).

Starting formulae for quarter 1

The remaining entries for column B, the first quarter, and the sales growth/decline formulae in C4 and C9 are detailed in Figure 11.2. Further explanation of the entries is given in the following paragraphs.

Starting with the Sales Revenue entry in B5, the formula is:

+B4*$B$28

where the calculator price is 'absolutely' addressed, i.e. the $ signs ensure that when copied, the price term does not change and the resulting formula always 'looks to' cell B28 for price. The resultant value displayed in this cell should be 52500.

Similarly, the Variable Costs entry in B6 is:

+B4*$B$29

where the calculator cost is absolutely addressed to ensure that it is unchanged when copied across the spreadsheet. The value displayed is 35000.

Since contribution is defined as Sales Revenue less Variable Costs, the Contribution expression in B7 is:

+B5-B6

In the same way, the formulae for digital watches can be entered. When these are complete, like entries are aggregated to get the expressions for Total Sales (i.e. sales of calculators and watches), Variable Costs, and hence Contribution. These are keyed into B15, B16, and B17.

Moving down column B past the Fixed Costs and Promotion entries, Profit (in B21) is obtained from:

+B17-B18-B19 i.e. Contribution less Fixed Costs and Promotion.

Contribution expressed as a percentage of sales in B23 is:

100*B17/B15.

Notice that this entry (and also the %Profit/Sales entry in B24) are calculated as percentage points rather than proportions.

Check that the numerical values you have obtained tie up with those in Figure 11.3. Having completed the entries for the first quarter, it is only necessary to enter four expressions in column C before copying across.

Sales growth/decline formulae

The formula for the growth in sales of calculators in C4 is:

	A	B	C	J	K
1	ORBIT ELECTRONICS		QUARTERLY	TOTAL	TOTAL
		1	2	Year 1	Year 2
3	CALCULATORS				
4	Sales Volume	3500	+B4*(1+$B$30)	@SUM(B4..E4)	@SUM(F4..I4)
5	Sales Revenue	+B4*$B$28		@SUM(B5..E5)	@SUM(F5..I5)
6	Variable Costs	+B4*$B$29		@SUM(B6..E6)	@SUM(F6..I6)
7	Contribution	+B5-B6		@SUM(B7..E7)	@SUM(F7..I7)
8	WATCHES				
9	Sales Volume	5300	+B9*(1+$B$33)	@SUM(B9..E9)	@SUM(F9..I9)
10	Sales Revenue	+B9*$B$31		@SUM(B10..E10)	@SUM(F10..I10)
11	Variable Costs	+B9*$B$32		@SUM(B11..E11)	@SUM(F11..I11)
12	Contribution	+B10-B11		@SUM(B12..E12)	@SUM(F12..I12)
14	PROFIT & LOSS				
15	Total Sales	+B5+B10		@SUM(B15..E15)	@SUM(F15..I15)
16	Variable Costs	+B6+B11		@SUM(B16..E16)	@SUM(F16..I16)
17	Total Contributn	+B7+B12		@SUM(B17..E17)	@SUM(F17..I17)
18	Fixed Costs	20400	+B18	@SUM(B18..E18)	@SUM(F18..I18)
19	Promotion	6000	+B19	@SUM(B19..E19)	@SUM(F19..I19)
21	Profit (PBIT)	+B17-B18-B19		@SUM(B21..E21)	@SUM(F21..I21)
23	%Contribn/Sales	100*B17/B15		100*J17/J15	100*K17/K15
24	%Profit/Sales	100*B21/B15		100*J21/J15	100*K21/K15
26	Planning	Values			
27	-------------------------------				
28	Calculator Price	15			
29	Calculator Cost	10			
30	CalculatorGrowth	0.02			
31	Watch Price	12			
32	Watch Cost	6			
33	Watch Growth	-0.10			

Figure 11.2 Main formulae in Orbit model before 'copying'

+B4*(1+\$B\$30)

where the growth rate expressed as a proportion (say .02 for 2 per cent growth) is stored in B30. (Thus sales in the second quarter will be 1.02 times sales in the first quarter, i.e. 2 per cent higher than the first quarter's sales.)

Similarly the expression for sales growth/decline in watches in C9 is:

+B9*(1+\$B\$33)

where the growth factor is addressed absolutely. Notice that if the entry in B33 is a negative quantity (say −.10), the effect will be a decline: sales will be .9 (or 90 per cent) of their previous level.

The formulae for growth/decline in C4 and C9 can now be copied across from column D to column I.

Fixed costs and promotion

Since the fixed costs in the second quarter (and successive quarters) are equal, enter the following formula in C18:

	A	B	C	D	E	F	G
1	ORBIT ELECTRONICS		QUARTERLY	PROFIT	FORECASTS		
		1	2	3	4	5	6
3	CALCULATORS						
4	Sales Volume	3500	3570				
5	Sales Revenue	52500					
6	Variable Costs	35000					
7	Contribution	17500					
8	WATCHES						
9	Sales Volume	5300	4770				
10	Sales Revenue	63600					
11	Variable Costs	31800					
12	Contribution	31800					
14	PROFIT & LOSS						
15	Total Sales	116100					
16	Variable Costs	66800					
17	Total Contributn	49300					
18	Fixed Costs	20400	20400				
19	Promotion	6000	6000				
21	Profit (PBIT)	22900					
23	%Contribn/Sales	42					
24	%Profit/Sales	20					
26	Planning	Values					

28	Calculator Price	15					
29	Calculator Cost	10					
30	CalculatorGrowth	0.02					
31	Watch Price	12					
32	Watch Cost	6					
33	Watch Growth	-0.10					

Figure 11.3 Numerical values in Orbit model

+B18

and then copy this formula across the cell range D18.I18.

This method of modelling equal entries proves useful if we want to change the fixed costs at a later stage. It is simply necessary to change the entry in B18 to reflect the changed level of quarterly fixed costs.

Promotion can be treated in the same manner as fixed costs. So in C19, enter the formula:

+B19

and then copy this formula across the cell range D19.I19.

At this point, the formulae in column C have been copied across the worksheet. It remains to copy the column B formulae for the sales revenue, variable costs, etc. for calculators, watches and the combined sales, costs, etc. for both products from column B to the range from column C to I.

The two performance ratios, %Contribution/Sales and %Profit/Sales in B23 and B24 can be copied from column B to the range from column C to K since they apply to annual contribution and annual profit figures as well as each of the quarters.

Annual totals

Lastly, the formulae shown in Figure 11.2 for the Year 1 and 2 Totals are entered into J4 and K4 and copied down the worksheet to row 21.

This completes the ORBIT model: the numerical results should now tie up with those in Figure 11.4. It would be prudent to save the worksheet before proceeding with the sensitivity analysis. However, if your model differs substantially from Figure 11.4, you may wish to load in the datafile called ORBIT1.

The effect of the decline in watch sales can be seen by studying the Profit line (row 21) and the two performance measures. The %Contribution/Sales ratios (row 23) show the effect on contribution of the changing product mix as watch sales drop. The %Profit/Sales ratios (row 24) show that despite the increasing sales of calculators the profitability of the business is declining.

11.3 Sensitivity analysis for Orbit

The structure of the Orbit model with quarterly revenues and costs expressed in terms of the planning values makes it easy to carry out 'sensitivity analyses'. For example, if the cost of one or other of the products increases, it is merely necessary to change the values(s) in B29 and/or B32. 1-2-3's recalculation facility shows the effect on profits over the two years almost instantaneously. Figure 11.5 shows the effect of increasing the cost of each product by one pound.

Another way of quickly assessing the effect of changing assumptions is to view the results graphically. Figure 11.6 shows a simple graph comparing the quarterly profits for the original set of assumptions (the 'base case') with those for the case with increased costs (the 'current case'). It is useful to be able to carry out 'what-if graphing' in this way and also to have a benchmark (the base case results) for comparison purposes.

	A	B	C	D	E	F	G	H	I	J	K
1	ORBIT ELECTRONICS		QUARTERLY	PROFIT	FORECASTS					TOTAL	TOTAL
		1	2	3	4	5	6	7	8	Year 1	Year 2
3	CALCULATORS										
4	Sales Volume	3500	3570	3641	3714	3789	3864	3942	4020	14426	15615
5	Sales Revenue	52500	53550	54621	55713	56828	57964	59124	60306	216384	234221
6	Variable Costs	35000	35700	36414	37142	37885	38643	39416	40204	144256	156148
7	Contribution	17500	17850	18207	18571	18943	19321	19708	20102	72128	78074
8	WATCHES										
9	Sales Volume	5300	4770	4293	3864	3477	3130	2817	2535	18227	11959
10	Sales Revenue	63600	57240	51516	46364	41728	37555	33800	30420	218720	143502
11	Variable Costs	31800	28620	25758	23182	20864	18778	16900	15210	109360	71751
12	Contribution	31800	28620	25758	23182	20864	18778	16900	15210	109360	71751
14	PROFIT & LOSS										
15	Total Sales	116100	110790	106137	102078	98556	95519	92923	90726	435105	377724
16	Variable Costs	66800	64320	62172	60324	58749	57420	56316	55414	253616	227899
17	Total Contributn	49300	46470	43965	41753	39807	38099	36608	35312	181488	149825
18	Fixed Costs	20400	20400	20400	20400	20400	20400	20400	20400	81600	81600
19	Promotion	6000	6000	6000	6000	6000	6000	6000	6000	24000	24000
21	Profit (PBIT)	22900	20070	17565	15353	13407	11699	10208	8912	75888	44225
23	%Contribn/Sales	42	42	41	41	40	40	39	39	42	40
24	%Profit/Sales	20	18	17	15	14	12	11	10	17	12
26	Planning	Values									
	------------------	--------									
28	Calculator Price	15									
29	Calculator Cost	10									
30	CalculatorGrowth	0.02									
31	Watch Price	12									
32	Watch Cost	6									
33	Watch Growth	-0.10									

Figure 11.4 Orbit after entering numerical values

	A	B	C	D	E	F	G	H	I	J	K
1	ORBIT ELECTRONICS		QUARTERLY	PROFIT	FORECASTS					TOTAL	TOTAL
		1	2	3	4	5	6	7	8	Year 1	Year 2
3	CALCULATORS										
4	Sales Volume	3500	3570	3641	3714	3789	3864	3942	4020	14426	15615
5	Sales Revenue	52500	53550	54621	55713	56828	57964	59124	60306	216384	234221
6	Variable Costs	38500	39270	40055	40857	41674	42507	43357	44224	158682	171762
7	Contribution	14000	14280	14566	14857	15154	15457	15766	16082	57703	62459
8	WATCHES										
9	Sales Volume	5300	4770	4293	3864	3477	3130	2817	2535	18227	11959
10	Sales Revenue	63600	57240	51516	46364	41728	37555	33800	30420	218720	143502
11	Variable Costs	37100	33390	30051	27046	24341	21907	19716	17745	127587	83710
12	Contribution	26500	23850	21465	19319	17387	15648	14083	12675	91134	59793
14	PROFIT & LOSS										
15	Total Sales	116100	110790	106137	102078	98556	95519	92923	90726	435105	377724
16	Variable Costs	75600	72660	70106	67902	66015	64414	63074	61969	286269	255472
17	Total Contributn	40500	38130	36031	34175	32541	31105	29849	28756	148836	122252
18	Fixed Costs	20400	20400	20400	20400	20400	20400	20400	20400	81600	81600
19	Promotion	6000	6000	6000	6000	6000	6000	6000	6000	24000	24000
21	Profit (PBIT)	14100	11730	9631	7775	6141	4705	3449	2356	43236	16652
23	%Contribn/Sales	35	34	34	33	33	33	32	32	34	32
24	%Profit/Sales	12	11	9	8	6	5	4	3	10	4

	Planning	Values	DATA TABLE	Calc Cost v Watch Cost				Watch Cost
26			Calc. cost					
28	Calculator Price	15	4	4.00	5.00	6.00	7.00	8.00
29	Calculator Cost	11	8.00	26	23	20	17	14
30	CalculatorGrowth	0.02	9.00	22	19	16	13	10
31	Watch Price	12	10.00	18	15	12	9	5
32	Watch Cost	7	11.00	14	11	8	4	1
33	Watch Growth	-0.10	12.00	10	7	3	0	-3

% Profit/Sales for different watch and calculator costs

Figure 11.5 Orbit worksheet for increased product costs (each product cost £1 more). Data Table showing effect on % profit/sales (year 2) for different product–cost combinations

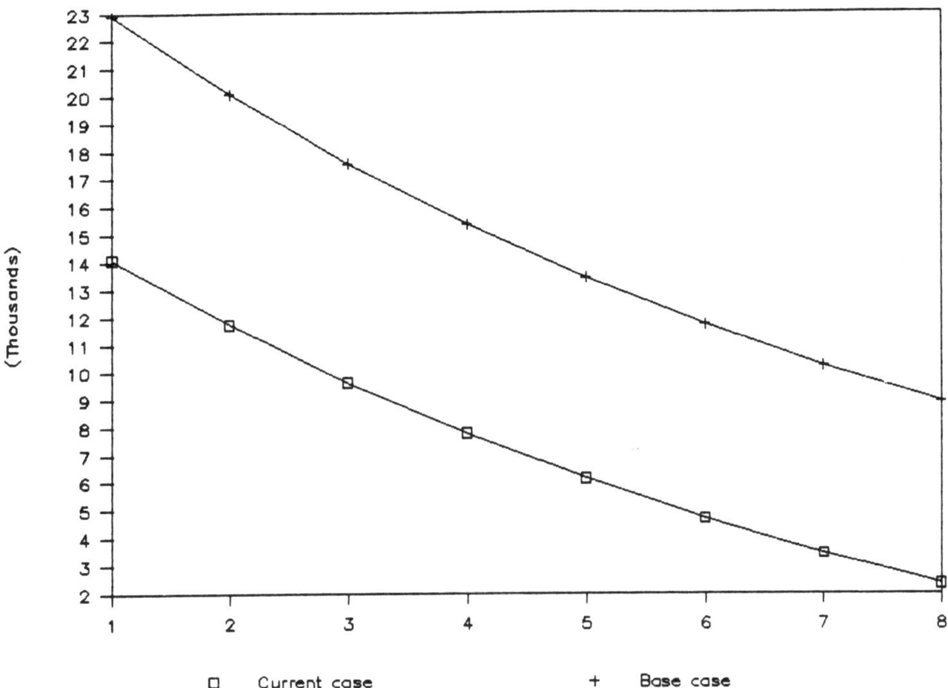

Figure 11.6 Comparison of profits: increased costs v. base case values

To construct a comparison graph of this type, carry out the following steps. From the Graph menu, specify the X range as B3.I3 and the A range as B21.I21 and View the graph.

Return to READY mode, change some planning values and press the Graph key (f10) to see the effect on profit. Although the changes in profit are highlighted by graphing, some of the difference is lost because of 1-2-3's automatic scaling. However, if the base case profit figures are retained in the spreadsheet, their values can be superimposed on the graph. The problem is the changing nature of the entries in the profit row cells.

The Range Value command can be used to retain the numerical values associated with a range of formula cells. The values in a range of formula cells are 'copied' to a 'storage' area. Let us suppose that row 40 is to be used for storing the 'base case' profit values.

Return the planning values to their original values, so that the spreadsheet contains the 'base case' assumptions.

With the pointer on cell B40, type:

/ Range Value B21.I21

and then point to cell B40 as the destination for copying. The result should be the transference of the profit values for the base case to row 40 of the spreadsheet. Put a suitable label (Profits—base case) in cell A40 for reference.

Return to the Graph menu, and specify the B range as B40.I40. If the graph is viewed the profit lines for the current case and the base case are one and the same. However, when some of the assumptions are changed, the two different profit lines should be visible as in Figure 11.6.

The Data Table command is useful in carrying out sensitivity analyses systematically. This was described in Chapter 4. The Orbit model has several measures of performance, e.g. the two ratios %Contribution/Sales and %Profit/Sales for each of two years and also the absolute profit figures. One approach would be to see how these measures change as the cost of producing a watch (in B32) changes. The Data Table with one 'Input' cell, namely B32, would be the appropriate 1-2-3 routine.

However, if we concentrate on one measure of performance at a time, say %Profit/Sales in Year 2 (in K24), we can use the Data Table with two 'Inputs'. For example, the effect of increasing or decreasing the costs of calculators as well as watches on the %Profit/Sales ratio can be studied using / Data Table 2. The '2' refers to the two Input cells: the first Input cell is the calculator cost, B29, and the second the watch cost, B32. The insert at the foot of Figure 11.5 shows the Data Table for Year 2 %Profit/Sales ratio (+K24). For instance, the results in the Data Table show that if the product costs could each be reduced by a pound (to 9 and 5 pounds respectively) then the %Profit/Sales ratio would go up to 19 per cent (from the base case 12 per cent).

Incidentally, the profit measure in the Data Table can be changed. For example, replace the entry in cell C28 (currently +K24) by +K23 say. The effect of changing product costs on the Year 1 %Contribution/Sales ratio can be seen in the Data Table by pressing the (f8/Table) key and WAITing till the contribution measure has been calculated for all the combinations.

One suggestion for improving sales of watches is to increase the promotion expenditure. For example, suppose doubling the promotional effort will halt the decline in sales. What effect will these changes have on profitability? The answer can be obtained by simply changing B19 to 12000 and B33 to 0. The entire worksheet is recalculated and the profitability is much improved as is shown in Figure 11.7.

Another plan is to improve the packaging of the watches and promote the products still further. This means that the cost of a watch will increase to 6.50 pounds because of increased packaging costs, etc. Promotional expenditure is to be trebled (18,000 per quarter) and watch sales are expected to expand at a rate of 5 per cent per quarter. Calculator sales will be affected by the promotion and the rate of growth of sales is expected to rise to 3 per cent per quarter. Figure 11.8 shows the effect on the spreadsheet of changing these values.

These are some examples of the kind of sensitivity analyses that can be carried out easily with 1-2-3. The extra effort of building a 'general' model such as the one for Orbit most often pays off because of the ease with which all kinds of sensitivity analyses can be undertaken.

Before leaving this exercise, you may wish to explore the ORBIT1 datafile on your CM disc. Several graphs have been 'named' and saved with spreadsheet ORBIT1. To view these named graphs, type:

/ G N V   to Use the Named Graphs.

Graph G1 is the comparison graph shown in Figure 11.6. Graphs G2 and G3 show the contributions from the different products and the performance measures. Graphs such as these can be used as a dramatic alternative to the usual tables of numbers.

	A	B	C	D	E	F	G	H	I	J	K
	ORBIT ELECTRONICS		QUARTERLY	PROFIT	FORECASTS					TOTAL	TOTAL
		1	2	3	4	5	6	7	8	Year 1	Year 2
14	PROFIT & LOSS										
	Total Sales	116100	117150	118221	119313	120428	121564	22724	123906	470784	488621
	Variable Costs	66800	67500	68214	68942	69685	70443	71216	72004	271456	283348
	Total Contributn	49300	49650	50007	50371	50743	51121	51508	51902	199328	205274
	Fixed Costs	20400	20400	20400	20400	20400	20400	20400	20400	81600	81600
19	Promotion	12000	12000	12000	12000	12000	12000	12000	12000	48000	48000
		↖Changed from 6000									
21	Profit (PBIT)	16900	17250	17607	17971	18343	18721	19108	19502	69728	75674
23	%Contribn/Sales	42	42	42	42	42	42	42	42	42	42
24	%Profit/Sales	15	15	15	15	15	15	16	16	15	15
26	Planning	Values									

28	Calculator Price	15									
29	Calculator Cost	10									
30	CalculatorGrowth	0.02									
31	Watch Price	12									
32	Watch Cost	6									
33	Watch Growth	0.00 ← Changed from -0.10									

Figure 11.7 Orbit worksheet with promotion doubled

	A	B	C	D	E	F	G	H	I	J	K
	ORBIT ELECTRONICS		QUARTERLY	PROFIT	FORECASTS					TOTAL	TOTAL
		1	2	3	4	5	6	7	8	Year 1	Year 2
14	PROFIT & LOSS										
	Total Sales	116100	120855	125816	130993	136395	142033	47918	154060	493764	580407
	Variable Costs	69450	72223	75113	78126	81267	84542	87958	91520	294911	345288
	Total Contributn	46650	48633	50704	52867	55128	57491	59960	62540	198854	235119
	Fixed Costs	20400	20400	20400	20400	20400	20400	20400	20400	81600	81600
19	Promotion	18000	18000	18000	18000	18000	18000	18000	18000	72000	72000
		Changed from 1200									
21	Profit (PBIT)	8250	10233	12304	14467	16728	19091	21560	24140	45254	81519
23	%Contribn/Sales	40	40	40	40	40	40	41	41	40	41
24	%Profit/Sales	7	8	10	11	12	13	15	16	9	14
26	Planning	Values									

28	Calculator Price	15									
29	Calculator Cost	10									
30	CalculatorGrowth	0.03 ← Changed from 0.02									
31	Watch Price	12									
32	Watch Cost	6.5 ← Changed from 6.0									
33	Watch Growth	0.05 ← Changed from 0.00									

Figure 11.8 Orbit worksheet with promotion up to 18000 and watch cost increased

11.4 Fortuna Stores

We will develop the idea of the Budget Worksheet in the context of the planning problem facing the manager of the Fortuna Store. He is required to prepare budgets for each of the following three months and an overall quarterly budget. Fortuna is part of a large retail chain whose central office handles all financial reporting and paying of tax. Fortuna's budget is therefore drawn up on a pre-tax basis. The main information available at Jan. 31st 1989 on actual and forecast sales and the Balance Sheet are shown in Figure 11.9.

```
FORTUNA STORES

BALANCE SHEET        JANUARY 31st 1989  Actual and Budgeted Sales, 1988/89
                          (£000s)                    (£000s)
NET FIXED ASSETS            100          Dec           200
                                         Jan           150
                                         Feb           100
Cash                          8          Mar           100
Debtors                     110          Apr           150
Stock                        55          May           200
CURRENT ASSETS              173          June          200
                                         July          250
Creditors                    55
Overdraft                     0
CURRENT LIABILIIES           55

NET CURRENT ASSETS          118

EQUITY                      218
```

Figure 11.9 Balance sheet and budgeted sales

Only about 20 per cent of Fortuna's sales are for cash: the rest are for credit. 75 per cent of the credit sales are paid for in the month following sale. The remaining 25 per cent are paid for two months after sale. Thus the figure of 110,000 pounds for debtors shown in the Jan. 31st Balance Sheet consists of credit sales solely from December and January calculated as follows:

$.25 \times .8 \times 150{,}000 + .8 \times 100{,}000 = 30{,}000 + 80{,}000 = 110{,}000$ pounds.

Fortuna sells goods such that the average gross profit rate is 45 per cent, that is, the 'cost of goods sold', COGS, is 55 per cent. Purchases of merchandise each month are matched exactly to the forecast sales requirement of the following month. They are paid for in cash in the month following purchase.

Various other cash payments are made monthly. There are the fixed expenses which cover rent, rates and insurance, etc. which total 5000 pounds per month. Variable expenses covering employees' commission and fringe benefits account for approximately 25 per cent of current sales and other operating expenses account for a further 5 per cent of sales.

Depreciation of fixtures is 1000 pounds a month. There are no plans for acquiring any new assets in the next quarter.

It is company policy that Fortuna should start the month with a cash balance of 8000 pounds. Any deficit below 8000 pounds is made good by arranging overdraft facilities with the local bank. The rate of interest is currently 12 per cent, i.e. 1 per cent per month.

11.5 The budget worksheet

The main building block in modelling Fortuna is the 'Budget Worksheet' for one month's transactions. The worksheet highlights the interrelationships between the Balance Sheet, the Profit and Loss Account and the Cash Flow. It permits a unified development of the financial projections required period by period in planning.

Figure 11.10 shows a Budget Worksheet appropriate for the types of transaction made by Fortuna Stores. Columns represent the different Balance Sheet items with headings for Fixed Assets, Stock, Cash, etc. Rows represent the different types of transaction, e.g. Pay Creditors, Debtors Pay, etc. Figure 11.10 shows the worksheet ready for modelling February's transactions. The units are thousands of pounds. The Opening Balances for February are shown as Fixed Assets of 100, Stock at 55, Debtors at 110, Cash at 8, Creditors at 55, etc.

The object of the exercise is to model Fortuna's performance over the February to April period on the basis of different assumptions. In the case of Fortuna, the assumptions concern sales over the coming months and factors like the cost of goods sold, the proportion of sales for cash, etc. These are the 'planning values' discussed earlier in this chapter and in Chapter 4. As in the earlier treatment, they are located in a separate part of the worksheet, in this case to one side of the main calculation area of the worksheet in column L.

The sales estimates are set out first. The notation used is Sales (−2) to denote sales two months ago (i.e. December's sales), Sales (−1) to denote last month's sales (January), Sales (0) to mean sales in the current month (February), Sales (1) for March sales, etc. Then come factors such as the cost of goods sold proportion (Cogs Pr in L11), the proportion of sales for cash (CshSales in L12) and the credit sales proportion (CrSalesPt in L13). Notice that these values are expressed as proportions, e.g. .55 to represent the Cost of Goods Sold of 55 per cent.

In modelling Fortuna, the aim is to express its monthly transactions in terms of the planning values as far as possible. With the layout of Figure 11.10, it is easy to change the planning values and quickly gauge the effect on the transactions.

The main steps in modelling Fortuna are:

1. Setting up the Budget Worksheet for Fortuna Stores.
2. Modelling the transactions for February.
3. Rolling the February worksheet forwards for March and April.
4. Summarizing the quarters' performance via financial statements.
5. Carrying out sensitivity analysis.

Each of these steps will now be described in detail.

11.6 Setting up the budget worksheet for Fortuna

This consists of entering into the computer the template shown in Figure 11.10, and keying in the formulae for the Closing Balances and the expressions for 'row balancing' in the Profit & Loss column.

Start by loading the Fortuna Stores datafile called FORTUNA into the computer, typing:

```
     A        B        C        D        E         F        G        H        I    J      K          L       M
 1   FORTUNA  STORES   BUDGET   WORKSHEET                                                                            1

 3   FEBRUARY F Assets    Stock  Debtors   Cash Overdraft   Crs   Equity   P&L    Planning Values                    3
 4   --------------------------------------------------------------------------------------------------------
 5   Open Bal       100       55       110      8        0     55      218      0    Sales(-2)      150 December
 6   Sales                                                                           Sales(-1)      100 January
 7   Cogs                                                                            Sales(0)       100 February
 8   MiscExpsV                                                                       Sales(1)       150 March
 9   MiscExpsF                                                                       Sales(2)       200 April
10   Deprn                                                                           Sales(3)       200 May
11   Purchases                                                                       Cogs Pr       0.55
12   Pay Crs                                                                         CshSales      0.20
13   Drs Pay                                                                         CrSalesPt     0.75
14   Interest                                                                        VarExp Pr     0.30
15   Overdraft                                                                       IntRate       0.01
16   P & L                                                                           Fixed Exp        5          0
17   Close Bal                                                                       CashCalc         0 NO O/D=0
     --------------------------------------------------------------------------------------------------------
```

Figure 11.10 Budget worksheet for Fortuna Stores

/ F R FORTUNA   to Retrieve the File.

(Alternatively, key in the Budget Worksheet as laid out in Figure 11.10.)

The screen display is restricted to columns A to H but the full spreadsheet is similar to Figure 11.10. Press the Tab key once to 'jump a page' horizontally to see the P&L column and the planning values in column L. (The Shift and Tab keys pressed together jump you back to the first 'page'.)

Notice that row and column labels (Titles) are frozen (do not scroll off screen). This helps in building the February spreadsheet but will be 'cleared' in rolling the model forwards. Also, the screen display is to the nearest integer (F0) with the exception of some of the planning values which are shown to two decimal places (F2). The 'global' format was imposed by using the Worksheet Global Format Fixed command and the individual cells were formatted using the Range Format Fixed command.

The formulae for Closing Balances are entered first. For example, in the Fixed Assets column:

Closing Balance = Opening Balance plus entries in column B.

This is true for all Closing Balances in row 17. So in cell B17, enter the formula:

@SUM(B5.B16)

Copy this formula across row 17 to I17 in the P&L column.

The Closing Balances equal the Opening Balances at this stage since no numerical entries for transactions have been made yet. Notice that these @SUM formulae can be entered in advance of the entries which make up the formula. In general, formulae can be entered before or after the cells they address are 'filled'.

Entries in P&L column (column H) act to 'balance' asset entries against liability side entries. In any row, the P&L entry is the sum of the entries on the 'assets' side of the spreadsheet (i.e. columns B to E) minus the entries on the 'liabilities' side (i.e. columns F to H). So enter a general formula into cell I5, namely:

@SUM(B5.E5)−@SUM(F5.H5)

and Copy it (From I5) down column I, i.e. To cell range I6.I15.

These formulae cells all display zeroes because none of the numerical entries have been made yet.

This completes the layout and general formulae for the Budget Worksheet. Figure 11.11 shows what the worksheet should look like at this stage. The Opening Balances for February have been entered already so the next step is to model the transactions for February.

11.7 Modelling February's transactions

Next we work down row by row entering February's transactions in the appropriate columns. These entries are expressed in terms of FORMULAE based on the planning values where possible. It is important to model the transactions in this manner, so that the assumptions can be changed easily at the 'what-if' stage.

In contrast to the method of modelling used for Orbit, no cells will be 'absolutely addressed'. In rolling the worksheet forwards for March and April, the planning values will be rolled forwards and adjusted. The method will become clear as we

```
       A          B        C        D         E         F        G        H          I  J        K           L      M
 1   FORTUNA  STORES   BUDGET   WORKSHEET

 3   FEBRUARY F Assets     Stock  Debtors   Cash Overdraft  Crs    Equity    P&L    Planning Values
     -----------------------------------------------------------------------------------------------------------------
 5   Open Bal       100       55       110      8          0   55       218   0     Sales(-2)       150 December
 6   Sales                                                                 ↗  0     Sales(-1)       100 January
 7   Cogs                                            @SUM(B5.E5)-@SUM(F5.H5) 0     Sales(0)        100 February
 8   MiscExpsV                                                                0     Sales(1)        150 March
 9   MiscExpsF                                                                0     Sales(2)        200 April
10   Deprn                                                                    0     Sales(3)        200 May
11   Purchases                                                                0     Cogs Pr        0.55
12   Pay Crs                                                                  0     CshSales       0.20
13   Drs Pay                                                                  0     CrSalesPt      0.75
14   Interest                                                                 0     VarExp Pr      0.30
15   Overdraft  @SUM(B5.B16)                                                  0     IntRate        0.01
16   P & L          ↓                                                               Fixed Exp         5          0
17   Close Bal      100       55       110      8          0   55       218   0     CashCalc          0 NO O/D=0
     -----------------------------------------------------------------------------------------------------------------
```

Figure 11.11 Worksheet with formulae for closing balances and P&L items

carry out the modelling. The point to notice at this stage is that no dollar signs are used in the cell addresses of planning values in contrast to Orbit and that this is deliberate.

Starting with row 6, Sales in February are forecast to be 100 (in L7) of which 20 per cent (in L12) will be cash sales. So the entries in the Sales row are:

+L12*L7 in E6 in the Cash column and

(1−L12)*L7 in D6 in the Debtors column.

Notice that the formula in I6 gives the 'balancing' entry (100) for the Sales row of the P&L column.

Continuing with the Cost of Goods Sold row, in C7 we need to deduct the COGS proportion (in L11) of February sales (in L7), i.e. enter the formula:

−L11*L7 in C7 in the Stock column.

Notice the balancing entry for Cost of Goods Sold in I7 of the P&L column.

For Miscellaneous Variable Expenses, we need to deduct a fixed proportion (in L14) of current sales, so enter:

−L14*L7 in E8 in the Cash column.

The Miscellaneous Fixed Expenses of 5 (thousand pounds) are deducted from Cash by keying the value −5 in E9 in the Cash column. Similarly, Depreciation is accounted for by deducting 1 from the Fixed Assets column in cell B10. The balancing entries for Miscellaneous Expenses and Depreciation can be seen in the P&L column (column I).

Since Fortuna purchases stock exactly in line with the next month's sales (in L8), for Purchases, enter:

+L8*L11 in C11 in the Stock column

where L11 is the Cost of Goods Sold. The Creditors Balance increases by the same amount, so type:

+C11 in G11 in the Creditors column.

The next transaction, Pay Creditors, concerns paying for goods bought on credit last month, so enter the formula:

−G5 in E12 in the Cash column and an equal entry to reduce the outstanding Creditors' Balance, namely:

+E12 in G12 in the Creditor column.

Debtors Pay is a comparable transaction involving an inflow to the Cash Column and a reduction of the Debtors Balance. The Debtors who pay consist of the remaining 20 per cent (i.e. 25 per cent of 80 per cent) of December sales who have still not paid, and the 60 per cent (75 per cent of 80 per cent) of the January sales. So enter the formula:

−(1−L13)*(1−L12)*L5−L13*(1−L12)*L6
from December from January

in D13 in the Debtors column and the balancing entry:

−D13 in E13 in the Cash column.

(Using the current planning values, the above formula translates into

−(.25) * (.8)*150 −7.5*(.8)*100)

December January

Interest (at the monthly rate given in L15) on any Overdraft outstanding at the start of February (in F5) must be paid, so enter the formula:

−L15*F5 in E14 in the Cash column.

The formula should be entered at this stage even though no Overdraft exists at the beginning of February.

If the Cash Balance in E17 is lower than 8 it is necessary to obtain additional overdraft facilities. On the current transactions for February this is not the case. However, we make the necessary entries at this stage so that the February formulae can be used to model other months. The necessity for additional overdraft is shown by the formula labelled 'CashCalc' in L17, namely:

@SUM(E5.E14)−8 which has the value 20 for February.

This is the surplus cash above the required Cash Balance of 8 for starting March's business activity. In cell M16 nearby, a logical function:

@IF(L17> =0,0,1)

displays 1 or 0 according to whether additional overdraft is required (1) or not (0). (L17 is the surplus cash: if the condition (L17> =0) holds, the expression is evaluated as 0, if (L17> =0) does not hold, i.e. cash is needed to start next month with a Cash Balance of 8, the expression is evaluated as 1.) The product of the contents of cells L17 and M16 gives the required overdraft whatever the circumstances with respect to cash.

Hence the entry for the Overdraft row is:

−L17*M16 in E15 of the Cash column and

+E15 in F15 of the Overdraft column.

To close off the Profit and Loss column, any profit at bottom of P&L column (displayed as 9 in I17) is withdrawn from P&L and put into Equity (or Retained Earnings). Profit is given by @SUM(I5.I15). So the entry in I16 is:

−@SUM(I5.I15)

and in H16 the balancing entry is −I16.

This concludes the modelling of February's transactions. All the formulae for the February transactions and the resulting values are shown in Figure 11.12.

The Balance Sheet for February can be read off from row 17 where the Closing Balances are located. Similarly, the Profit and Loss account for February can be seen in column I and the Cash position (with the Overdraft requirement) is shown in column E.

	A	B	C	D	E	F	G	H	I	J	K	L	M	
1	FORTUNA	STORES	BUDGET	WORKSHEET										
3	FEBRUARY	F Assets	Stock	Debtors	Cash	Overdraft	Crs	Equity	P&L		Planning Values			
5	Open Bal	100	55	110	8	0	55	218	0		Sales(-2)	150	December	5
6	Sales	(1-L12)*L7 →		80	20 ←	+L12*L7			100		Sales(-1)	100	January	6
7	Cogs	-L11*L7 →	-55						-55		Sales(0)	100	February	7
8	MiscExpsV	-L14*L7 →			-30				-30		Sales(1)	150	March	8
9	MiscExpsF				-5				-5		Sales(2)	200	April	9
10	Deprn	-1							-1		Sales(3)	200	May	10
11	Purchases	L11*L8 →	83				83 ←	+C11	0		Cogs Pr	0.55		11
12	Pay Crs				-55		-55 ←	+E12	0		CshSales	0.20		12
13	Drs Pay	see text →		-90	90	-D13			0		CrSalesPt	0.75		13
14	Interest	-L15*F5 →			0				0		VarExp Pr	0.30		14
15	Overdraft	-L17*M16 →			0	0	+E15		0		IntRate	0.01		15
16	P & L							9 -I16	-9 ←		Fixed Exp	5	0	16
17	Close Bal	99	83	100	28	0	83	227	0		CashCalc	→ 20	NO O/D=0	17
									@SUM(I5.I15)		@SUM(E5.E14) -8	@IF(L17>=0,0,1)		18

Figure 11.12 Worksheet for February's transactions with formulae

Before modelling the transactions for March and April, we will start to build up the financial statements.

11.8 Profit & loss and balance sheet for February

The file FORTUNA1 on your CM disc contains the model for February together with a template for the Budget Profit and Loss Account and Balance Sheet. After filling in entries for February's statements, you may wish to continue with your own worksheet. For this reason, save your file before retrieving FORTUNA1, that is, type:

/ F S MODEL to Save your File called MODEL (say)

/ F R FORTUNA1 to Retrieve the File FORTUNA1.

The structure of the whole FORTUNA1 worksheet is illustrated in Figure 11.13. There are blocks for each month's transactions spreading down the worksheet and to the left of the February worksheet, a Budget Profit and Loss Account and a Balance Sheet. When first retrieved, the February worksheet is displayed. Press the Tab key twice to jump the pointer across to Q1, the start of the Budget P&L Account. The worksheet labels in columns Q and R are shown in Figure 11.12.

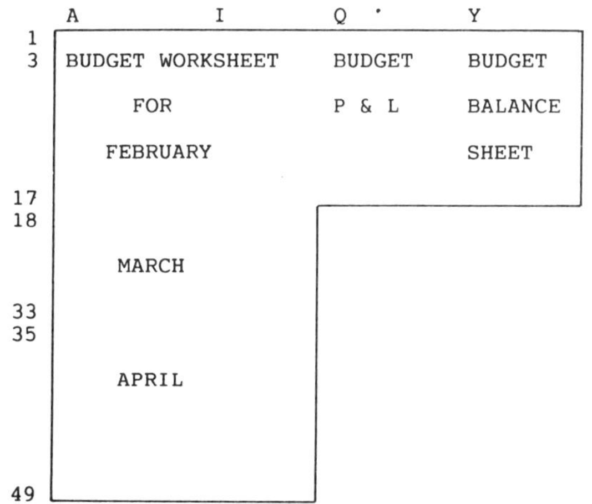

Figure 11.13 Layout of Fortuna1 worksheet

Enter the addresses of the P&L items (from column I of the February worksheet) in Column S as shown in Figure 11.14. For example, the Sales reading for February comes from cell I6, the Cost of Goods Sold from I7, etc. Key in the other formulae for Gross Profit and Net Profit as shown. This completes the P&L Account for February.

Similarly, move the pointer across to Y1 where the Budget Balance Sheet starts. The January entries come from the Balance Sheet in Figure 11.9. Again, enter the addresses

```
        Q      R                S          T           U        V
    FORTUNA  STORES
    BUDGET P&L                 FEB       MARCH       APRIL  QUARTER
    -------------------------------------------------------------
 4  Sales                      100 ← +I6
 5   less COGS                 -55 ← +I7

 7  GROSS PROFIT                45 ← +S4+S5

     less:
10   MiscExpsV                 -30 ← +I8
11   MiscExpsF                  -5 ← +I9
12   Depreciation               -1 ← +I10
13   Interest                    0 ← +I14

15  Total Expenses             -36 @SUM(S10.S13)

17  NET PROFIT                   9 ← +S7+S15
```

```
       Y          Z          AA          AB         AC          AD
    FORTUNA     STORES
    BUDGET BS                JAN         FEB       MARCH       APRIL
    -----------------------------------------------------------
 4  N FIXED ASSETS           100          99     ←    +B17

 6    Cash                     8          28     ←    +E17
 7    Debtors                110         100     ←    +D17
 8    Stock                   55          83     ←    +C17
 9  CURRENT ASSETS           173         211   @SUM(AB6.AB8)

11    Creditors               55          83     ←    +G17
12    Overdraft                0           0     ←    +F17
13  CURR LIABILITIES          55          83     ←    +AB11+AB12

15  NET CURR ASSETS          118         128     ←    +AB9-AB13

17  NET ASSETS               218         227     ←    +AB4+AB15

19  EQUITY                   218         227     ←    +H17
```

Figure 11.14 Layout of P&L and balance sheet

of the appropriate Closing Balances for February from row 17 as indicated in Figure 11.4. When the Budget Worksheets for March and April are complete, the remaining columns of the Budget Balance (and the P&L Account) can be completed.

11.9 Rolling forwards for March and April

Figure 11.13 shows the suggested positions in the worksheet for the March and April transactions. It is relatively simple to duplicate the worksheet already developed for February, putting 'copies' into rows 19 to 33 for March and rows 35 to 49 for April. The details are set out in the Note at the end of this chapter. You will need to use the file MODEL you saved at the beginning of Section 11.8.

An alternative approach is to use the template already set up for you in the FORTUNA1 worksheet. The transaction labels for the March and April Worksheets and the planning values have been copied into position. To explore this part of the spreadsheet, move the pointer to A19 and then down to A35. Figure 11.15 shows the template for the March and April transactions.

MARCH	F Assets	Stock	Debtors	Cash	Overdraft	Crs	Equity	P&L	Planning Values		
Open Bal	99	83	100	28	0	83	227	0	Sales(-2)	100	January
Sales									Sales(-1)	100	February
Cogs									Sales(0)	150	March
MiscExpsV									Sales(1)	200	April
MiscExpsF									Sales(2)	200	May
Deprn									Sales(3)	NA	
Purchases									Cogs Pr	0.55	
Pay Crs									CshSales	0.20	
Drs Pay									CrSalesPt	0.75	
Interest									VarExp Pr	0.30	
Overdraft									IntRate	0.01	
P & L									Fixed Exp	5.00	0
Close Bal	99	83	100	28	0	83	227	0	CashCalc	20	NO O/D=0

APRIL	F Assets	Stock	Debtors	Cash	Overdraft	Crs	Equity	P&L	Planning Values		
Open Bal	99	83	100	28	0	83	227	0	Sales(-2)	100	February
Sales									Sales(-1)	150	March
Cogs									Sales(0)	200	April
MiscExpsV									Sales(1)	200	May
MiscExpsF									Sales(2)	NA	
Deprn									Sales(3)	NA	
Purchases									Cogs Pr	0.55	
Pay Crs									CshSales	0.20	
Drs Pay									CrSalesPt	0.75	
Interest									VarExp Pr	0.30	
Overdraft									IntRate	0.01	
P & L									Fixed Exp	5.00	0
Close Bal	99	83	100	28	0	83	227	0	CashCalc	20	NO O/D=0

Figure 11.15 Template in Fortunal file for March and April transactions

Notice that formulae for Opening Balances have been entered, e.g. in cell B21, the formula +B17 makes the Opening Balance for March's Fixed Assets equal to February's Closing Balance. Also the formulae for the Closing Balances for March and April are already entered.

The transactions in March are the same in kind as those in February. They differ only in as much as the Opening Balances and the planning values for March differ from those for February. Therefore, the formulae in the February Worksheet can be copied down as they stand for March and April. So, Copy from range B6.I16 to cell B22 for March's transactions, and then Copy the same range again, B6.I16, to cell B38 for April's transactions. The results are shown in Figure 11.16.

11.10 Completing the financial statements

The Budget Profit and Loss account can now be completed using values in the P&L column (that is column I) for March and April. Similarly, the Budget Balance Sheet requires the addition of items from the Closing Balances for March and April in rows 33 and 49 respectively.

Before proceeding to the next section, remember to save your model at this stage, calling it MODEL1 say.

11.11 Sensitivity analysis for Fortuna

Having completed the model for Fortuna Stores, we can investigate the effect on profits, overdraft requirements, etc., if some of the assumptions made in modelling Fortuna Stores change. To carry out these sensitivity analyses, it helps to see the planning values adjacent to the Budget P&L account or Balance Sheet. Splitting the Worksheet Window and scrolling the two sides independently helps us achieve this.

(i) Continue with your own model if it ties up with Figure 11.16. If there are big discrepancies, you are advised to retrieve the FORTUNA2 file.

(ii) Position the pointer in the third column from the left hand side of the screen. Type:

/ W W V — to split the Worksheet Window Vertically and

/ W W U — for Unsynchronized scrolling.

You can jump the pointer from left to right window with the (f6/Window) key.

(iii) By pointer moves, get K1 in top left hand corner of left window; and get Q1 in top left hand corner of right hand window.

You should now have the planning values lined up by the Budget P&L projections.

The model of Fortuna Stores is now ready for answering a range of 'what-if' questions. For example, what happens to profits if the Cost of Goods Sold increases from 55 per cent to 65 per cent or even higher? What happens if sales are 15 per cent higher than forecast, or 10 per cent lower than forecast?

Let us focus first on the Cost of Goods Sold Proportion. Change the value of L11, to .65 and watch the effect on say the Net Profit (cells S17 to V17) or the Overdraft requirement

	A	B	C	D	E	F	G	H	I	J	K	L	M
19	MARCH	F Assets	Stock	Debtors	Cash	Overdraft	Crs	Equity	P&L		Planning Values		
21	Open Bal	99	83	100	28	0	83	227	0		Sales(-2)	100	January
	Sales			120	30				150		Sales(-1)	100	February
	Cogs		-83						-83		Sales(0)	150	March
	MiscExpsV				-45				-45		Sales(1)	200	April
	MiscExpsF				-5				-5		Sales(2)	200	May
	Deprn	-1							-1		Sales(3)	NA	
	Purchases		110				110		0		Cogs Pr	0.55	
	Pay Crs				-83		-83		0		CshSales	0.20	
	Drs Pay			-80	80				0		CrSalesPt	0.75	
	Interest				0				0		VarExp Pr	0.30	
	Overdraft				3	3			0		IntRate	0.01	
	P & L							17	-17		Fixed Exp	5.00	1
33	Close Bal	98	110	140	8	3	110	244	0		CashCalc	-3	NO O/D=0
35	APRIL	F Assets	Stock	Debtors	Cash	Overdraft	Crs	Equity	P&L		Planning Values		
37	Open Bal	98	110	140	8	3	110	244	0		Sales(-2)	100	February
	Sales			160	40				200		Sales(-1)	150	March
	Cogs		-110						-110		Sales(0)	200	April
	MiscExpsV				-60				-60		Sales(1)	200	May
	MiscExpsF				-5				-5		Sales(2)	NA	
	Deprn	-1							-1		Sales(3)	NA	
	Purchases		110				110		0		Cogs Pr	0.55	
	Pay Crs				-110		-110		0		CshSales	0.20	
	Drs Pay			-110	110				0		CrSalesPt	0.75	
	Interest				·0				0		VarExp Pr	0.30	
	Overdraft				25	25			0		IntRate	0.01	
	P & L							24	-24		Fixed Exp	5.00	1
49	Close Bal	97	110	190	8	28	110	267	0		CashCalc	-25	NO O/D=0

Figure 11.16 Completed worksheets for March and April

(cells AB12 to AD12). Other values can be substituted to gauge the sensitivity of results to changes in margins.

Turning to Sales, it is worth introducing a Factor (for multiplying by) to model changes such as 15 per cent increase or 10 per cent decrease. (The alternative is to multiply the current and future sales estimates by 15 per cent or whatever.) Put the value 1 for this Factor in L1, format it to 2 decimal places and put an explanatory label such as 'Factor' in K1. Change the entries for Sales from the current month onwards by the Factor in L1, e.g. in L7 change the entry from 100 to

100*L1

Make this amendment to the entries in cells L7 down to L10. Since the current value of the Factor is 1, these changes should have no effect on the numerical values.

Now change the value of the Factor to 1.15 (for a 15 per cent rise in the sales estimates) or .9 (for a 10 per cent reduction). Again watch the effect on items such as Net Profit in the P&L and Cash Overdraft in the Balance Sheet.

Note: Optional exercise
Modelling March and April from February's worksheet

Having developed the model for February up to the end of Section 11.7, retrieve your file (MODEL or whatever) and proceed as follows:

'Unfreeze' the titles (/ Worksheet Titles Clear)

Copy the entire Budget Worksheet for February down into rows 19 to 33 and adjust it for March. That is, type:

/ C A3.I18 to A19

Change the label FEBRUARY to MARCH

Make Opening Balances for March equal Closing Balances for February, i.e. in B21 enter the formula:

+B17 and copy it across the range C21.I21.

Adjust the planning values.

First copy down all the labels from K3.K18 to K19. (Some minor additions of dotted lines, etc. may be needed as well.) To adjust the sales so that the current month is March, and hence Sales (−2) contains January sales, with the pointer on L21, enter the formula:

+L6 and copy this down to L22.L25

To ensure that the sales figures for 3 months ahead in L26 is not wrongly interpreted as zero, put the special 'not available' function in this cell:

@NA in cell L26

so that the cell displays the NA or 'not available' message.

Copy the remaining planning values from L11 to L16 down to L27 and below. In doing this it is important to set up a relation with the first set of planning values so that it is only necessary to change their values in one set of cells to see the effect on profit. So type the entry:

+L11 in cell L27 and display it to 2 decimal places (F2) using the Range Format Fixed command. Copy the formula down to range L28.L32.

Next copy the CashCalc formula in L17 down to L33 so that the formula in L33 appears as

@SUM(E21.E30)−8

Also copy the formula and label in range M16.M17 to M32 and M33. The values displayed should indicate that an overdraft of 3 thousand pounds is required (−3 in L33, and 1 in M32 meaning overdraft needed).

The formulae for March's transactions have the same structure with respect to the planning values and opened balances as those for February. So the March transactions should now be displayed from rows 21 to 33.

Similarly April's transactions can be obtained by rolling March's formulae forwards in exactly the same manner. Figure 11.16 shows the results for March and April. You may wish to check your Closing Balances for March before producing the worksheet for April.

```
     Q       R          S              T                U
 1   FORTUNA  STORES
 2   BUDGET P&L         FEB            MARCH            APRIL
 3   ------------------------------------------------------------
 4   Sales              +I6            +I22             +I38
 5    less COGS         +I7            +I23             +I39

 7   GROSS PROFIT       +S4+S5         +T4+T5           +U4+U5

      less:
10    MiscExpsV         +I8            +I24             +I40
11    MiscExpsF         +I9            +I25             +I41
12    Depreciation      +I10           +I26             +I42
13    Interest          +I14           +I30             +I46
14
15   Total Expenses     @SUM(S10..S13) @SUM(T10..T13)   @SUM(U10..U13)

17   NET PROFIT         +S7+S15        +T7+T15          +U7+U15
```

```
     Y       Z             AB             AC               AD
 1   FORTUNA       STORES
 2   BUDGET BS             FEB            MARCH            APRIL
 3   ---------------------------------------------------------------
 4   N FIXED ASSETS        +B17           +B33             +B49

 6    Cash                 +E17           +E33             +E49
 7    Debtors              +D17           +D33             +D49
 8    Stock                +C17           +C33             +C49
 9   CURRENT ASSETS        @SUM(AB6..AB8) @SUM(AC6..AC8)   @SUM(AD6..AD8)

11    Creditors            +G17           +G33             +G49
12    Overdraft            +F17           +F33             +F49
13   CURR LIABILITIES      +AB11+AB12     +AC11+AC12       +AD11+AD12

15   NET CURR ASSETS       +AB9-AB13      +AC9-AC13        +AD9-AD13

17   NET ASSETS            +AB4+AB15      +AC4+AC15        +AD4+AD15

19   EQUITY                +H17           +H33             +H49
```

Figure 11.17 Formulae in budget P&L and balance sheets

If your model tallies with that shown in Figure 11.16 for March and April, all is well. If not, you may prefer to Retrieve the File called FORTUNA1 and work through Section 11.9.

The summary financial statements can now be completed by adding the addresses of the P&L items from column I and the Balance Sheet items from row 33 for March and row 49 for April. The labels and formulae are shown in Figure 11.17 and the results in Figure 11.18. Your model is now ready for the sensitivity analyses described in Section 11.11.

	Q	R	S	T	U	V
1	FORTUNA	STORES				
2	BUDGET P&L		FEB	MARCH	APRIL	QUARTER
3	------------	------------	------------	------------	------------	------------
4	Sales		100	150	200	450
5	less COGS		-55	-83	-110	-248
7	GROSS PROFIT		45	68	90	203
	less:					
10	MiscExpsV		-30	-45	-60	-135
11	MiscExpsF		-5	-5	-5	-15
12	Depreciation		-1	-1	-1	-3
13	Interest		0	0	0	0
15	Total Expenses		-36	-51	-66	-153
17	NET PROFIT		9	17	24	49

	Y	Z	AA	AB	AC	AD
1	FORTUNA	STORES				
2	BUDGET BS		JAN	FEB	MARCH	APRIL
3	------------	------------	------------	------------	------------	------------
4	N FIXED ASSETS		100	99	98	97
6	Cash		8	28	8	8
7	Debtors		110	100	140	190
8	Stock		55	83	110	110
9	CURRENT ASSETS		173	211	258	308
11	Creditors		55	83	110	110
12	Overdraft		0	0	3	28
13	CURR LIABILITIES		55	83	113	138
15	NET CURR ASSETS		118	128	146	170
17	NET ASSETS		218	227	244	267
19	EQUITY		218	227	244	267

Figure 11.18 Budget P&L and balance sheets

CHAPTER 12

Investment Appraisal

Like profit planning, investment appraisal is another important area of financial analysis for which spreadsheet modelling is the ideal tool. Generally speaking, each investment project requires its own model. Much the most difficult part of the exercise is estimating the costs and benefits that contribute to the final projected cashflow for the investment project. However, once these costs and benefits have been decided, the spreadsheet model can be constructed. There are various well-known measures of an investment's profitability: net present value, internal rate of return, payback period and return on capital employed, etc. Most of these measures are easy to calculate in the spreadsheet. In particular, net present value and internal rate of return are measures based on the idea of discounting future benefits back to the same time base. These are the so-called discounted cash flow (or DCF) measures. Since they are frequently evaluated, 1-2-3 has special functions, @NPV and @IRR, for this type of financial analysis.

Investment appraisal is a subject in its own right with its own extensive literature, much of which is devoted to fairly complex arguments of principle (and even economic theory) as to which costs and benefits should be included in different situations. We shall not venture into these controversial areas, but will illustrate the approach with some examples. First, the concept of discounted cashflow is explained and then net present value (NPV) and internal rate of return (IRR) are introduced. Their use is demonstrated by analysing the proposal by the small Dowty Publishing Company to purchase a word processor.

12.1 Present and future value

Most of us are aware of the important idea that the value of money is time-dependent. By this, we understand that one pound (£1) now is worth more than one pound in a year's time or at some other date in the future. This 'discounting' of the value of money in the future is the result of various factors. For example, risk and uncertainty mean that although today's pound exists and can be realized, tomorrow's pound may be subject to uncertainty. Then there are investment possibilities that make today's pound yield more wealth if it is invested. There is also inflation at work, which reduces the purchasing power of money over time. Therefore, in analysing and comparing cashflows generated by different means, it is customary to adjust future cashflows for the time value of money, that is, future cashflows are discounted.

Let us assume we can evaluate the risk-free rate of interest, i, which can be used to calculate the 'future value' of £1 invested now. To simplify the argument, questions about the effect of inflation and uncertainty on value are put on one side. Again, to simplify the text, the rate is referred to in the following paragraphs as the discount rate. Since this is not a treatise on finance, we deliberately side-step round the controversy as to the exact definition of the appropriate rate used for discounting. Having decided on the discount rate, we proceed to adjust the cashflows accordingly.

Suppose we invest a sum of £100 for 6 years at a compound interest of 10 per cent. At the end of year 1, the value of the investment is the original sum multiplied by factor 110% or (1+0.10) = 1.10. Figure 12.1 shows the 'future values' of the investment at the end of each year. (Datafile FUTURE on your CM disc contains a spreadsheet version of Figure 12.1 if you want to follow the calculations in 1-2-3). After 6 years, the future value, FV(6), of the investment is given by

FV(6) = 100*(1 + 0.10)^6 = £177.16

The notation '^' means 'to the power'. Here the factor (1 + 0.10) is raised to the power 6, i.e. the investment of 100 is multiplied by the factor 6 times. The notation '^' is also used in Lotus 1-2-3 for obtaining powers of expressions.

	A	B	C	D	
1	FUTURE VALUES OF AN INVESTMENT				
2					
3	Year	Amount	Interest	Future	
4		beg. year	factor	Value	
5					
6	1	100.00	1.10	110.00	
7	2	110.00	1.10	121.00	
8	3	121.00	1.10	133.10	
9	4	133.10	1.10	146.41	
10	5	146.41	1.10	161.05	
11	6	161.05	1.10	177.16	= FV(6)
12					
13	Investment		100	= PV	
14	Discount rate		10%		
15					

Figure 12.1 Future values of an investment over 6 years

From this, it follows that the 'present value', PV, of £177.16 received at the end of year 6 (which we know to be £100) is obtained from the expression:

PV = FV(6) / (1 + 0.10)^6

As an exercise with file FUTURE, check that the future value of £2000 after 4 years at interest rate 8% is approximately £2721.

In general, the future value of an investment P after n years using the discount rate i is therefore:

$FV(n) = P*(1 + i)\hat{}n$

Similarly, the present value of a cashflow F at the end of the nth year using the discount rate i is given by:

$PV = F/(1 + i)\hat{}n$

Using these concepts, it is possible to evaluate a present value for any future cashflow and by aggregating to calculate a present value for a sequence of future cashflows. We apply these definitions to obtain the present value of a hypothetical investment proposal.

12.2 Net present value and internal rate of return

Suppose that an initial investment of £200 gives rise to cash inflows (benefits) of £70, £80, and £130 at the end of years 1, 2, and 3 of the project. Suppose the discount rate is 10 per cent. Figure 12.2 shows a spreadsheet layout for the calculations to get the net present value of this proposal. The associated datafile, called DCFLOW, is on your CM disc and can be retrieved at this juncture.

```
         A         B         C         D                 G         H         I
 1 DISCOUNTED CASHFLOW CALCULATIONS                 Lotus @functions:
 2
 3     Year Cashflow        PV       NPV       A. @NPV(rate,cashflowrange)
 4
 5        0     -200   -200.00   -200.00          +B5+@NPV(C13,B6..B8)
 6        1       70     63.64   -136.36
 7        2       80     66.12    -70.25            gives      27.42
 8        3      130     97.67     27.42
 9                                             B. @IRR(guess,cashflowrange)
10      SUM    80.00     27.42
11                                                @IRR(12%,B5..B8)
12
13 Discount rate           10%                      gives      16.84%
14
```

Figure 12.2 DCF calculations compared with Lotus @NPV and @IRR

The cashflows are shown in column B and the discount rate in cell C13. Column C contains the present value of each cashflow discounted back to the start of the project. For example, the cashflow of £80 at the end of year 2 is divided by factor (1 + rate)^2 to give the formula for its PV in cell C7 as:

80/(1 + C13)^2 = 80/(1.10)^2 = 66.12

When the present values for the cashflows at the ends of years 1, 2 and 3 are summed and the initial investment at the start of the project is differenced off, we obtain the 'net present value' (or NPV) of the project. In Figure 12.2, this sum is in cell C10.

The value, 27.42, arises from the formula in cell C10, namely:

@SUM(C5 . . C8)

(Additionally, column D contains cumulated sums of present values, so that the NPV of the cashflows at some intermediate time point can be obtained.)

In practice, it is not necessary to evaluate the present values for each individual year of the project because 1-2-3 has a special @ function that carries out the NPV calculations. To compare results, this @NPV function is used in the expression in cell H7. The exact formula for the NPV of the proposal as stored in cell H7 is:

+B5+@NPV(C13,B6 . . B8)

where C13 is the location of the discount rate and range B6 . . B8 contains all the cashflows that require discounting and B5 contains the initial investment.

It is important to note that the Lotus @NPV routine applies discounting to *all* the cells in the specified range. As the initial investment of £200 does not require any discounting, since it is essentially a 'present value', it is not included in the @ function range of cashflows.

If you have retrieved the datafile DCFLOW, explore the formulae in column C, in particular, cells C6 to C10, to make sure that you understand NPV and compare this with the expression for NPV in cell H7.

Next look at the effect on NPV of changing the discount rate. In succession, try discount rates of 15 per cent, 16 per cent and 17 per cent, etc. (by entering .15 or 15%, etc., but not 15).

As the discount rate increases, the NPV of the investment decreases. For a rate just less than 17%, the NPV changes from a positive to a negative amount. In fact, the 'internal rate of return' is the discounting rate for which the NPV of the cashflows equals zero. Rather than establish the value as we have done by trial and error, the @IRR function can be used. This is shown in cell H13 of the spreadsheet. The displayed value, 16.84%, is the rate of discounting that makes the NPV for this project zero. (Try it out in cell C13 and check that the ensuing NPV value in cell C10 (or D8 or H7) is approximately zero).

The expression for the IRR in cell H13 is:

@IRR(12%,B5 . . B8)

where 12% is a guess for the IRR value and the range B5 . . B8 contains all the cashflows in the project. The first quantity (in B5) must be negative (a cash outflow) and corresponds to the initial investment at the start of the project. (In calculating the NPV, the B5 term is not discounted.) Notice the subtle difference in the range of cashflows in the @IRR versus the @NPV expressions.

The general syntax for this @ function is:

@IRR(guess,range)

The 'guess' is a number between 0 and 1, say .12 (or a percentage, say 12%), which is your rough estimate of the IRR, and which can be gauged to some extent by inspecting the NPV of the project. The @IRR function works iteratively. If it cannot get to within .0000001 of the answer, after 20 iterations, an error message (ERR) is displayed. If this occurs, the simplest approach is to edit the @IRR expression, typing in a different guess.

When using the @NPV (and the @IRR) formula in Lotus, consistency is important. If the cashflows are annual ones, then the discount rate is an annual one. If the cashflows refer to any other time period, the interest rate must be adjusted accordingly. Notice also, that the discount rate or the 'guess' in the IRR function is keyed in as a decimal (.20 to indicate a rate of 20% but not 20). The rate may of course be displayed in a cell as a percentage (using Range Format Percent) or alternatively, entered into the formula as a percentage using the % symbol (i.e. entered as 20% but not 20).

12.3 General definition and discussion of NPV

For completeness, we give below general definitions for the NPV and IRR. The definitions use the algebraic notation used in the Lotus Reference Manual. Notice that the cashflows are always assumed to occur at the ends of periods.

General definitions of NPV and IRR

The net present value, NPV, of an investment project is equal to the sum of the present values of each of the future cashflows less the initial investment. Putting this algebraically, suppose the investment project involves an initial investment I which gives rise to a stream of cash flows V_1, V_2, ...V_n in subsequent periods. Then the net present value of the investment is given by:

$$\text{NPV} = \frac{V_1}{(1+i)} + \frac{V_2}{(1+i)^2} \ldots \frac{+V_t}{(1+i)^t} \ldots \frac{+V_n}{(1+i)^n} - I$$

where V_t is the cash flow at the end of period t, i the discount rate, I the initial investment, and n the project's life.

As the discount rate rises, the NPV falls. It is usually possible to find a value for the discount rate that results in zero for the NPV. At this rate, called the internal rate of return, the present value of the future cashflows equals the initial investment.

Having evaluated the NPV, what do we do with it? What decision is taken on the basis of the NPV or the IRR? One argument says that if the discounting rate, i, is equal to the rate for raising an equivalent sum on the capital market, then any project for which the NPV is positive is financially worthwhile. Another argument uses a so-called hurdle rate (a required rate of return). If a project is discounted at the hurdle rate and its NPV is positive, then it makes money when judged against the hurdle rate. If there is no shortage of capital, the project should be undertaken. A variant of this approach involves recognizing that projects carry differing degrees of risk in their returns. A hurdle rate is stipulated for each risk class. For low risk projects, the hurdle rate could be 10 per cent, whereas for more risky projects the hurdle rate could be higher, say 15 per cent. Finally, in comparing equally risky projects, where say there is a shortage of capital, the project with the highest NPV should be chosen if profits are to be maximised.

12.4 Dowty Publishing's proposal to buy a word processor

We now apply the the ideas of NPV and IRR to Dowty Publishing Company's proposal to invest in a new word processor. The aim is to compare the profitability of the investment with the status quo. Hence, we look at the costs and benefits that are additional to remaining with the existing system. If the NPV of these cashflows is positive, then it is more profitable for Dowty to buy the word processor than remain with their existing arrangements.

The capital cost of the word processor and peripheral equipment is known to be about £5000. Dowty expect to get savings in office and secretarial expenses for about 5 years, services which are currently being provided by a bureau. The initial level of savings is estimated at about £1500 in the first year. However, bureau costs have been rising by 8 per cent per year recently, so the savings associated with the word processor are likely to increase over the years. Dowty plan to borrow the money to buy the word processor from the bank. A 3-year loan has been agreed and this will entail interest payments of 17 per cent of the outstanding loan per year. One further cost must be allowed for in judging whether the investment will be profitable or not. An annual maintenance cost of £100 will be incurred in the first year if the word processor is installed, and this is likely to rise by 10 per cent in future years.

The datafile called DOWTY on your CM disc contains a starting layout for the NPV calculations. Use File Rctrieve to load DOWTY into memory and explore the spreadsheet.

The layout is shown in Figure 12.3, with labels for the main calculations in rows 5 to 19 and assumptions stored in the area below row 21. In the upper part of the spreadsheet, there are calculations to work out the outstanding loan on which interest payments must be made and then further calculations to work out the net cashflow. The NPV and IRR of the project will be displayed in G23 and G24 when the cashflows have been evaluated.

Initial formulae:

Rather like the budget worksheet in Chapter 11, most of the entries in the Year 1 and Year 2 columns have to be keyed in individually. Thereafter, the spreadsheet can be extended to future years by Copying.

The first few entries involve preliminary calculations to get the Repayment amounts, and average Loan balances, etc.

Loan (start yr)

In cell C5, enter the starting loan:

+C23

In Year 2, the loan at the start of the year will be identical to the loan at the end of Year 1. Hence in cell D5, the formula is:

+C7

```
             A            B      C          D          E          F          G
 1 DOWTY INVESTMENT APPRAISAL:
 2 -------------------
 3       Calculations:        Year 1     Year 2     Year 3     Year 4     Year 5
 4
 5 Loan (start yr)
 6 Repayment
 7 Loan (end yr)
 8 Mid Year Balance
 9
10   Project Cashflow:
11
12 Cap. repayment
13 Maintenance
14 Interest
15 Bureau saving
16
17 Operating Savings
18
19 Net Cashflow
20
21 Planning Values:                              Investment Appraisal Measures:
22
23 Capital cost                £5,000            NPV @ discount rate
24 Bureau saving               £1,500            Int Rate Return
25 Bureau cost incr p.a.           8%
26 Maintenance cost             £100
27 Mtce cost incr p.a.            10%
28 Interest                       17%
29 Loan term (years)               3
30 Discount rate                  10%
31
```

Figure 12.3 Layout for Dowty's investment appraisal

Repayment

The full capital cost (C23) must be repaid over 3 years (C29), hence repayments are C23/C29 for the first 3 years. In fact, repayments cease as soon as the outstanding loan is zero or less. The expression (C5 > 0) can be used as a multiplier to make the Repayment term zero. The value of a logic expression such as (C5 > 0) is 1 if true: 0 if false. Hence, the formula in cell C6 is:

($C$23/$C$29)*(C5>0)

Loan (end yr)

This is simply the difference between the Loan (start yr) and the Repayment, so the formula in cell C7 is:

+C5−C6

Mid Year Balance

Suppose that the level of interest on the outstanding loan is to be based on the Mid Year Balance. The formula for this balance in cell C8 is:

(C5+C7)/2

The next set of entries reflect the different factors making up the cashflow for the project.

Capital repayment

Since these have already been modelled in row 6, the formula in C12 is:

−C6

Maintenance

This is another cost against the project. The first year amount is £100 stored in cell C26, thereafter costs increase by 10 per cent per year, given in cell C27. Hence, the formula in cell C13 is:

−C26

and in the adjacent cell D13:

+C13*(1+$C$27)

Interest

Interest of 17 per cent (in cell C28) is another cost against the project. It is payable on the Mid Year Balance (row 8), hence the formula in cell C14 is:

-C8*$C$28

Bureau saving

The saving in Year 1 is £1500 in cell C24 and the annual percentage increase, 8%, is in cell C25. So the formula for Year 1 in cell C15 is:

+C24

and in Year 2 in cell D15:

+C15*(1+$C$25)

Operating savings

These are defined as Bureau savings less (Maintenance and Interest charges). The corresponding formula in cell C17 is:

@SUM(C13 . . C15)

Net cashflow

Cashflow is the difference between the Operating Savings and the Capital repayments. Hence the formula in cell C19 is:

+C17+C12

This completes the initial formulae. They can be copied across to Year 5 to get the cashflow for the project. The figures should correspond to those shown in Figure 12.4.

It is useful to be able to show the effect on cashflow of changing assumptions graphically. Figure 12.5 shows the cashflow range of cells (C19 . . G19) plotted over the 5 years (C3 . . G3) as a Bar chart. If you have used the same layout for your entries as in Figure 12.4, you should be able to view a graph similar to Figure 12.5 simply by pressing the Graph key. Try changing some of the planning values in READY mode and then pressing the Graph key to see the effect on cashflow. (The datafile DOWTY contains a preset graph which displays the cashflows as soon as the formulae are entered in row 19).

Before proceeding, remember to return the Planning values to their original values, as shown in Figure 12.4.

Investment appraisal measures

The net effect of the investment on Dowty's cashflow is shown in the cell range C19 . . G19. Initial outflows are replaced by healthy inflows once the loan on the word processor has been paid off. The net present value at the assumed discount rate of 10 per cent (cell C30) is calculated in cell G23 with the formula:

@NPV($C$30,C19 . . G19)

which evaluates to £874. Thus, at this discount rate, the acquisition of the word processor is justified.

Given that the NPV is relatively large when the discount rate is 10 per cent, we could guess that the internal rate of return is likely to be at least 20 per cent. Using this value as a first guess, the formula in cell G24 for the IRR is:

	A	B	C	D	E	F	G
1	DOWTY INVESTMENT APPRAISAL:						
2	--------------------						
3	Calculations:		Year 1	Year 2	Year 3	Year 4	Year 5
4							
5	Loan (start yr)		£5,000	£3,333	£1,667	£0	£0
6	Repayment		£1,667	£1,667	£1,667	£0	£0
7	Loan (end yr)		£3,333	£1,667	£0	£0	£0
8	Mid Year Balance		£4,167	£2,500	£833	£0	£0
9							
10	Project Cashflow:						
11							
12	Cap. repayment		(£1,667)	(£1,667)	(£1,667)	£0	£0
13	Maintenance		(£100)	(£110)	(£121)	(£133)	(£146)
14	Interest		(£708)	(£425)	(£142)	£0	£0
15	Bureau saving		£1,500	£1,620	£1,750	£1,890	£2,041
16							
17	Operating Savings		£692	£1,085	£1,487	£1,756	£1,894
18							
19	Net Cashflow		(£975)	(£582)	(£180)	£1,756	£1,894
20							
21	Planning Values:				Investment Appraisal Measures:		
22							
23	Capital cost		£5,000		NPV @ discount rat		£874
24	Bureau saving		£1,500		Int Rate Return		28%
25	Bureau cost incr p.a.		8%				
26	Maintenance cost		£100				
27	Mtce cost incr p.a.		10%				
28	Interest		17%				
29	Loan term (years)		3				
30	Discount rate		10%				
31							

Figure 12.4 Completed NPV calculations for Dowty

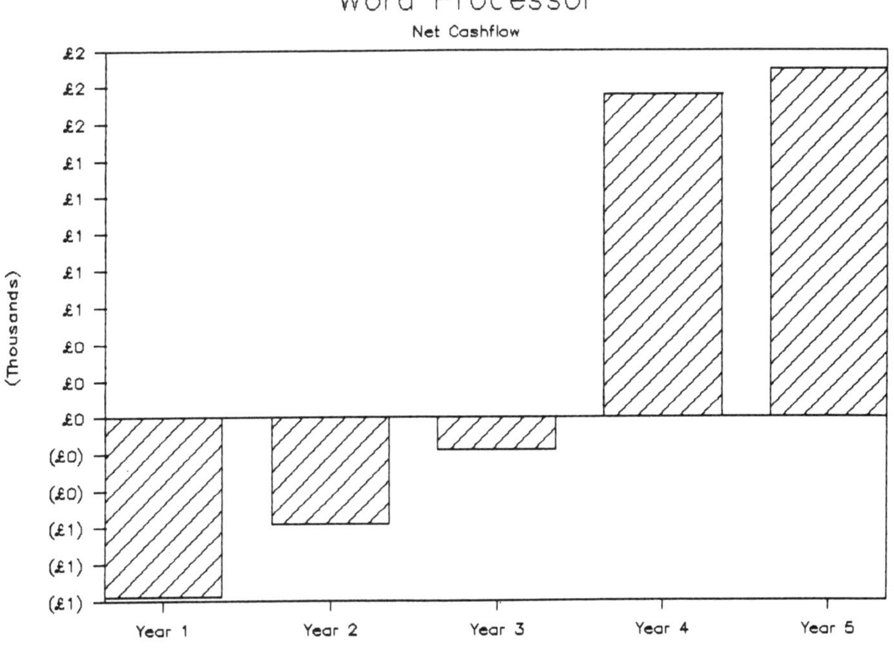

Figure 12.5 Net cashflow for word processor project

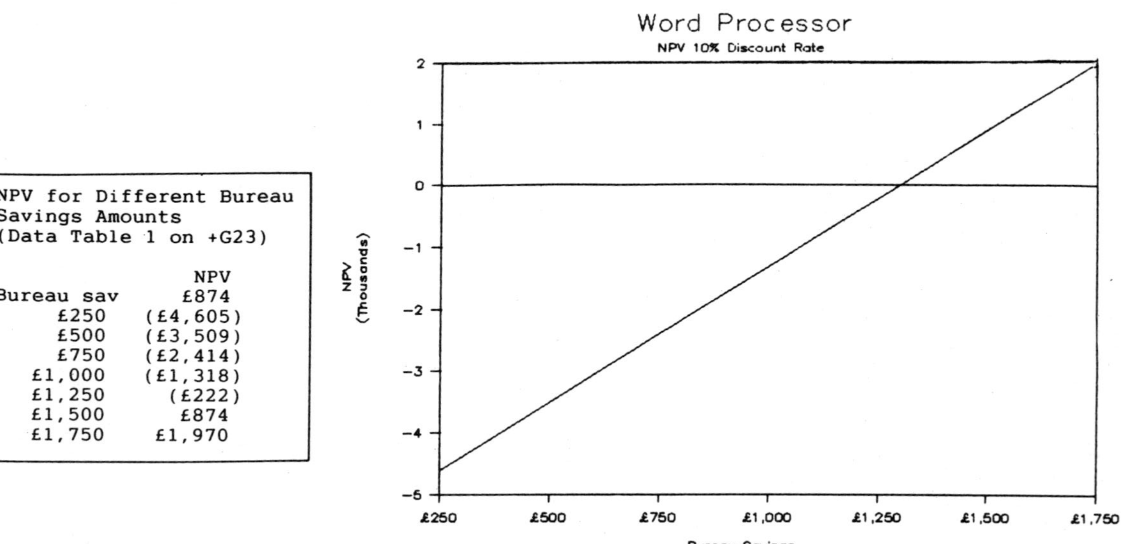

NPV for Different Bureau Savings Amounts
(Data Table 1 on +G23)

Bureau sav	NPV £874
£250	(£4,605)
£500	(£3,509)
£750	(£2,414)
£1,000	(£1,318)
£1,250	(£222)
£1,500	£874
£1,750	£1,970

Figure 12.6 NPV for word processor project for different levels of bureau savings

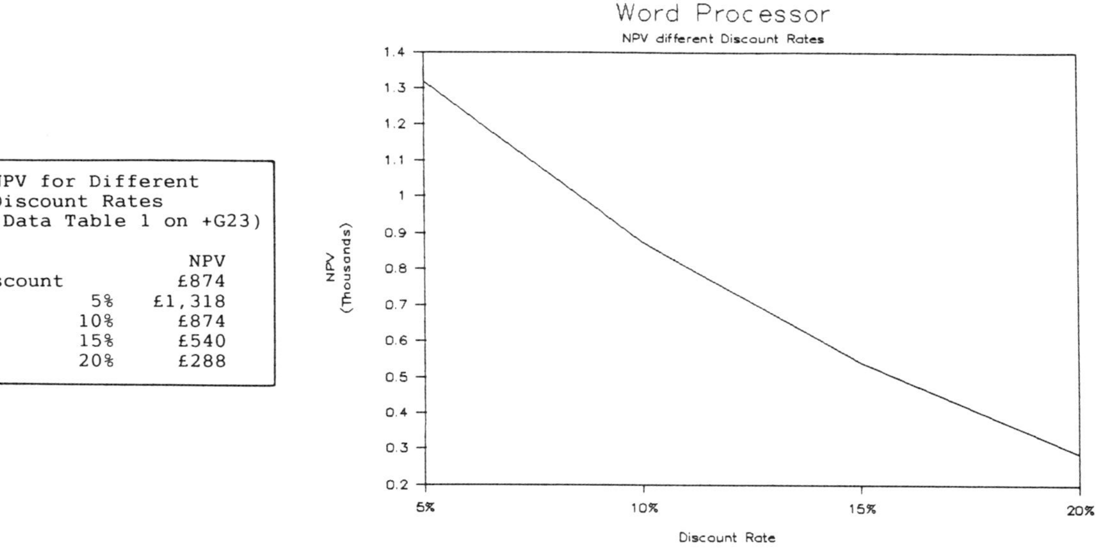

NPV for Different
Discount Rates
(Data Table 1 on +G23)

Discount	NPV
	£874
5%	£1,318
10%	£874
15%	£540
20%	£288

Figure 12.7 Effect on NPV of changing the discount rate

@IRR(0.2,C19 . . G19)

which in fact evaluates to 28 per cent.

Here both financial functions are applied to the same range of cashflows C19 . . G19 because the Year 1 cashflow must be discounted in both cases.

12.5 Further analysis using the model

As with several of the applications in this book, the model forms the basis for sensitivity analysis. The idea is to use the Planning values to enter and change the variables that affect the outcome. In this case, Dowty may well want to examine how the project looks under different assumptions as to possible loan terms, interest charges, and cost inflation.

For example, Figure 12.6 shows the effect on NPV of different assumptions as to the size of the saving in Bureau costs. These figures have been obtained in a Data Table based on the NPV formula in cell G23. Similarly, Figure 12.7 shows the size of the NPV of the project if the discount rate is taken at different values.

The results of such sensitivity analyses can often be very effectively displayed as a graph, as shown here. To plot these, choose the Graph menu and specify the X range and A ranges as the cell ranges of the Data Table. When both variables connected in the Data Table are numeric, choose the XY type of graph.

Your CM disc contains the datafile DOWTY1, which contains the completed analysis described in this section. When you explore the model, look at the Data Tables in rows 37 and below on which the graphs in Figures 12.6 and 12.7 are based. From the Graph menu, 'name' and 'use' the preset graphs, which display the values in the Data Tables.

Index